THE INTIMATE TOUCH

CONSULTANT
Dr GLENN WILSON

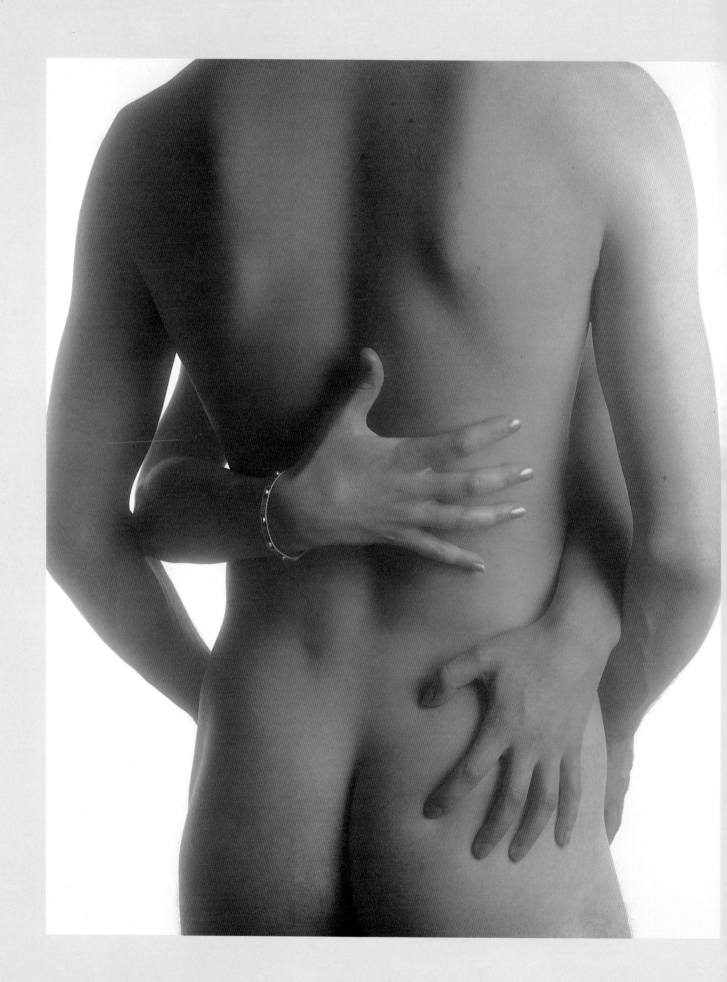

THE INTIMATE TOUCH

CONSULTANT
Dr GLENN WILSON

A GUIDE TO MORE ACTIVE LOVEMAKING FOR YOU AND YOUR PARTNER

Macdonald Illustrated

A Macdonald Illustrated BOOK

Editor Joey Chapter
Art Editor Gordon Robertson
Production Deborah Cracknell

Macdonald & Co (Publishers) Ltd
Orbit House, 1 New Fetter Lane, London EC4A 1AR

First published in Great Britain in 1990 by
Macdonald & Co (Publishers) Ltd
London & Sydney

A member of Maxwell Macmillan Pergamon
Publishing Corporation plc

First printing 1990
1 2 3 4 5 6 7 8 9   99 98 97 96 95 94 93 92 91 90

Concept, design and production by
Marshall Cavendish Books Limited,
58 Old Compton Street, London W1V 5PA

Original text copyright
© Marshall Cavendish Limited 1990
This edition copyright
© Macdonald & Co (Publishers) Ltd 1990

British Library Cataloguing in Publication Data
Wilson, Glenn, *1942–*
   The intimate touch.
   1. Man. Sexual intercourse. Techniques
   I. Title
   613.96

ISBN 0–356–19199–0

Typeset by J&L Composition Ltd, Filey,
North Yorkshire

Printed and bound in Hong Kong

Although the artworks in this book do not depict men wearing condoms, we do recommend the use of them, especially in a new relationship, or where you have not known your partner very long.

CONTENTS

INTRODUCTION

Good sex helps to keep us healthy and happy; and good health and fitness inevitably ensure a good, active sex life. It is therefore surprising how little thought some people give to the sexual side of their nature. It is the most natural form of exercise you can take; but that is not to say that a little care and attention cannot do wonders for you, giving you more energy, making you more supple, and giving full rein to the sensuality that lies within you.

While the aim of this book is to point out ways in which you can improve or maintain your sexual activity, the one aspect of your life which is perhaps most vital to your well-being cannot be taught –

and that is the joy of a close, loving relationship. The feeling of being important to somebody else, and the knowledge that someone else cares about our problems, gives us strength. Being loved enables us to override crises and deal effectively with stress. And needing and wanting someone, knowing we are not just living for ourselves, is the best source of happiness that there is.

What helps us to stay happy and healthy in relationships? The equation is simple – good relationships make you feel valued and appreciated, and bad relationships make you feel the opposite. It follows, therefore, that the most important element in keeping your relationship healthy and, by extension, keeping yourself and your partner

healthy too, is making your partner feel valued and loved and hoping that the expressions of appreciation and caring will be returned.

Good sex is part of most good relationships. Again, this cannot be learned just by reading a book – good sex happens when the chemistry is right. But it can still be worked on; you can ensure that your body and your surroundings are at their best for loving. Tension, irritability, moodiness or just general lethargy can destroy sexual desire and arousal. Leave time in your life for both exercise and relaxation – by yourself and with your partner. It is amazing how many of us have to learn to relax, much as we learn to exercise – but the benefits are incalculable.

The guidelines here are gentle and simple. We can all benefit from a sensible attitude to our bodies, our food, our way of life. But to love and to be loved, to care and to be cared about – these are the most potent recipes for health. And it is the basis upon which this book is based, for intimacy can only be truly complete between partners who love and care for each other. Indeed, the couple who know each other intimately, and whose lives are based on receptiveness and commitment, can make lovemaking new, fresh and fulfilling every time. With love and responsiveness, familiarity can only breed contentment. And with these foundations, good sex becomes wonderful sex, simply because it is the deepest expression of feeling that two people can share.

A BETTER BODY

When you're feeling healthy and happy, your whole life benefits – and no aspect of it more so than your sexual relationships. Some gentle exercises, the ability to relax properly, and learning how to get in touch with each other's bodies will result in more vitality and a deeper appreciation of your physical nature

EVERYDAY EXERCISES

*Exercising need not be strenuous to be doing you good.
With a few simple exercises you can correct postural faults,
look better, feel fitter and improve your health*

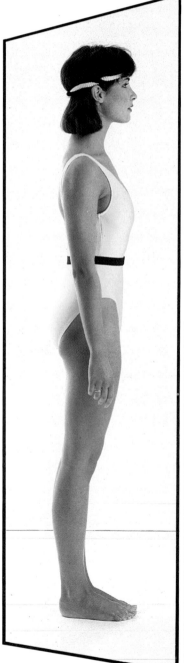

Standing correctly (left) may require some re-training of your body, but the benefits to both looks and health are well worth the effort

(Below) When your body is supple and free from aches or stiffness, your lovemaking is all the more fulfilling

All too often, people have no awareness of their body until it fails them. They use it and abuse it thoughtlessly. Only when it becomes run down, a source of pain or chronically ill, do they stop to consider what went wrong and how best to steer it back to health.

SERVICING OUR BODIES
It seems that because we are issued with our bodies free of charge, we ignore them. Where money has changed hands, such as when we buy a car, we are much more careful. But unlike cars, bodies actually thrive on being used. So, far from wearing out with repeated actions, your muscles actually improve with use and exercise.

BODY POTENTIAL
Before you start a programme of exercise, it is important that you establish certain criteria that will make it effective for you. You must gauge your own body potential and lifestyle in order to choose a programme

which is both realistic and enjoyable. It will only be of value if it can become as much a part of your everyday life as cleaning your teeth and brushing your hair.

Exercise is not going to make you slim and lithe if you are short and stocky, but it will make the very best of your body, both in terms of how it looks and how it functions.

BODY AWARENESS

We so easily get into the habit of standing or sitting badly that we are completely unaware that we are doing it. Indeed, altering our posture very often feels awkward and unnatural at first.

This is why it is important to use a full-length mirror while exercising, in order to see that you are working in the correct position. Gradually, you will learn to feel when your body is properly aligned, so that eventually you will be able to find the correct position automatically, without the help of the mirror.

But it is no good looking at the symptom – the way you hold your body – without looking at the cause. You did not start off life with a bad posture. Unless you

TYPICAL POSTURAL FAULTS (STANDING)

TYPE A Head poking forwards, chin slightly lifted (squeezing the back of the neck). Shoulders up and rounded. Sway back and tummy sticking out (squeezing lower spine). Knees swayed back or turning in (knocked) or both. Feet turned slightly in and rolling onto inside edge.

TYPE B Head tilted to one side. One shoulder up, one shoulder down, arms folded. Standing with one leg bent, the other straight so that one hip is up and one is down.

TYPE C Chin lifted (military bearing). Shoulders right back and chest pushed forwards. Back arched – bottom stuck out. Knees locked back.

TYPE D Neck curved forwards. Rounded shoulders. Pelvis swayed forward.

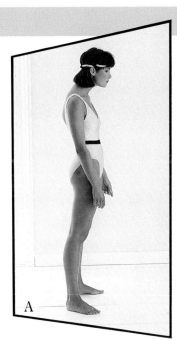

A

B

C

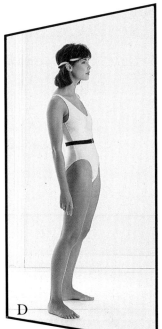

D

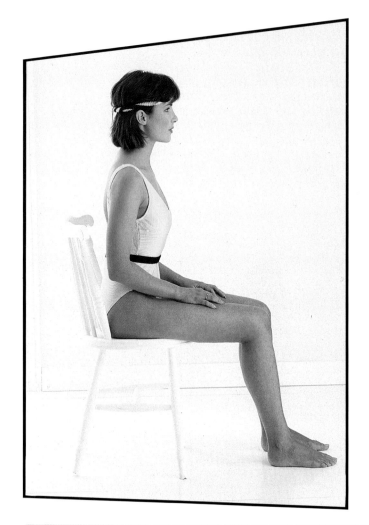

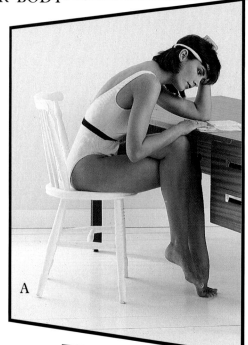

TYPICAL POSTURAL FAULTS (SEATED)

TYPE A Sitting at a desk, hunched forwards, shoulders up, neck stuck out. Feet under chair or legs crossed.

TYPE B Chair too high so legs dangling, toes resting on the floor. Tensed-up body and tight hands.

TYPE C Completely slumped in an armchair or bed, with legs curled up and body squashed.

have had an accident or congenital defect, it is very unlikely that your body will be structurally imbalanced.

MUSCLES AND MOVEMENT

Think of your spine as a tent pole with your head balanced on top. Your arms and legs connect to your spine through your shoulder and pelvic girdles.

This is your basic structure. Movement is made by muscles pulling on joints. Muscles tend to work in pairs, so that the muscles on one side of a joint will shorten and pull while those on the other side of the joint must relax to allow the movement.

If you bend your body over to the right side, the muscles on the right will shorten and pull you to the right while those on the left will relax. The muscles on the left will then 'pull' you back to your neutral upright position, where you will be held in place by a light all-round tension in your muscles.

Good muscle tone means that a muscle must have both the strength to pull and the flexibility to release. In order to hold your spine as upright as a tent pole, the muscles must exert a light balanced hold like guy ropes. If the tension in the muscles becomes imbalanced over a period of time, with one set of muscles constantly held in a tight pull with the opposing muscles slack, your body will be pulled in such a way that it is permanently out of alignment.

This misalignment will in turn put an extra strain and uneven wear on the joints and ligaments that hold them in place. The deterioration will often cause pain and, in extreme cases, loss of mobility. There are many causes for the development of poor posture, from a job which makes you sit or stand awkwardly, to emotional factors.

THE BODY/MIND CONNECTION

Imagine you are told to mime someone who is angry, anxious, very sad or very happy, using your whole body rather than just your face. When you are angry or anxious, you react as if you were under attack. Your shoulders rise, your fists clench and your chin juts forward aggressively.

In a real situation, your body also undergoes chemical changes which prepare you for action. This is often referred to as your 'fight' or 'flight' reaction, which was our ancestors' way of dealing with an attack – either to fight physically or to run away.

In our world, however, it is rarely possible either to flee from the source of our anxiety or to attack it – everything has to be bottled up inside. If nothing is resolved, your body tends to stay primed for fight or flight.

The same applies to sadness and depression. When you are depressed, you will find that you hold yourself in a protective way, body curled inwards,

PURPOSE
To relax shoulders and base of neck. These seem to bear the brunt of tension for most people and can be a constant source of discomfort.

HOW TO DO IT
1 Start by lifting your shoulders up towards your ears.
2 Then relax them down. Repeat this eight times, slowly.

arms folded, legs crossed and tucked under, whereas when you are happy your whole body opens out.

BODY ARMOURING
The way in which you protect yourself against emotional attack is sometimes referred to as body armouring. Sooner or later, we all armour ourselves against emotional attack, but this does not usually last for long and we return quickly to a relaxed state.

For those people who have a low tolerance to stress, or who are under attack through circumstances beyond their control, the physical armouring can become a way of life. If your mental state can cause a muscular reaction, then releasing tens muscles can help release mental strain and help you deal with the cause of your distress.

THE COMPENSATION SYSTEM
When you are standing straight, your shoulders should hang evenly and your hips should be level so that if you drew a line through them they would be parallel. If you stand with one leg bent and the other straight, as in Type B (p 11), your body would have to compensate for the unevenness of your hips to make your shoulders level.

So, if your left hip was up, your right shoulder would have to lift to compensate. This would cause a

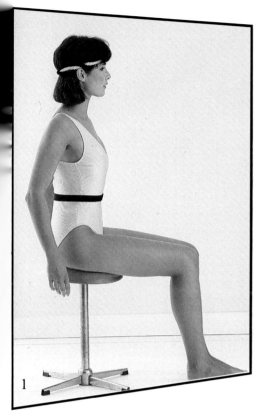

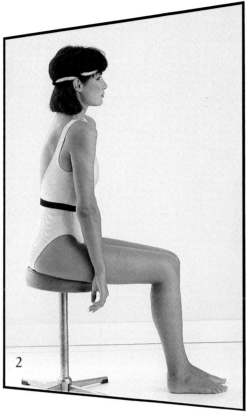

HOW TO DO IT

1, 2 With your shoulders relaxed downwards and centred, move them smoothly forwards and backwards eight times. Come back to the centre.

NECK

PURPOSE

To strengthen your neck and help keep your head upright.

HOW TO DO IT

Place your hands behind your head, elbows relaxed (left). Gently but firmly, press your head back into your hands so that you feel the muscles at the back of your neck tighten as you press back.

Press and release slowly and smoothly eight times, making sure that you do not lift your chin or press your head forwards.

PURPOSE

To release muscles at back of neck.

HOW TO DO IT

Tilt your head forwards until your chin rests on your chest (right). Take a deep breath in and, as you sigh your breath out, try to relax the muscles at the top of your shoulders and up the back of your neck. Hold for 10 to 30 seconds and then bring your head up slowly, lengthening from the base of your neck. Full head circles can increase neck tension and grind your vertebrae together. It is better just to semi-circle your head in the forwards position.

sideways curvature of your spine, and if you consistently stood with the same hip lifted, this curvature could become permanent.

If, when sitting, you always cross the same leg over the other, this can cause one hip to push forwards further than the other. If you always carry your bag on the same shoulder you will find that eventually you have one shoulder higher than the other. If your job entails always working in a certain position, you will find you always tend towards that way of holding your

UPPER BACK EXERCISE

PURPOSE
The muscles of your upper back have a tendency to become weak. Chest muscles can also become too tight so that your shoulders are pulled forwards and your upper back rounds and you tend to slump forwards. Eventually this will inhibit breathing and digestive processes.

HOW TO DO IT
1 To strengthen upper back muscles and open up your chest, take your arms behind you and rest your hands on your lower back, elbows bent, shoulders down.
2 Using your upper arms, squeeze your shoulder blades together and then release. As you pull back your chest will open. Do not straighten your arms nor arch your back as you perform the shoulder squeeze.

body and may develop all kinds of tensions and pains.

To compensate for these you must first become aware of the way in which you hold yourself. The next step is to strengthen the muscles which have become slack and weak, and stretch and release those which have become tight and over-tensed.

STANDING WELL

Imagine you have a string pulled up through your spine from your tail bone to the crown of your head.

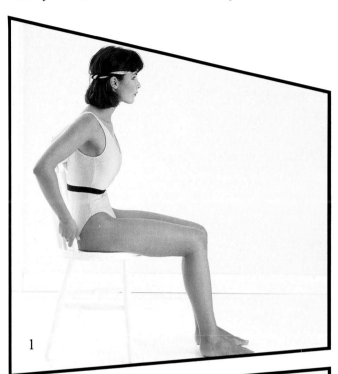

1

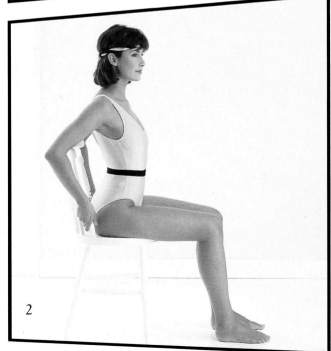

2

LOWER BACK

PURPOSE
To mobilize lower back muscles.

HOW TO DO IT
1 Try gently rocking your pelvis backwards and forwards. Pull in your abdominal muscles so that your hip bones tilt back, without rounding your upper back or slumping. Now lift, back to an upright position.
2 Gently push your hip bones forwards so that your back lightly arches, and come back to the centre.

Repeat, this time breathing in before you start, then breathing out as you tilt back. Breath in as you smoothly roll your hip bones forwards and then breath out as you tilt back again.

Repeat slowly and smoothly eight times.

ABDOMINALS

PURPOSE
To develop the strength of your abdominal muscles.

HOW TO DO IT
1 Start with your hands holding lightly onto the sides of your chair. Tilt your hip bones back and then lift your right knee up to your chest and then lower it.

2 Now, lift your left knee up to your chest and lower it.

Repeat slowly and smoothly four times with each leg, trying to control the speed of the movement all the way through. You should only feel the weight of your leg in your abdominals as you lift it. Your abdominals should not strain nor should you feel anything in your lower back.

1

2

Pull up from the crown of your head and you will immediately feel the back of your neck lengthen, making your chin level in front and stretching your spine.

Relax your shoulders down away from your ears. Do not let them droop forwards. Keep them down and back, but without pushing out your chest in front.

Try to centre your body. Tuck your bottom under so that your tummy is lightly held in. Balance your weight through your heels and the balls of your feet. Keep your knees soft – they should be neither braced back nor bent.

SITTING WELL
When you are sitting, try to keep the same length through your spine as in your standing position. If you have to sit for long periods, it helps if you can sit back in your chair so that your spine is supported, but you should also be able to rest your feet comfortably on the floor.

Try to keep your thighs parallel and do not cross your legs or tuck them under your chair if possible as this restricts your circulation as well as causing an imbalance.

EASY BASICS
Exercising can be simple. Indeed, there are many exercises which can be incorporated into your daily routine which can be done sitting down. These are particularly good if you have a weight or a joint problem, since they allow the spine, hips, knees and ankles to be supported.

Choose a firm, level chair or stool to work on. If your feet do not easily touch the floor, place some large books under your feet to raise the 'floor' level so that your legs are relaxed.

Initially, concentrate on the neck, shoulders and back, as these are the areas most likely to be tense and held in the wrong positions out of habit. The other exercises can follow on.

These few simple exercises can be fitted into your day at any time and will help to keep your body well aligned as well as helping you to develop a good body awareness. In time it will become second nature for you to stand, sit and walk correctly.

By holding yourself well, and strengthening your back and abdominal muscles, every move you make will become a beneficial exercise and you will look and feel in better shape.

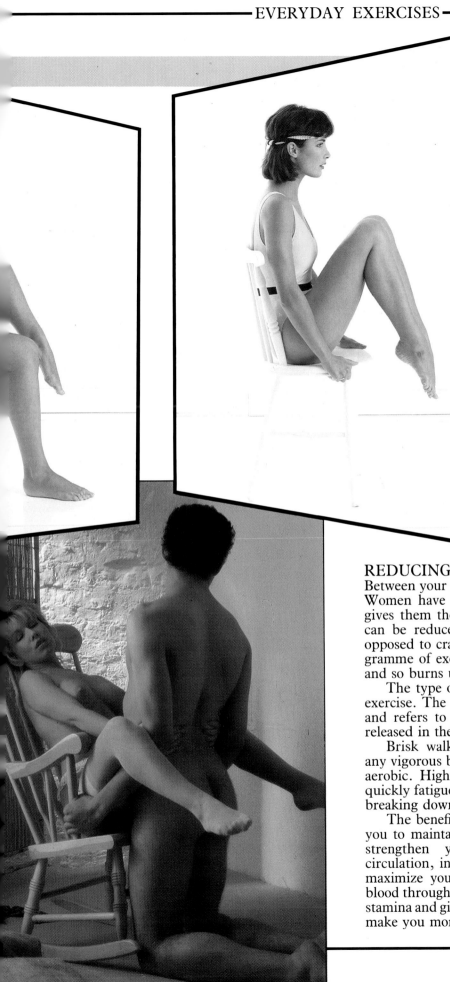

PURPOSE
Also, to strengthen abdominal muscles.

HOW TO DO IT
Once you feel comfortable with the previous exercise, you can add more weight by lifting both legs together in the same way.

Make sure that you hold your tilt and that your abdominals are pulled right in all the time. Try to breathe out as you lift your knees up to your chest and in as you lower them. It helps if you start with an in-breath and then breathe out and lift. If you cannot manage the breathing with the exercise, breath normally but do not hold your breath.

REDUCING FAT
Between your skin and your muscles lies a layer of fat. Women have 9 per cent more fat than men, which gives them their softer, more curvaceous shape. Fat can be reduced by a combination of long-term (as opposed to crash) dieting, in conjunction with a programme of exercise which speeds up the metabolism and so burns up body fat.

The type of exercise best suited to this is aerobic exercise. The word aerobic means, literally, with air, and refers to any form of exercise where energy is released in the presence of oxygen.

Brisk walking, jogging, bicycling, swimming or any vigorous but low intensity exercise will be mainly aerobic. High intensity exercise, where you become quickly fatigued, is called anaerobic and is not good at breaking down fat.

The benefits will be many – the exercise will help you to maintain your correct body weight, tone and strengthen your heart muscle, improve your circulation, increase the efficiency of your lungs and maximize your capacity for distributing oxygenated blood throughout your body. It will also build up your stamina and give you a feeling of well-being. And it will make you more sensual and supple for sex.

EXERCISES FOR BETTER SEX

A gentle warming-up drill will prepare you for some later stretching exercises. Knowing how to relax your thigh and back muscles will make you more supple and your lovemaking more enjoyable

If your thighs and back are stiff, you may well find that lovemaking can be difficult and uncomfortable for you. Your general health may also suffer since your blood vessels run through your muscles and if your muscles are very tight this may push up your blood pressure. It makes sense, therefore, to learn to loosen up your muscles and lose this stiffness.

1 Stretch your left leg out behind you

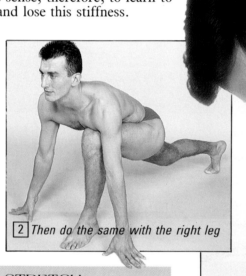

2 Then do the same with the right leg

FRONT OF THIGH STRETCH

PURPOSE
To release any stiffness in the front thigh muscles. Stretch each leg six times, building up to two minutes for each leg.

HOW TO DO IT
1 Place your right leg in front of you, with your knee bent and your foot resting flat with its heel on the floor. Make sure that your knee is directly above your ankle. Push your left leg out directly behind you keeping it as straight as possible, knee facing downwards, so that the ball of your left foot is resting on the floor. Support your body by placing your palms flat on the floor on either side of your bent knee. You should feel the stretch in the front of your left thigh. Allow at least 30 seconds in this position, lengthening your body over your right thigh without letting your right knee move.
2 Change legs and repeat the exercise.

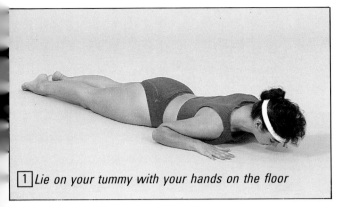

1 Lie on your tummy with your hands on the floor

2 Slowly pull your head and trunk up off the floor

3 Lower slowly to your original position

SUPPLING THE SPINE

PURPOSE
To make the spine more flexible so that it can bend backwards.

Try this three or four times at first, gradually working up to eight times a session.

HOW TO DO IT
1 Lie on your tummy, and place your hands flat on the floor below your shoulders with your elbows tucked in at your sides.
2 As you breathe in, very slowly and carefully pull your head and trunk upwards off the floor, keeping your shoulders down and your hands and hips on the floor. Only go as far as you can without straining, and try to lengthen the spine upwards and forwards.
3 Breathing out, lower slowly to original position. Rest for a few seconds and repeat.

It is not just your sex life that will benefit from learning to relax and tone your muscles; your general health will improve too

OPEN THIGH STRETCH

PURPOSE

To open up the muscles around your hips and groin so that the blood flow to your genital area is increased. This can lead to faster arousal and greater feeling during lovemaking.

Try doing this slowly, and hold for 30 seconds at first, gradually building up to two minutes. Once you have done some slow press downs with your knees, try bouncing them out gently.

HOW TO DO IT

1 Sit on the floor with the soles of your feet together and your back as straight as possible. If your knees come up very high, then sit on a small cushion or folded towel to lift you. This will also help to straighten your back. You can also put your hands behind you for support.
2 Keeping your back straight, gently ease your thighs downwards without forcing them towards the floor. Feel the stretch on the inside of the thigh and into the groin. Hold for 30 seconds, then release.
3 Once your thighs are sufficiently open, you will be able to tilt your body forwards from the hips,

1 *Sit with the soles of your feet together*

2 *Ease your thighs down towards the floor*

3 *Tilt your body forwards from the hips*

4 *Bending forwards increases the stretch*

keeping your back straight. Bending forwards from the hips will help you to increase the stretch on the insides of the thighs still further.

You will find it easier to experiment with a whole variety of lovemaking positions if your back and thigh muscles are flexible and relaxed

WHAT CAUSES STIFFNESS?

Your muscles may be stiff for one of several reasons. Sometimes the cause is hereditary – in a number of people the depth of their joint sockets and the tightness of the ligaments which help to stabilize the joints limit their range of movements to some extent. In some people muscles just tighten up from lack of use, especially if you spend most of your day slumped in a chair or over a desk and you are generally inactive.

Tight muscles may also have an emotional cause. Some therapists believe that for every stiff muscle there is a blocked feeling or emotion. Just think how your body tightens and stiffens when you are angry or frightened, and how the words 'relaxed' and 'happy' go together. If you are constantly under stress, your muscles will be continually tensed and unrelaxed, even though you may not be aware of it. This will eventually result in stiffness and loss of mobility.

Stretching exercises will help to release tight muscles and to counteract stiffness, as well as increasing their flexibility. This will not only extend your range of movements and promote better circulation, but may also help to remove some of your emotional blocks. If, however, you have any joint or back problems, it is advisable to check first with your doctor before attempting any of the exercises.

INNER THIGH STRETCH

PURPOSE

To loosen the inner thigh muscles so that you can move your legs apart easily and comfortably during lovemaking.

When you have mastered the exercise you can gradually increase the length of time you hold the stretch from half a minute to two minutes.

HOW TO DO IT

1 Sit up straight with your legs as far apart as is comfortable. Make sure that your knees are facing upwards, not rolling inwards. Straighten your back as much as you can, putting your hands behind you for support. Getting your back straight and your pelvis centred will depend on how tight your lower back muscles are. When your back is in the correct position you will feel your two sitting bones. Relax your feet.

2 Sling a scarf around each heel, holding the ends in your hands.

3 Tilt forwards from the hips, keeping your back straight. Hold for at least 30 seconds.

1 Sit up straight with your legs apart

2 Hold ends of scarves put round each heel

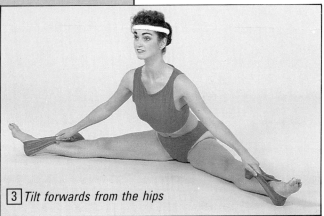

3 Tilt forwards from the hips

KEEPING WARM

When stretching, always make sure that you are really warmed up. Either do some gentle jogging or have a warm bath before doing the exercises. Wear warm clothing which is also loose and unrestricting. Never try to force a muscle to stretch. You are trying to relax your muscles so that they will release to their full length.

Try to hold your stretches for at least 30 seconds so that the muscles have time to release. Breathe normally through your nose while stretching. Do not hold your breath. Stretching can feel uncomfortable at first, but you should not experience pain. Releasing tight muscles takes time, and must be done slowly and gently to be effective.

LITTLE AND OFTEN

All exercise is best done frequently and in small amounts. Instead of making a big thing of putting aside time for your stretching exercises, try to incorporate the ones you can do on your own into your daily life. The thigh exercises, for example, can easily be done while watching television, and the standing stretches when taking a hot shower.

THIGH EXERCISES TO DO WITH YOUR PARTNER

These thigh exercises which are designed for you to do with your partner serve basically the same purpose as those you can do on your own – they will loosen up your thighs and hips so that sex can become more varied and enjoyable. But they are more fun – and more effective – because you are using extra weight to stretch the muscles.

All these partner exercises should be done very gently. Apply pressure slowly, and never try to force a movement. Try to relax into the stretches, and stop immediately if you feel any pain.

INNER THIGH STRETCH

HOW TO DO IT

Once you are both able to sit up straight in this position, you can practise gently pulling each other forwards, and holding each stretch for 30 seconds.
1 Sit opposite your partner, each with your legs spread as wide apart as is comfortable. Place your feet together – or, if one of you is less flexible, he or she can rest the soles of the feet on the inside of the partner's legs. Hold each other's hands or wrists and gently try to draw yourselves up straight.

2 As you become looser you should slowly draw your partner towards you in the stretch position so that he or she increases the stretch by moving the body forwards from the hips.
3 Then your partner can gently draw you forwards to increase your stretch from the hips. Alternate the pulls, keeping your back straight.

1 Sit opposite your partner with your legs apart

2 Slowly draw your partner towards you

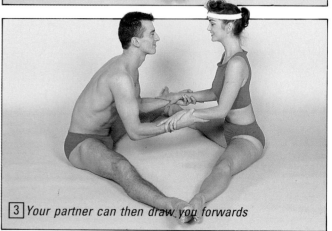
3 Your partner can then draw you forwards

HAMSTRING STRETCH

Gradually increase the stretch time for each stage of the exercise from 30 seconds to two minutes for each leg.

HOW TO DO IT

1 Lie on your back with your left leg straight and the right knee bent level with your chest

2 Your partner should hold your left leg firmly at the knee to keep it down, and to prevent it from turning outwards. The other hand should be placed on the knee of the right leg, and the leg gently pressed towards your chest. Hold for 30 seconds, then release. Change legs and repeat.

3 Then try raising the right leg as far as it will comfortably go, keeping your thigh as close to your chest as posible. Bend your knee so that your right foot is pointing upwards. Keeping one hand on the knee of your straight leg, your partner should, with the other hand, hold the ankle of your raised leg, and push the leg gently away from him until you feel the stretch without distorting your body. Hold for 30 seconds, then release. Change legs and repeat.

4 Now you can try straightening and raising your right leg, keeping your thigh close to your chest. Using one hand to anchor the right leg, your partner should use the other hand to hold your raised leg just above the ankle, and very gently push the leg away from him. Try to hold this position for 30 seconds, then change legs and repeat.

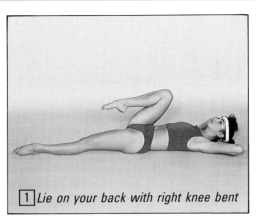

1 Lie on your back with right knee bent

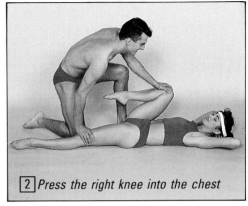

2 Press the right knee into the chest

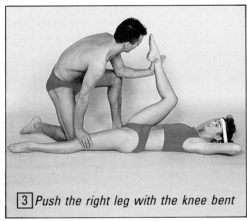

3 Push the right leg with the knee bent

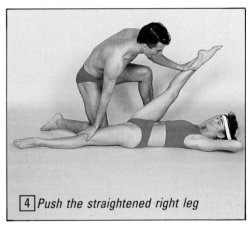

4 Push the straightened right leg

1

2

STRONGER AND SEXIER

Using music and movement you can create better body balance by strengthening thigh, back and tummy muscles. This will help to make you healthier, shapelier and sexier

Keeping your muscles well toned will not only contribute to greater physical pleasure during lovemaking, but will also help to improve your appearance. Strengthening exercises will develop your muscles and make you more shapely, but not if there is a thick layer of fat obscuring the underlying structure.

FIRST FIGHT FLAB

If you are overweight, you need to deal with this problem first while starting your muscle-strengthening exercises. Carrying too much weight can put an enormous strain on your heart and blood circulation. The best way of losing weight is to combine a sensible eating programme with some form of vigorous aerobic exercise, such as brisk walking, swimming or cycling two, three or four times a week about 20 minutes on alternate days. This will also make you feel more relaxed and self-confident, give you more energy, and help to eliminate stress which tends to diminish your sex drive.

If you are overweight you should avoid jarring ex-

CUSHION SQUEEZE

PURPOSE
To tone up the abductor muscles on the insides of the thighs.

Start by repeating the exercise eight times slowly, and then eight times quickly. As your muscles strengthen repeat the sequence.

HOW TO DO IT
1 Lie on your back with your knees bent up and your feet flat on the floor. Place a firm cushion between your inner thighs, and squeeze them firmly together.
2 Then release your thighs and the cushion.

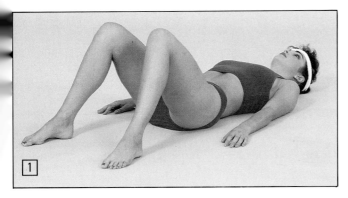

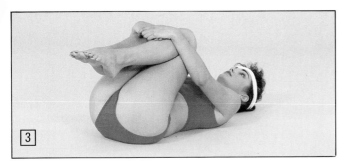

ercises such as jogging, running and other activities which are likely to put too much strain on your weight-bearing joints.

BEING SELECTIVE

Although you should try to work on all the muscles in your body, those which you will use most when making love are in the thighs, abdomen, buttocks and in the lower part of your back.

Strengthening exercises work the muscles against resistance which can be body weight and/or gravity. It is important that you follow the correct technique for each exercise very carefully to make sure that you exercise each muscle exactly in the way described. If, for example, you exercise a bulging tummy muscle by adding weight to it, then the muscle will bulge still more. If, however, you pull in the muscle when you add the weight, it will develop in this way.

BALANCED OUTLINE

Watch also how you place your thighs so that you do not overdevelop one set of muscles and leave another set weak. This could alter the whole shape of your legs and the way you hold your body. The thigh exercises on pp 20–24 are designed to balance the muscles in the front and the back, and in the inside and the outside of the thighs.

BUTTOCKS LIFT AND SQUEEZE

PURPOSE

To strengthen the gluteal muscles in the buttocks and the hamstrings at the backs of the thighs. Squeeze and release as many times as you comfortably can, but so that you really feel the muscles working. This will increase as your muscles grow stronger.

HOW TO DO IT

1 Lie on your back with your knees bent, legs parallel, and feet flat on the floor. Tilt your pelvis back so that your tummy is pulled in and your lower back is lengthened and touching the floor. Keep your arms by your sides.
2 Lift your buttocks a few inches off the floor and squeeze them strongly together, pushing upwards from underneath. Then release. Do not push up too far. Your lower back should not arch up at any time. Repeat several times, making some of the movements slow and some faster.
3 Bend your knees into your chest to release the back muscles when you finish this exercise.

THE CURL

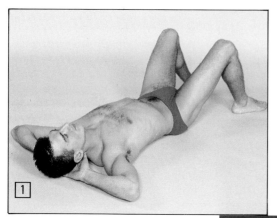

PURPOSE
To strengthen the tummy muscles. Do the forwards curl eight times, then two curls in each direction.

HOW TO DO IT
1 Lie on your back with knees bent and feet flat on the floor. Pull your tummy muscles in tightly and tilt your pelvis back.
2 Lift your head from the floor and curl your head and shoulders up slowly, keeping the back of your neck lengthened and your shoulders down. Slowly curl your body back down to the floor again.
3 Then try curling up to the right and to the left. After the exercise, bend your knees into your chest to release the muscles.

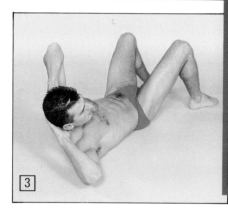

THE CURL

PURPOSE
To strengthen the tummy muscles.

HOW TO DO IT
This is done in the same way as the curl exercise you can do on your own, but getting your partner to hold your feet down.

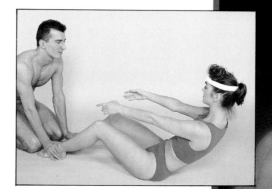

LEG LOWERING

PURPOSE

To strengthen the tummy muscles.

Start off with 24 leg changes, and gradually build up to 64.

HOW TO DO IT

1 Lie on your back with your arms by your sides and your knees bent in towards your chest. If your lower back or tummy muscles are weak, place a small cushion under your pelvis to keep it tilted back.
2 Keeping one leg bent towards your chest, straighten the other and extend it in the air. Your straightened leg will act as a weight for your tummy muscles to work against.
3 Now change legs in a bicycling movement. While each leg is straight up in the air it provides little resistance to your tummy muscles.
4 Add more resistance as the muscles strengthen, by straightening your leg out at a lower angle. Breathe normally throughout the exercise, and remember to hold in your tummy muscles all the time. When your tummy muscles get tired, bend your knees into your chest, clasp your hands round them and pull them in towards you to release your back and leg muscles.

When you stretch a tight muscle to loosen it, it is important to go gently at first and hold the stretch for several seconds. When you strengthen a muscle, however, it is better to do this by making a movement rather than by holding a contraction which may leave the muscle in spasm and restrict your circulation, pushing up your blood pressure.

If you have any trouble at all with your muscles or joints, consult your GP before attempting to do any of these exercises.

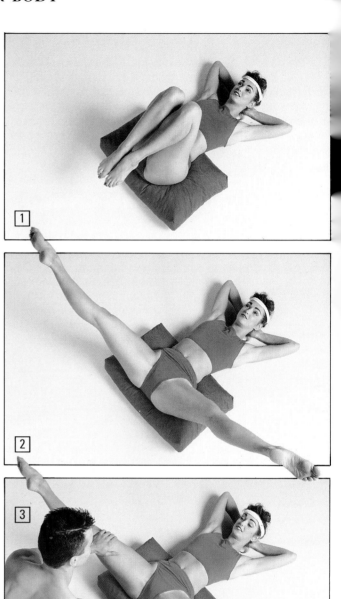

LEGS APART IN THE AIR

PURPOSE

This also tones up the muscles on the insides of the thighs.

Try doing this exercise two or four times.

HOW TO DO IT

1 Lie on your back with your knees bent up towards your chest. Place a small cushion under your pelvis to help maintain a pelvic tilt.

2 Straighten your legs up into the air, then turn them outwards from the hip sockets and allow them to open as far as they can without forcing.

3 Your partner should

BACKWARDS HINGE

PURPOSE
To strengthen the quadriceps muscles at the front of the thighs. It is also good for weak knees.

Do the backwards hinge two to four times each to begin with, eventually working up to eight times.

HOW TO DO IT
1 Both you and your partner kneel on an oblong cushion facing each other, and clasping each other's hands or wrists. Pull in your tummy muscles tightly so that your buttocks are well tucked under (as for the pelvic tilt, p 32).

2 Lean backwards from the knees keeping your back and thighs in a straight line until you feel the front of your thighs taking your weight. Your partner stays in the upright position to help hold you. Do not go too far back at first, and keep the movement slow and smooth.

3 Come up slowly as your partner leans backwards in the same way. To release the muscles follow this with a front thigh stretch.

place his or her hands on the insides of your knees to provide resistance as you try to bring your legs together. Your partner should not try to force your legs apart, but add just enough resistance to make bringing them together exercise your inner thigh muscles. Bend your knees up towards your chest when you have finished the exercise, and follow this with the inner thigh stretch before working on your partner in the same way.

THE PELVIS

The pelvis is the focal area for sexual activity, yet it is one of the most neglected parts of the body. Learning how to keep the pelvis in good shape not only helps you stand, sit and feel better, but can also improve your lovemaking

The pelvis is the powerhouse of sexual activity. Its bone structure, the pelvic girdle, encases and protects the sex organs – when the muscles which control it are fit and flexible, it allows for greater variety of movement and positions in lovemaking. And the muscular 'pelvic floor' plays a major part in the sensations of sex.

PELVIS ALIGNMENT

If the pelvis is positioned correctly, there is an equal pull between the abdominal muscles which extend from the breast bone to the pubic bone at the front of the pelvic girdle, and the muscles which run down either side of the spine.

When the abdominal muscles are weak, the rib cage moves down towards the pelvis, causing the tummy to protrude, and forcing the back to take the extra strain. The back muscles tighten in an attempt to support or

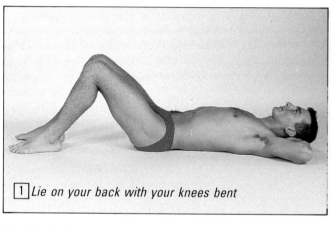
1 Lie on your back with your knees bent

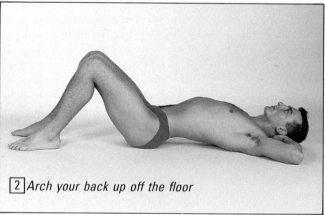
2 Arch your back up off the floor

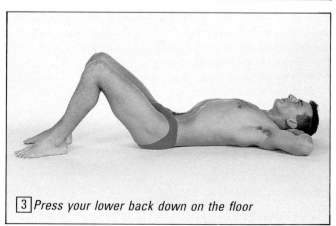
3 Press your lower back down on the floor

THE PELVIC TILT

PURPOSE

To release tightness in the pelvic area and to strengthen abdominal muscles. This will increase the suppleness of the pelvis and lower back, and allow for greater mobility and flexibility.

Start by doing six or eight of these exercises a day. Once you have mastered the pelvic tilt backwards and forwards, you can move on to the pelvic clock exercise.

HOW TO DO IT

1 Lie on your back on the floor with your knees bent, thighs parallel, and feet flat on the floor.
2 Breathe in deeply as you gently try to arch your back up off the floor. Your back muscles are shortening, and your tummy muscles are releasing and lengthening.
3 Now breathe out as you pull in your tummy muscles so that your lower back presses down on the floor. As the tummy muscles shorten they pull the pubic bone up towards you, so that your tummy scoops into a hollow. Go back to 2 and repeat.

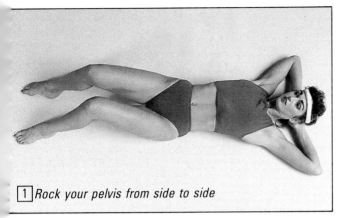

1 Rock your pelvis from side to side

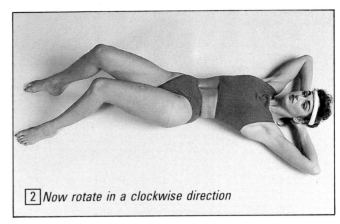

2 Now rotate in a clockwise direction

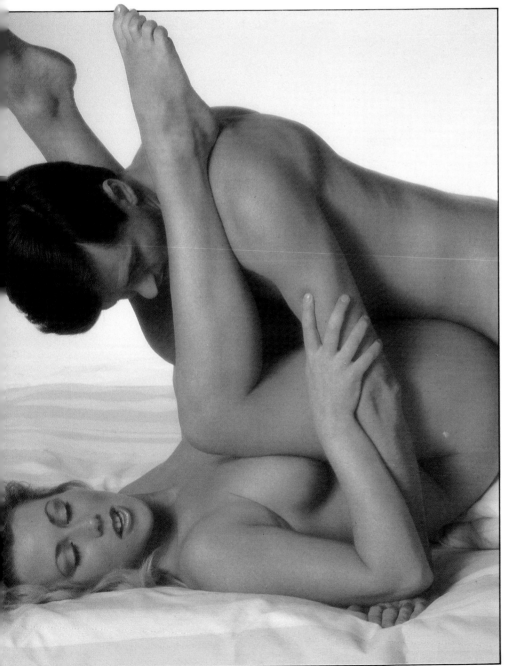

THE PELVIC CLOCK

PURPOSE
To develop a full range of movement in the pelvic area so that you have a wider choice of lovemaking positions without encountering stiffness or pain. Make sure the movements are very slow and precise, and do the exercise twice in each direction every day.

HOW TO DO IT
1 Lie on the floor in the same position as for the pelvic tilt, then slowly roll your pelvis from side to side, keeping your legs still.
2 Now imagine that there is a clock drawn across the back of your pelvis. Start at 12 o'clock and slowly rotate your pelvis round through one and two o'clock to three o'clock on the right side of the pelvis. Then go on to four, five and six o'clock. Continue on with seven, eight and nine o'clock on the left side of the pelvis, and then back to 12 o'clock via 10 and 11.

KNEES TO CHEST

PURPOSE
To release the lower back muscles and the hamstrings, making them stronger and more flexible.

Repeat this exercise four times a day, making sure that your breathing is slow and deep.

HOW TO DO IT
1 Lie on your back on the floor with your legs together straight out in front of you, feet relaxed.
2 Bend your knees towards your chest, clasping your hands round them.
3 As you breathe out, squeeze your knees into your chest without moving your bottom up from the floor. Then release the pressure, breathing in as you do so.

'splint' the spine, which not only puts pressure on the spine itself, but also pulls the pelvis out of alignment.

Many people have such tight back muscles and slack tummy muscles that their ability to move their pelvic area is severely restricted.

THE PELVIC FLOOR
The pelvic floor is a group of thin, sheet-like muscles slung like a hammock across the base of the girdle. It forms a continuous layer – except where there are openings for the urethra and the anus – and, in women, the vagina.

Rings of muscles, known as sphincters, are arranged around these openings in a figure-of-eight loop

1 Lie on your back with your legs straight

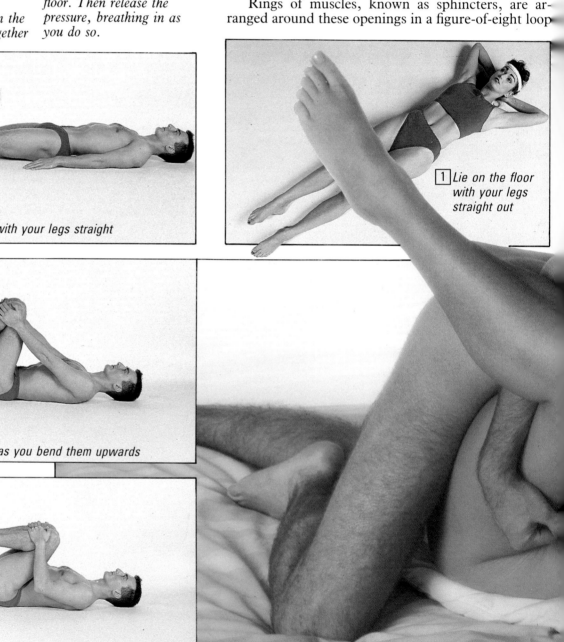

1 Lie on the floor with your legs straight out

2 Clasp your knees as you bend them upwards

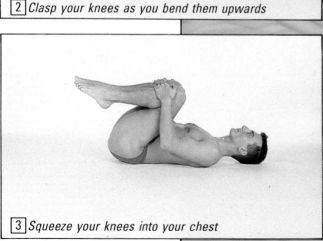

3 Squeeze your knees into your chest

- the front loop passing around the urethra (and vagina in women), the stronger back loop passing around the anus. The sphincter muscles are integrated with the rest of the pelvic floor muscles, so the whole muscular area works as one unit.

PELVIC EXERCISES

Since the pelvic floor cannot be seen, it is necessary to identify it before you start exercising, so that you can be sure that you are actually working on the pelvic floor muscles – not those of the tummy or the buttocks.

The various muscles work as if they were a single unit, so if you identify one particular element you will have found the whole floor. The easiest part to focus on is the loop of muscles around the urethra.

FINDING THE LOOP

You can find this front loop in your pelvic floor when you are passing water. To do this, you start to urinate, then squeeze your muscles tightly to try and stop the flow. When you squeeze the front loop, all the pelvic floor muscles will be pulled in too. This will help you to recognize the sensation of the pelvic floor muscles being pulled in and up. And it will give you some idea of how strong they are – depending on whether you manage to stop the flow, or only to decrease it. When the pelvic floor muscles are healthy, a woman's vaginal muscles tighten and relax more effectively during sex, which can enhance the pleasure of both partners; and in men, good pelvic muscle tone makes it easier to achieve and maintain an erection.

2 Stretch your right leg down as far as possible

3 Then do the same with your left leg

HIP LIFT

PURPOSE

To loosen the lower back and to exercise the waist muscles giving them greater strength and mobility.

Do six right and six left hip lifts to begin with, gradually increasing the total daily number to ten on each side.

HOW TO DO IT

1 Lie on your back on the floor with your legs together straight out in front of you.
2 Stretch your right leg down as far as you can so that your left hip tilts in towards you.
3 Then stretch out your left leg so that your right hip tilts up. Continue the movements slowly and rhythmically.

PELVIC FLOOR PULL-UPS

PURPOSE

To strengthen the pelvic floor muscles. This will increase sexual pleasure by toning up a woman's vaginal muscles and helping a man to maintain his erection longer.

Practise this little and often at first as under-used muscles will tire easily. Give yourself a rest between every two or three squeezes and build up to ten. Always end with a contraction to return the muscles to their supportive resting state.

Once you get used to this exercise, try to do 50 pelvic floor pull-ups a day – you can do a few at a time while standing in the bus queue or sitting at your desk, for example. Your contractions may be weak or fleeting at first, but with practice they will become stronger and last for longer.

It is a good idea to combine this exercise with the pelvic tilt so that you get the feeling of everything pulling in.

HOW TO DO IT

1 Lie on your back with your legs slightly apart, knees bent and feet flat on the floor. Put your right hand on your pubic bone to help you to concentrate on your internal muscles.
2 Breathe out as you draw up your pelvic floor muscles. Contract them until you feel the inside passages tighten up. Hold for two or three seconds then release, slowly breathing in as you do so. You can do several quick contractions then rest, but always end up with a contraction.

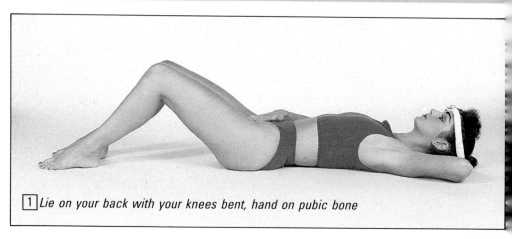

1 Lie on your back with your knees bent, hand on pubic bone

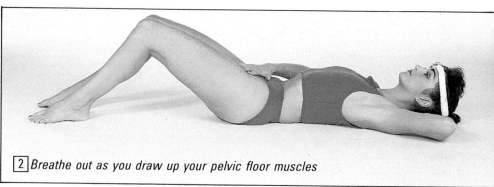

2 Breathe out as you draw up your pelvic floor muscles

THE LIFT (WOMEN ONLY)

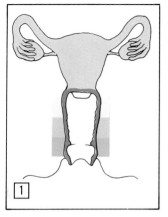

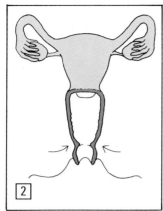

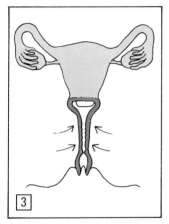

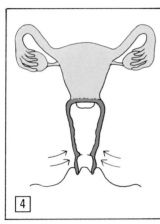

TOWEL POWER (MEN ONLY)

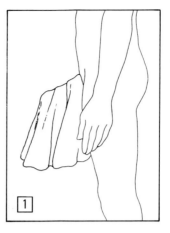

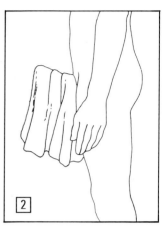

PURPOSE

To tone up the pelvic floor muscles to achieve stronger erections. Try this exercise two or three times at first, increasing the number to ten times.

HOW TO DO IT

1 Hang a light towel or scarf over your erect penis.
2 Lower and raise the penis by releasing and contracting your pelvic floor muscles.

PURPOSE

To increase control over the vaginal muscles so that during intercourse the vagina maintains firm contact with the penis.

This is difficult to do at first, and will need a certain amount of practice. Begin with two sets of contractions and do them three times a day, gradually working up to five sets of contractions three times a day.

HOW TO DO IT

1 This exercise can be done in any position, but it is easier to try it lying down at first, once you have got the hang of it you can do the exercise sitting up.
2 Imagine that there is a lift going up your vagina from the opening to the top. Tighten your muscles as if it were going up from the ground floor, through the middle part of the vaginal canal and then smoothly on to the top.
3 Try to hold a contraction at this level for three seconds, then lower the lift slowly and smoothly back to the 'ground floor' position. Do not worry if you cannot hold the contraction at first; this will come with practice.
4 Always finish by pulling back up to the middle level to complete the exercise with a toning action.

RELAXATION

Learn to combat the effects of stress with your partner by using pleasant and simple relaxation techniques

Tension and stress, in the right places, are essential parts of life. Active sex, obviously, involves plenty of muscular tension and heart-thumping. The aim of relaxation is not a lifestyle free of the thrills and excitements that can make you tense. Nor will your ideal be to loosen each of your 620 muscles until you are a quaking jelly on the floor. Stress, indeed, is not the real enemy – it is the wrong reaction to stress that does the damage.

HOW THE BODY REACTS TO STRESS

You know how swiftly and powerfully your heart reacts to a sudden threat like a missed foothold or car backfiring, but did you also know that your pupils dilate to see the danger more clearly and that your neck and shoulder muscles hunch to ward off a blow? Your breathing speeds up in case you have to run for it and sweat erupts from your pores to keep your skin cool in the 'battle' to come.

Meanwhile your liver releases energy in the form of sugar to nourish your muscles. And powerful hormones – adrenalin and noradrenalin – flood into the bloodstream to regulate the whole programme. Other key systems close down for the duration – digestion is not a priority in a battle situation so, while the emergency lasts, your digestive system switches off. Signals go to the sphincter muscles that control the bladder and bowels and order them to shut (in cases of extreme alarm those signals are overpowered and switch the sphincters open, with the well-known results).

For those whose lifestyle is one long series of strain and stress, the signs of living with a body permanently on alert are painfully obvious.

SIGNS OF TENSION

Stressed people are the ones with permanent worry lines and the hunched shoulders of anxiety. Fists unconsciously clenched, they fight against life's tide and a host of minor ailments. Obviously, with a digestive system switched to limbo, they have digestive disorders. Rashes and minor infections are rife, since the counter-infection agents of the body's defences are not properly on duty.

DEALING WITH STRESS

Physically, relaxing is not easy. You know perfectly well, for example, that when someone says 'just relax, this is not going to hurt', it is probably time to start

Getting your partner to help you relax completely at the end of a tough day can be a blissful and rewarding experience

running. More seriously, you actually do not have direct knowledge of what your muscles are up to.

Although not widely known, this fact is crucial to understanding your 'struggle' to relax. In many relaxation classes, you will be told 'relax that muscle'. In one notable scientific experiment, members of a relaxation class were asked if they felt this or that muscle was relaxed or not. Mostly, they claimed that muscles were relaxed when the instruments showed they were not.

TENSING AND RELAXING

Most experts now agree that the key to teaching yourself to relax is to work on each muscle group in turn. *Increase* its state of stress, then 'let go' and let yourself feel the difference. It is a pleasant and rewarding routine to enjoy and share with your partner, and may well end with a relaxing bath together – and bed. It may seem odd that successful relaxation should begin by increasing your muscle tension – but the principle is easy to grasp.

Try this test. Say to yourself: 'Relax your shoulders'. What happens? Not much. You are simply giving a command that your body does not really know how to respond to. Now try hunching your shoulders up towards your neck. Push up hard for around eight seconds. Then simply 'let go'. What happens? You will feel your shoulders drop further down than they were originally. Do not move. Savour the feeling of their new position and enjoy the sense of relaxation it brings.

RELAXATION PROGRAMME

To begin a relaxation programme there is no need to seek out a specially quiet situation or unusual equipment. The aim is to live a more relaxed life in the real world. Many ante-natal relaxation classes have been held in noisy clinics. And, once you have mastered the routines involved, you can even conduct your own relaxation session at the office.

At home, find enough space to swing a cat in, loosen your clothing, and choose an easy chair with arm rests or lie on your back on the floor.

WORKING ON THE MUSCLE GROUPS

What you are going to do is talk yourself through each important muscle group. If your partner is available to help, get them to give you the sequence and commands. Their task is not to encourage or monitor your performance, however. They should stick simply to the key words involved, talking quietly.

The sequence of muscle groups often recommended is *arms, legs, breathing, head, face*. Once learned, never vary it. You need a routine that allows you to concentrate entirely on the information your body gives to your brain.

Although your muscles are not wired up to inform your brain if they are relaxed or not, your joints and your skin are linked to the brain by millions of nerve impulses. In a relaxation routine, it is the joints that get the orders. You are going to instruct your joints to move in ways that bring a key muscle group into ten-

ARE YOU TENSE?

Checking your neck tension is a good way to find out how tense you really are. Lie on your back and get your partner to stand with one foot on either side of your body. Ask them to lift your head and shoulders by pulling your arms up. If you are fully relaxed, your neck will be able to stretch easily until your head almost touches the floor. But if you are tense, you will find that your head does not roll back easily.

sion. You are going to concentrate on how that state of tension feels. Then you are going to stop the movement that has led to tension. And finally you are going to feel what sensations your new relaxed state reveals.

Again, you and your partner should memorize a simple routine of commands, and never vary it. One leading expert in relaxation techniques recommends keeping to the formula *move and feel, stop, feel.*

ARMS AND LEGS

Thus, the arm exercise that begins the sequence means tensing your muscles, by stretching your fingers out as far as they go, while pressing your elbows into the chair or floor. Hold that position about eight seconds. Feel for what your joints and fingertips are telling you about the sensation of tension. Then stop – let go. The muscles relax. Your arms and hands take up a new position. Feel what this one is like – and take some 15 seconds to do so, for this is the relaxed position you want your body to learn.

SHOULDER TEST

Hunch your shoulders as far up towards your neck as possible 1. Hold this position for eight seconds. Then let them drop 2. Without moving, savour the new feeling of relaxation this simple exercise brings

Go through a similar sequence for the legs, by pushing your feet into the floor while curling your toes downward. Then let go.

RELAX YOUR BREATHING
Next is breathing. Breathe through your nose and not deeply – the aim is to feel what is happening in that area between your waist and your lower ribs at the front. Feel this area expanding and lifting the ribs upwards and out. Stop by letting your breath out, and feel the ribs fall.

Then push your whole body against its support points on the chair, or if you are lying down let your body press into the floor. Stop by letting every muscle go, and feel your body supported in a subtly new way – this is a routine of great value to those who go to bed tense and lie rigid as boards, unable to sleep.

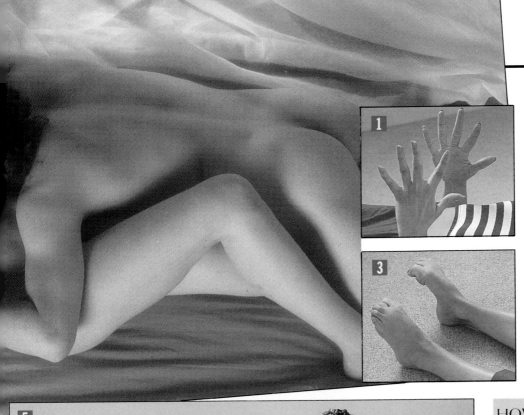

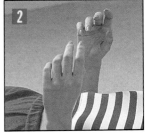

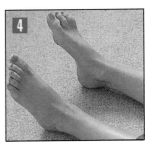

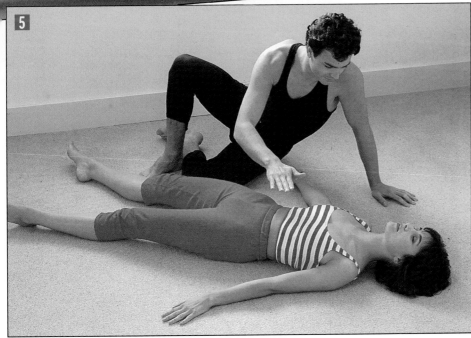

HOW TO RELAX

Choose a sequence of muscle groups to work through, for example, arms, legs, breathing, head, face – and never vary it. Then ask your partner to go through the commands: move and feel, stop, feel. If starting with the arms, stretch your fingers as far as possible 1, and press your elbows into the ground. Count to eight. Then let go. Feel the new relaxed position of the arms and hands 2. Do the same for the legs, by curling your toes tightly and pushing your feet into the floor 3. Then let go and savour the feeling 4. Press your whole body into the ground 5. Then relax every muscle and enjoy the restful feeling

HEAD AND FACE

The head is one of the most difficult parts to relax, since in every waking position the neck muscles are at work. The trick here is to press the head against the support – the back of the chair or the pillow beneath you on the floor. Then stop pushing and feel the support taking the weight for you.

Finally, for the face, squint your eyes, clench your jaws, and grimace. Stop and feel your jaw drop, your lips heavy and your face relaxed.

It all sounds simple and it is. The sensations involved are complex. Once you have relaxed each muscle group in turn you will end in a state of pleasurable and peaceful ease. Savour the experience. Watch your partner after a relaxation session and take note of the way their limbs lie, how restful they are.

Of course, the routine can be adapted or used in part when conditions require. In office, aeroplane, or a car in a jam, concentrate on that part of the body that is taking the most strain.

YOGA

The basic principle, learning by tension followed by letting go, is not a new one. Many exercises known to yoga demonstrate that. Yoga (the word means union or communion) is an Indian science that offers many skilful paths to relaxation. Indeed, Air India once produced a booklet especially designed to help business passengers relax after international flights.

One effective exercise is to raise both hands above

RELAXING YOUR FACE

Most of us are not aware when our faces are tense. Try this simple experiment. Tense all of your facial muscles – squint your eyes, clench your jaws, pull your mouth wide open and grimace for eight seconds. Let go and feel the relaxed heaviness in your jaw, cheeks and lips

USING YOGA

Raise both hands above your head and crook your left thumb into your right, hanging your body from your right thumb 1. Feel your body weight being supported by your arm. Bend double at the waist, your upper body hanging and supported by your legs and thighs 2

your head – crook your right thumb into your left and 'hang' your body from your left thumb. Feel the weight of your body against the strength of your arm supporting it. Then 'let go' and reverse your thumbs.

Another simple technique is to let yourself bend double at the waist. Hang the weight of your upper body from the pillar of strength in your legs and thighs.

Yoga is an ideal path to relaxation that partners can share together. Classes conducted by experts feature in many evening class programmes worldwide. But it can be as enjoyable to learn yoga by taking turns between each partner acting as instructor, checking the student's position and performance in an exercise sequence against illustrated cards or an instruction manual.

Relaxation should come easily to us, once the right mental attitude to the subject is achieved. Yet, old routines die hard and people seem reluctant to abandon their old familiar habits that cause stress and tension. Some of the world's largest and most far-sighted firms are now devoting time and money to efforts that, hopefully, will persuade valuable workers to relax more and live longer.

Take a glance at the tense faces and hunched shoulders in the next rush hour to work. Decide, right now, to set time aside to keep your mind and body intact. With very little effort, you can relieve much of the stress of everyday life.

MASSAGE

Massage is an art. But if you are sensitive to what relaxes and gives pleasure, you can work miracles on someone who is feeling tired and tense

Massage is easy – and deeply satisfying – to learn and practise. Between friends and lovers it is an ideal therapy for relaxation and communication. Because massage puts us back in touch with ourselves and each other, one of its first benefits can be a powerful release of emotions. You may well, in an early experience of giving or receiving massage, feel a strong urge to weep. Let it happen. You are being led back to the first and most important language of infancy – the language of touch.

Many, especially in the West, are starved of 'touch' experience. And, say some psychologists, a poor opinion of oneself often comes from the frustration of that primitive need to be touched.

PRACTICAL BENEFITS
Massage brings immediately practical benefits too. As you pass your hands skilfully over someone else's skin, you are doing wonders for the largest of the body organs.

The skin, the organ of touch, responds to all the injuries that modern life throws our way. A dull skin can be the measure of inner and environmental stress bombarded by chemicals and bacteria in the atmosphere or poorly nourished by a sluggish circulation. Stimulated by massage, the skin comes alive and acquires a beautiful, healthy glow.

If you use some of the essential oils available as agents in massage, you may help to regenerate the skin cells, relieve aching muscles and aid the healing of wounds and bruised tissues.

The technique of using massage to heat and technically irritate the skin can relieve pain in tissues below skin level. The scientific explanation of 'rubbing it better' is that rubbing sends signals through the nerves' 'gateways' of communication to the brain faster than the pain signals coming along the same route.

Since the gateways (known as synapses) must open and shut to let messages through, the 'rubbing' messages serve to shut the door on the pain messages following behind.

BASIC TECHNIQUES

With a basic repertoire of strokes, you can alternate to give a relaxing and soothing massage.

Effleurage (1) Always begin and end your massage with this stroke. It is a light soothing movement. Stroke up both sides of the spine, then out across the shoulders, down the sides and the back to your original position.

Petrissage (2) Kneel at one side of your partner and grasp a handful of flesh, next to the spine. Squeeze it between your fingers and thumb and allow the flesh to slide into your palm. As you let go, pick up another handful close to it with your other hand. Repeat the grasping and releasing movements.

Circular frictions (3) This movement is used for specific areas of tension, such as either side of the spine. Use your thumbs, making small but deep penetrating circles.

Tapotement (4) This is a quick, light tapping movement made with the fingertips, or alternatively with lightly clenched fists.

Hacking (5) This is a chopping motion made with the edge of the hands to tone up the muscles.

Cupping (6) Similar in speed to hacking, this is a light, rhythmic movement using alternate hands. Cup your hands, keeping fingers together and thumbs tucked in, so that they make a hollow sound.

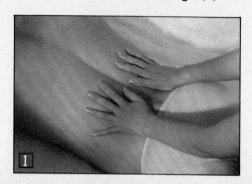

SURFACE MUSCLES

Below skin level – waiting to be reached by your massaging hands – are the muscles and joints that become tense under the short- and long-term stresses of daily life. Both the giving and receiving of massage can reveal these knots of tension to the conscious mind.

Gentle massage can help large muscle groups relax – and define specific knots of tissue that your hands, rightly applied, can sense and work on until the tension dissolves.

DEEP MASSAGE

Deep in the body's structure are the bones and ligaments that 'deep massage' reaches.

Techniques of deep massage include some – such as Rolfing – that require expert training. Rolfing involves powerful pressure that literally restructures deep body tissues.

You and your partner, however, need not go to such lengths. Although no one should attempt to 'cure' a chronic health problem by friendly massage (some back conditions can be worsened by over-enthusiastic amateur masseurs), you will find that many human ills will respond to the power of touch.

SETTING THE SCENE

In practical terms, begin by setting the scene for a massage and make your own personal journey together from there.

☐ A bed makes the least satisfactory site for a massage. It is too low and too soft – pressure will simply push your partner's body into the mattress. A table as high as the top of your thighs is the best choice – and the floor is the best alternative

☐ Massage is best experienced in the nude. So ensure that the room is warm

☐ If you are using oil, have it in a container that – when it inevitably does get knocked over – will not spill to excess. And have the oil ready to hand during a session

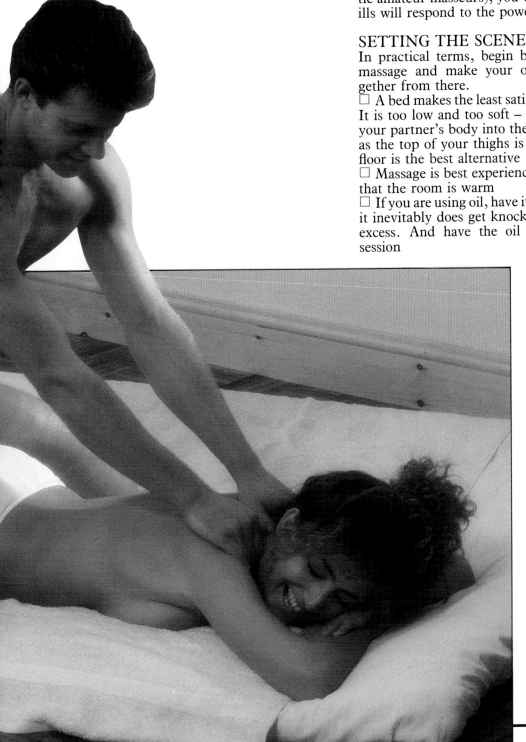

OILS

Vegetable-based oils are best for massage – and many 'essential' herbal oils have highly claimed benefits. 'Baby oil' – which is mineral based – is less suitable because it soaks into the skin swiftly.

Dilute 'esential oils' unless they are packed specially for direct use. Pregnant women, especially, should avoid undiluted oils.

Sweet Almond Oil Contains vitamins E & F
Apricot Oil contains vitamin A
Lavender Oil eases pain
Sandalwood moisturizes dry skin
Peppermint Oil is an aid to painful joints
Geranium Oil reduces swellings

☐ Once a massage session has started, you should aim to keep in body contact throughout – rest a forearm on your partner's body, for example, while replenishing the oil

☐ Do not pour oil directly onto your partner's skin as this is startling. Instead, pour a small amount into your palm and rub your hands to warm it. You are now ready to begin

☐ The back is the best starting point – both to learn massage and to receive it. The back tends to be the first place for the day's tensions and stresses to gather – and it is a large enough area for the beginner to approach with confidence. But do not attempt massage on anyone with acute back pain or a recent injury without taking medical advice as you could end up doing a lot more harm than good.

SIMPLE STROKES

With your partner lying face down, spread the oil over their back in gentle, long strokes from the base of the spine to the shoulders. Carry on these movements into the real strokes of massage.

You can choose to stand at your partner's head if he or she is lying on a table, or you can work from the base of the spine up. On the floor, you can even straddle your partner's thighs while massaging. Choose whichever way suits you best.

Whatever the starting position, aim to move your hands up the back to the shoulders, then return to the base of the spine by moving your hands down your partner's sides.

THE BEAR WALK

The 'bear walk' is so called because, tradition tells, bears were once trained to stroll up and down on stiff-backed East Europeans who were in search of relief. Your bear walk technique will be to apply pressure with the heel of your palm against your partner's back, while they lie face down, arms above the head, either on a table or on the floor.

Lean down with your body weight, taking care that your hand is positioned just to the far side of the spine. Put your other hand alongside and bring pressure to bear behind it while 'walking' the first hand down to the next step down. Repeat on the other side of the spine.

DO IT YOURSELF

If a partner is absent and you feel you need to relax, why not give yourself an expert massage work-out.

☐ **Hot foot** Sit. Rest one foot on the other thigh. Work over the tired foot with fingers and thumb, squeezing and pulling (1) to 'pop' the muscles.

☐ **Pain in the neck** Hang your head low. Find the base of your skull with your fingertips. Press and knead six times slowly (2).

☐ **Heart ache** Lie down. Press and knead your rib cage with your fingertips ten times slowly (3).

☐ **Belly ache** Circular motion by one hand is both instinctive and effective.

☐ **Sleepy head** When slumber threatens but you need to stay awake, try using an 'acupressure' remedy. Rubbing your right earlobe is a technique that has worked for many.

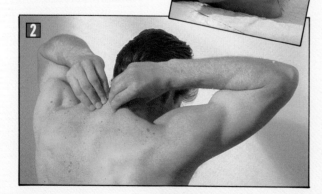

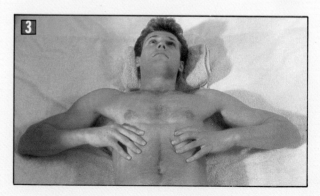

THE HEAD

It can make good sense to start learning massage with a part of the body none of us has any 'hang ups' about – the head.

Work out for yourself the most natural sequence of massage. It may be that you might begin kneeling behind your partner (who should be lying and not sitting, to reduce 'drag').

Rest your palms on their forehead (1). Imagine that some kind of power and understanding is passing between you. Do nothing for several moments. Then begin the sequence.

There is no right or wrong way. Rest your fingertips, for example, on your partner's temples. Squeeze slightly, and rotate them (2). Squeeze and knead the eyebrows two or three times. Apply gentle but firm pressure at two single points where the eyebrows are thickest (3) – a few seconds will suffice. Pressure, rather than movement, is the key to this part of the facial structure.

Move your fingers, a fraction of an inch at a time, around the bony eye socket and press gently as you pause.

Explore the other parts of the face following the same principles. Pressure the knot of the muscle at the hinge of the jaw. Press behind the ears and explore gently inside the ears. Lift and rotate the cheeks (4). Finally, massage the scalp, encouraging the skin to move as freely as possible over the bone.

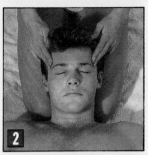

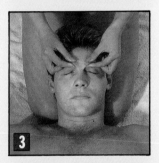

HAND MOVEMENTS

Your movements will be circular and rhythmic. Concentrate on feeling the contours of your partner's body beneath your hands. Imagine that your hands are moulded to the body beneath you. The skill that you need to develop is to be able to apply pressure with relaxed hands.

It goes against the body's normal habits to relax a part of the body while actually using it, and most of us have chronic tension in our hands as well. It will help you to get your hands working properly if you develop the understanding that massage is performed with the whole body, not the hands alone.

Lean the weight of your upper body on to your hands when you need to apply pressure – it is far less tiring and keeps you from tensing the muscles in your arms and wrists.

EXPLORING THE BODY

Close your eyes and feel the structure of the body you are touching. Let your fingertips, for example, trace the channel on each side of the spine. Discover the way the shoulders are put together. Experience the differences in body texture from the softness of the buttocks to the firmness of the lower back.

Exploring a body in this way is far more important than learning individual massage strokes in a 'textbook' fashion. Massage, essentially, is a part of a living relationship with a living body.

You will gain confidence as your partner tells you what degrees of pressure are most effective (you will find that the body can enjoy more pressure than you first imagined). Your hands will begin to tell you what is right too. Massage is like sex – as long as you both enjoy it, you're doing it right.

47

THE GENTLE APPROACH

It will come to you instinctively to adjust your approach to the more delicate parts of the body. Use your thumb to run lightly up and down the 'valleys' between the tendons to each toe. Probe gently for the little hollow immediately above where the cleft of the buttocks begins.

You will probably quite naturally discover the technique known as 'raking' when working on the backs of your partner's legs. Forming your hands into claws, pull them down the limbs, pressuring with your fingertips.

When giving a whole body massage, work steadily over all the body rather than concentrating on the parts that are particular focuses of tension. Do not 'jump about' from place to place, and do keep all movements fluid and confident.

It is possible to give a whole body massage in as little time as ten minutes, but far better to allow half an hour to build and sustain a mood.

MAKE YOURSELF COMFORTABLE

Your own comfort matters just as much as your partner's and you should pace yourself not to become overtired. Floor massage is more tiring than table massage. Always ensure that your floor covering gives you, the masseur, adequate space for your knees. Your partner will sense the stress in you if you are in discomfort.

Your aim is to achieve total relaxation for your partner – so allow yourself to finish the session well. A few feather-light strokes from top to toe make one nice ending – you can vary the 'rake' technique by actually using your fingernails to lightly stimulate the skin.

Where the object of massage is to ease and relax tension, it makes sense for the recipient to lie quietly

THE SHOULDER RUB

There are many individual massage techniques for all parts of the body. Simplest and among the most effective is the shoulder rub, a welcome soother at the end of a stressful day. There is no need to remove clothing or use oil. Simply loosen a tight collar and sit in an upright chair.

The partner giving the massage stands behind the chair and rests both hands on the other's shoulders. Pause a moment to establish the

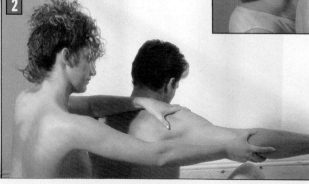

feeling of contact and calm. Then gently squeeze the shoulder muscles. Imagine you are loosening and spreading the tension there, outwards and away from the neck (1).

Next, while keeping

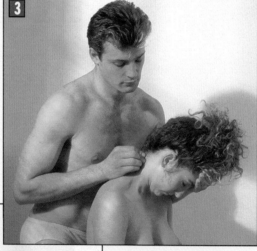

one hand on your partner's shoulder, raise that arm by the forearm and gently move the arm in a circle, starting forwards and then upwards (2). Be gentle and make the circle only as large as is comfortable. What you

are doing is loosening the shoulder joints and stretching taut tendons.

With both hands back on the shoulders again, let your thumbs explore for small knots of muscle tension. With circular movements, rub the tension out. This technique of circular friction is a valuable one for any specific area of muscle tension, as it eases away the knots.

The thumbs can probe for tension in the hollow behind the shoulder blade. Simple pressure helps to relieve stress there. Then apply pressure with both hands leaning down on your partner's shoulders before paying attention to their neck.

Finally, cradle or support your partner's forehead with one hand to encourage the neck muscles to relax (3). With your other hand, squeeze those muscles at the back of the neck in a finger and thumb grip, moving up the neck from the shoulders.

or a few minutes to enjoy the sensation once the session is over. Cover your partner with a sheet or blanket, as oiled skin feels the cold.

BETWEEN LOVERS
A good massage has psychological as well as physical benefits. Between lovers it can be a very creative way to renew the discovery of each other's bodies by approaching each other in a new physical context. For example, in the context of massage rather than foreplay, a man can cup his partner's breasts and rotate them very gently.

The experience of massage is highly sensual, but although it can happily lead to explicitly sexual activity there are real benefits of enjoying the virtues of massage in its own right. Give a massage to friends, as well as lovers.

Think about the benefits of a massage by two friends at the same time, working in harmony. Think, too, of the experience of massage in total darkness without words.

MASSAGE IN PREGNANCY
Although the abdomen, in pregnancy, needs the lightest touch, massage can help to prevent stretch marks, give relief to skin and muscles under strain – and help a father-to-be experience the magic of being in touch with two people at once.

One favoured technique is to use one hand to make continuing circular movements above the abdomen while the other makes semicircular movements around it. It is surprisingly difficult to do (practise on a flat surface) but pleasant to receive.

Equally satisfying are stroking movements from the abdomen towards the groin. Such light-as-a-feather techniques can be used until delivery itself.

SEXUAL HYGIENE

Cosmetic companies suggest that personal freshness depends on deodorants and scented sprays – but are there simple ways to be clean and sexy?

Following the success of deodorants and anti-perspirants in eliminating underarm odour, there was an effort to launch similar products to stop any odour in the vaginal area. Genital deodorants were never really successful in Britain, but their existence did stimulate debate about the nature of 'personal' odour, whether it is offensive, and whether there is any need to get rid of it or cover it up in the first place.

SEX SECRETIONS

As well as the endocrine glands which excrete the odourless liquid we call sweat, both men and women have apocrine or scent glands in certain parts of the body, which excrete a more milky fluid with a distinctive, but not unpleasant smell. The secretions play an important role in sexual attraction.

Women have considerably more of these glands than do men. In women, the apocrine glands are mainly situated around the nipples and umbilicus (navel), under the arms and in the genital area (on the labia minora). The actual odour of the secretions from these glands varies from woman to woman.

The secretions around the vagina are perfectly normal and healthy, and do not need to be eliminated by any special preparation. Indeed, because of the sensitivity of the tissues around the vaginal area, deodorants can cause irritation, generally doing more harm than good, and are best avoided in this delicate area.

DAILY ROUTINE

As long as your general hygiene includes proper washing of the genital area (the vaginal area for the woman and the penis for the man) there is no reason why unpleasant odours should build up at all. In addition, both men and women should change their underwear daily if they really want to be fresh and good to be near.

The usual cause of an unpleasant odour of the genital area, where there is no infection present to account for it, is the trapping of moisture from both the endocrine and apocrine glands, and the action of bacteria upon these secretions.

Overweight women may have more of a problem

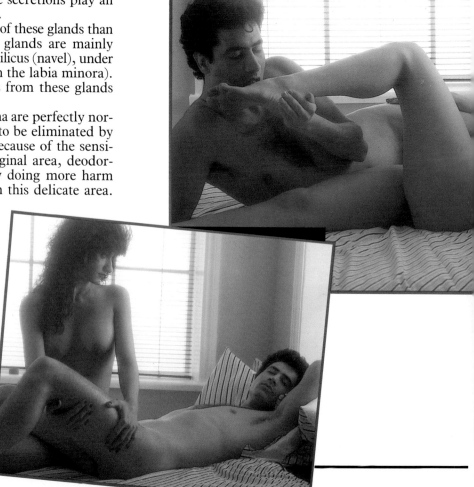

A clean body with its own unique scent is just as sexy as artificial perfume or cologne

because moisture becomes trapped among skin folds, and the wearing of tight, particularly nylon, clothing may also be a contributory factor.

The most effective way of reducing the risk of odour is a simple soap and water routine. This will wash away secretions and also cut down on the bacteria present on the skin.

It is important for women to wash carefully between the folds of the vulva to make sure the area is properly cleaned, either using some sort of washing cloth or simply with the fingers – well soaped.

SMEGMA

Particular care should be taken with the area between the inner and outer lips and around the clitoris. It is here that smegma (cellular debris) may have built up and this is a rather unpleasant 'cheesy' material.

In the same way, men may find a build-up of smegma around the penis. It is essential that the penis is washed thoroughly and carefully. Uncircumcised men should pull back the foreskin and wash away any secretions and bacteria lurking there.

Build-up of smegma is not only unpleasant, it can lead to inflammation if not washed away. However washing is done, it is a routine that should be carried out at least once a day. This applies to all men and women, whether they have sex regularly or not.

Always ensure that you are fresh and clean from head to toe before making love: a bath or shower together can be part of your foreplay

GOOD CLEAN SEX

It is a good idea for both of you to wash your genital area before and after intercourse. Men tend to be less fastidious in this, and may need a little encouragement. It is also advisable to pass urine after intercourse. Passing urine cuts down the growth of bacteria and may help to avoid the problems of cystitis in women and urethritis in men.

If you or your partner have any inflammation, sores, or any discharge in the genital area, refrain from intercourse and seek medical advice.

ORAL SEX

There has long been a widely held notion among the more puritanical, that oral-genital sex is dirty. It probably arises from the fact that such people actually think of the genitals as 'dirty' and so cannot accept the idea of mouth contact with them.

But there is no reason at all why the genitals should not be scrupulously clean – and you should make sure they are before you embark on this form of lovemaking. In terms of transmitting infections, oral-genital sex is no more hazardous than penis-in-vagina intercourse.

Some infections, such as gonorrhoea, can be transmitted from the genitals to the mouth or throat. Others such as trichomoniasis cannot.

Herpes can be transmitted from the mouth to the genitals and vice versa. So if either you or your partner have cold sores around the mouth, do not have oral sex until these have cleared up and disappeared. Likewise, if either of you suffers from inflammation, sores or discharge around the genital area you should also refrain from sex – including oral sex – and seek medical advice.

Some types of streptococcus are common in the mouth and throat, but not in the vagina. And a recurrent vaginal discharge can be caused by germs in your partner's mouth and throat.

DIAGNOSING DISCHARGES

While normal healthy secretions from the vagina are odourless, and only cause odour when bacteria work

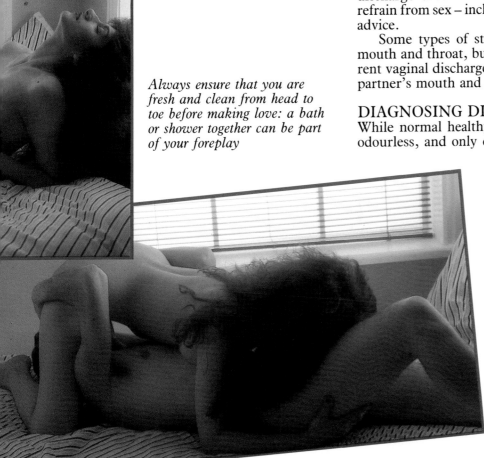

It is a mistaken belief that oral-genital contact is dirty. In fact, oral sex is just as clean as conventional intercourse, provided both partners are scrupulous about hygiene

on them, sudden discharges caused by infection are often characterized by a strong smell.

They are usually yellow or pink in colour, rather than white or clear – and they do need treatment. Women who develop a vaginal discharge should go to their doctor or special clinic for advice and diagnosis. Treatment is usually quick and straightforward.

If a woman suffers from a rather heavy vaginal discharge at certain times of her menstrual cycle, and she is free from infection, she may well feel more comfortable using some sort of disposable liner inside her pants, at the heaviest time.

CYSTITIS

Cystitis, which is inflammation of the bladder, can be caused by bacteria which normally live in and around the bowel opening. When they are carried to the urethra and bladder, they multiply and cause an inflammation of the lining of the bladder.

Cystitis is far more common in women than in men, partly because the anus, vagina and urethra are close together and partly because the urethra is much shorter in women, allowing germs easier access to the bladder.

Cystitis is often linked to beginning an active sex life. Because of this, it is sometimes referred to as 'honeymoon' cystitis. In such cases, the problem is often caused by lack of vaginal lubrication – using KY jelly or saliva, if necessary, should help.

The best precaution is for a woman to wash well before and after intercourse, and get her partner to do the same. It may also help to pass urine before and after intercourse. In rare cases the cause of cystitis has been found to have originated from bacteria living beneath the foreskins of uncircumcised men.

Another source of transfer of germs occurs when a woman wipes herself after going to the toilet. Always wipe your bottom from front to back, so that germs are not passed from anus to urethra.

If a woman is prone to attacks of cystitis, she should not use antiseptics, talcum powder, perfumed soap or deodorants in the area around the vagina. It is also advisable to avoid shampoo or oils in the bath if they are found to be irritants.

Any tight clothing can contribute, particularly synthetic fibres – so nylon pants should be avoided. Cotton pants and stockings rather than tights are ideal.

HYGIENE DURING MENSTRUATION

Periods differ greatly between women both in terms of how long they last and how much blood is lost. Some women are lucky enough to have only three days of bleeding while others may suffer blood loss for as many as eight days.

The menstrual fluid consists of blood, degenerated cells from the lining of the womb, and mucus from the glands of the cervical canal.

The fluid is entirely odourless when it is inside the uterus, but once it starts to flow down the vagina, bacteria begin to act on the blood content, and it is this which produces the characteristic menstrual odour

In order to prevent any odour becoming offensive it is important to wash or bathe frequently during a period and to make sure that tampons or sanitary towels are changed frequently.

Towels and tampons should be changed at least three to four times a day, and probably more often during the first few days of the period when the flow is

heaviest. Always make sure your hands are clean when inserting tampons, particularly those with no applicator.

TOXIC SHOCK SYNDROME
Frequent changing of tampons not only cuts down the risk of odour or infection, but also avoids the risk of toxic shock syndrome (TSS). A few years ago TSS, a potentially serious condition, was found to be linked with tampon use in the United States. As a result certain types were considered dangerous, and natural fibres preferred to the synthetic super-absorbent types.

The TSS infection is caused by *Staphylococcus aureus* and although it can occur in both men and women from various causes, it is most commonly linked with tampon use during menstruation.

As long as tampons are changed frequently, possibly using sanitary towels at night, and a low absorbency factor tampon is used, TSS is highly unlikely. Many women like to use a higher absorbency tampon at the start of their period and change to a less absorbent one after a day or so. A higher absorbency tampon should not be used as an alternative to frequent changing.

In the very rare event of your experiencing high fever, vomiting, diarrhoea, muscle pain or a skin rash, remove the tampon and contact your doctor immediately.

CONTRACEPTION AND PERIODS
Different methods of contraception can affect the amount of blood loss in a cycle. A woman taking the combined Pill will usually experience a lighter bleed each month, which eliminates the problems associated with heavy periods. Mini-pills (progestogen-only Pills) act differently from combined Pills, and women who take them may find they have break-through bleeding between their periods and may sometimes experience irregular periods.

Women who are fitted with an IUD (coil) tend to have heavier periods and sometimes intermittent bleeding, particularly when it has been recently fitted.

CAPS AND DIAPHRAGMS
The cap and diaphragm do not alter periods in any way, but do necessitate a slightly altered bathing routine. Bathing should be done before inserting the cap with spermicide applied to it. And to make sure that the spermicide is not flushed away, you should not have a bath until six hours after intercourse. This routine usually works well at night – a bath can be taken in the morning after the cap is removed. But it may not be so convenient if a couple want to have sex at other times of the day.

The cap itself should be properly looked after, and washed in warm water after each use. It should be dried thoroughly and kept in a cool, dry place. Caps should never be boiled or have disinfectants, detergents, talcum powder or lubricants applied to them.

Some women use a cap to make intercourse more pleasant when they are having a period. It is perfectly all right to do this, whether or not she is a regular cap user.

If the cap is being used as contraception as well as convenience (you can become pregnant from intercourse during a period), it should be left in place for six hours, then removed and a sanitary towel or tampon inserted. If the cap is being used merely to prevent a mess, it can be removed straight after sex.

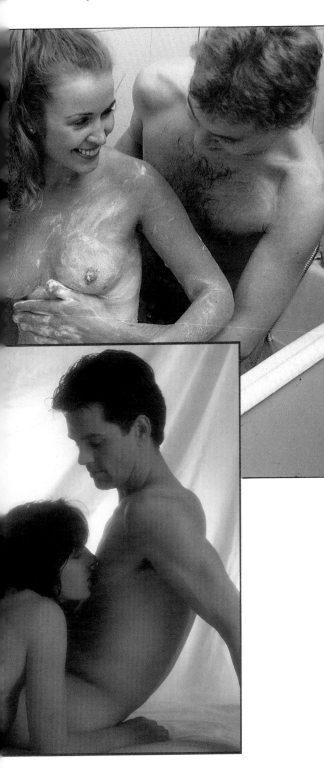

EXERCISES IN SEX

Anybody can enjoy making love – but the more supple and fit your body, the more sensual and varied can be your lovemaking. There are many ways in which you can ensure that conditions are ideal to make the best of your sex life – and for the imaginative and adventurous couple the horizons of sexual technique become virtually limitless

A ROOM FOR LOVING

The vast majority of lovemaking still happens in bedrooms, although many people make love in other places from time to time. Most couples give little thought to what their bedrooms are like for making love in, and then wonder why it is that so many things seem to conspire against them to reduce their sexual pleasure

With a little imagination, every aspect of a bedroom can make it altogether more conducive to sex.

In many – if not most – homes, the choice of which bedroom to occupy is fairly limited. Parents usually take the largest one, unless they have several children and need to put two or more of them in the same room. It makes sense to choose the largest bedroom you can spare for yourselves as this gives you a lot more scope when it comes to sex.

If you have a choice – and many young married couples do, because they have not yet started a family, or perhaps have a baby in one room and a spare room or two – try to organize it so that your bedroom has an empty room (or store room) next to it to act as a sound barrier.

Few people want lovemaking to be overheard. Whether it is the sweet nothings you talk, the giggles or the orgasmic cries, most couples prefer privacy, especially from children and other adults in the house.

SOUNDPROOFING
Heavy carpeting and good quality, thick curtains both help absorb sound, but it might be desirable to put sound-insulating board on the walls that adjoin other people's bedrooms.

If you think that all your personal sexual pursuits are being monitored by, or intruding on, the occupants of the adjoining room, it is not a good setting for good sex. Ask a builder to advise you if you have very thin walls that let all the sound through, or see if you can cover them with soundproofing boards on a DIY basis – it is not difficult.

Remember that a lot of sound travels up through the ceiling across to other rooms. A way round this is to insulate your ceiling.

ENSUITE BATHROOM OR SHOWER
If possible, it is both pleasant and practical to have some form of bathroom or shower as part of your bedroom set-up. Even a washbasin in the room is a good start.

An ensuite bathroom is ideal because you can use it for lovemaking in its own right, go to the toilet easily without waking other members of the household, wash easily after sex (especially if you make love while having a period), and can wash with a face flannel or use a bidet to freshen up before sex.

A large mirror in your bedroom is probably one of the best investments you can make for a novel and varied sex life

your bedroom. Instead of using a central light, try replacing it with lamps either on the walls or the floor, or by the bed. This kind of indirect lighting is much softer, and can be used to give a romantic effect.

If you cannot afford to do this, put a dimmer on your central ceiling light so that you can have a gentle glow or full light, according to your needs at the time. With good lighting and thick, light-tight curtains, you will be able to control the light level in your bedroom all year round.

DECOR

This will obviously be a matter of personal taste. Keep the colours muted and restful, but otherwise be guided by your personal feelings about colours. Warm colours are probably more conducive to feeling sexy.

HEATING

In a mainly cold country such as Britain, to be ready for sex it is essential to be able to heat up your bedroom quickly.

Ideally, central heating is best for background warmth, but you will need another sort of heater to warm up the room quickly so that it is comfortable to be naked in. Electric heaters are best, but make sure not to buy one with a fan. The droning and buzzing of the fan can be a turn-off for some. A powerful convector or radiant heater is best for instant heat.

Cure any obviously draughty windows with draught excluders, or with simple double glazing if necessary.

If you have a shower or bathroom ensuite, bathing or showering together can more easily become part and parcel of a lovemaking session. Also you need never wear night clothes or dressing gowns.

It is a good idea to have your ensuite bathroom completely separate from your bedroom – for example, with a door that can be closed – as many people say that they like to prepare for sex privately rather than in front of their partner.

Many individuals are put off by seeing or hearing their partner on the lavatory and some women are sensitive about being seen to shave their legs or bikini line. If the bathroom can be made completely private for such occasions it is certainly helpful.

LIGHTING

Few people enjoy lovemaking in a very bright artificial light, so it is worthwhile being able to dim the lights in

FURNITURE AND FURNISHINGS

When it comes to lovemaking, chairs can be a real help. It is useful to have a simple, armless chair, because the man can sit on it and the woman can easily face him, legs apart, and sit on his penis. The permutations are endless and you can fill many winter evenings with experimentation.

A low couch, bench, or chaise longue all take up much more space, but offer delights a bed does not. With a bench, the man can kneel in front of the woman who lies back, legs wide apart, for intercourse. Or she can kneel up on it and he can enter her from behind. Some women like their man to lie flat on such a low stool or chaise longue so that they can kneel comfortably in between his legs and fellate him.

Apart from a bed and some sort of chair or stool, it is probably best to keep the floor uncluttered to leave the maximum amount of room for lovemaking and moving about.

THE BED
This is the central piece of furniture in a couple's bedroom. Generally, most beds are poor, both for sleeping and for lovemaking. Here are some useful guidelines.

SINGLE OR DOUBLE
Without a doubt the best bed for lovemaking is a double bed – and preferably as large a one as you can afford, taking the size of your bedroom into consideration. Some couples prefer to sleep alone because they have very different tastes in mattresses, temperature and so on. Some individuals spread themselves all over a bed and are highly disruptive to sleep with. For such people (and their partners) single beds may well be the only answer.

However, from a sexual point of view a double bed is undoubtedly best. It gives more room for manoeuvre during intercourse, enables more adventurous positions to be taken up and means that after sex the couple can cuddle up and go to sleep in each other's arms.

HOW BIG?
Ideally a bed should be at least 15 cm (6 in) longer than the tallest occupant. This will mean that even when he or she is fully stretched out, their feet will not hang over the end. Have as wide a bed as you have space for.

MATTRESSES
Always choose a firm mattress and go for the best you can afford. They all become more saggy with age, so err on the side of buying too firm a mattress in the sure knowledge that within a year or so it will be a lot softer. The average life of a good quality mattress is about 10 years.

For lovemaking, the firmer the mattress the better – within reason. A saggy mattress means that the woman's pelvis sinks low into the bed and the angle of penetration of the man's penis is very different from that which occurs on the floor or a good mattress.

If you have a saggy mattress, putting a pillow under the woman's bottom can help overcome this problem to some extent, but it will still do both of your backs no good when you are sleeping.

An armless chair is a useful prop in lovemaking – the woman can crouch on the seat using the back for support and her partner is at a perfect height for rear entry

Lounging on a chaise longue, the woman can relax while her partner kneels at her feet, comfortably positioned, and kisses or caresses her vulval area with his tongue

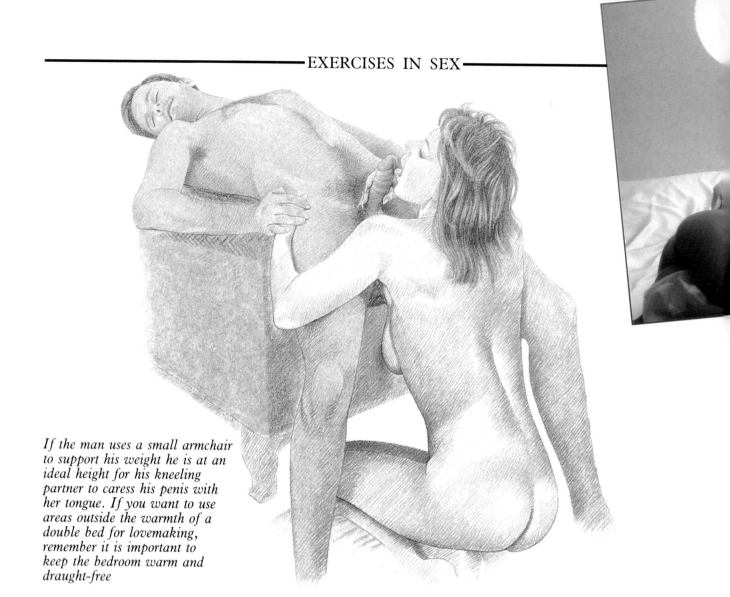

If the man uses a small armchair to support his weight he is at an ideal height for his kneeling partner to caress his penis with her tongue. If you want to use areas outside the warmth of a double bed for lovemaking, remember it is important to keep the bedroom warm and draught-free

SHEETS
There is little doubt that silk or satin sheets are the most sensual and sexy. They are, however, highly impractical for most people as they are expensive to buy and to keep clean. Pure linen sheets feel very comfortable but may need professional laundering, especially if they are big. They also need ironing, and look rather unkempt if they are simply tumble dried. Most people settle for poly-cotton sheets which, while not the nicest material to feel, are highly functional.

DUVETS OR SHEETS?
Sheets and blankets have their advantages as some people like the sensation of being 'tucked up tight', but duvets are far more practical when it comes to both sleeping and lovemaking. A duvet can easily be turned back or completely removed and placed on a chair so as to leave the entire bed clear for sex. Similarly, once lovemaking is over it can be easily replaced.

PRIVATE CUPBOARD
Most couples have contraceptives, erotic books or magazines, sex aids or sexy underwear that they would rather keep private. It therefore makes sense to have a cupboard or drawer with a lock in your bedroom, so

that you can keep prying fingers and eyes out of your personal belongings.

As children grow older, they become somewhat fascinated by their parents' sex life and many explore their parents' bedroom looking for signs of sexual activity. There are several ways to deal with this, but having a lockable, private place certainly helps overcome many of these problems.

FURNISHINGS
If you can possibly afford it, carpet your bedroom wall-to-wall. The advantages are:
☐ It is warmer in winter
☐ It deadens sound
☐ It makes the room cosier
☐ It is soft to lie on if you like making love on the floor

CURTAINS
Have the best-quality material you can afford. If they are made of heavy material they will absorb sound and keep out the light when you want to darken the room on summer evenings. They will also keep out the early morning sun in the summer and allow you to sleep in if you want to. Few people thrive, sexually or otherwise, on waking with the birds at 4.30 am.

Avoid harsh lighting in the bedroom – coloured bulbs will create a warm atmosphere for lovemaking. Also add a touch of sensuous luxury by using satin sheets – these have the added advantage of allowing you to move more freely and uninhibitedly across the bed

PICTURES
Think about having some sensual or erotic pictures or prints on your walls. Erotic pictures help set the scene for sex and are more likely to give lasting pleasure than pornographic pictures or pin-ups. Do not, however, confine yourself just to erotic pictures. How about other beautiful scenes that give you pleasure?

FANTASY AND MIRRORS
Perhaps a vivid scene that you enjoy fantasizing about would help turn you on and put you in the mood. No one else will realize that it is fantasy material for you

should they come into your room for any reason.

Some couples greatly enjoy having mirrors in which to watch themselves when making love. These can be on dressing tables, on the wardrobe doors, on the wall – or even the ceiling – depending on the size and shape of the room. If you opt for mirrors on your wardrobe, by opening the door to the exact position you can have greater control over what can and cannot be seen.

BOOKS AND MAGAZINES
The most readily available erotic material comes in the form of books and magazines. If you feel your sex

life could be improved by reading erotic literature, find out by trial and error what you both enjoy best and then always be sure to have suitable material at hand in your private cupboard or drawer.

Do not forget that what turns one of you on may well have little or no appeal to the other. As with so many sexual matters, it is give-and-take all the time.

Be vigilant to the needs of your partner for sexually

explicit turn-ons – even if they do nothing for you. Seeing them aroused is almost certain to affect you and you can, if you are sufficiently open, learn a lot about their desires from their fantasy material.

Sensible partners build such material into their sexual repertoire to arouse each other better and more quickly in the future.

For a woman-on-top position (above), an armless chair is an ideal support. The man sits, while the woman gently lowers herself on to his erect penis

If you can watch television in the privacy of your own bedroom, add a touch of excitement by hiring an erotic video. Not only will this increase your level of sexual excitement, it may also give you and your partner some new ideas to add to your sexual repertoire or allow you to talk more freely about what you might like your partner to do to turn you on

VIDEO, TV AND MUSIC

Once the lights are dimmed and the room is warm, many couples enjoy the added relaxation of music, television or a video. This need not be sexy or erotic, but it may help if it is. Making love while listening to a favourite piece of music can be bliss, and many couples enjoy the turn-on of a sexy film or video on TV before lovemaking.

Think carefully before putting a television in your bedroom, however. While it may start off being something you can watch together and which, especially used with a video, can greatly enhance the mood, it can easily become an incitement to laziness and avoiding sex altogether. If you find that this is the case, then do not have one.

TISSUES

After sex, and especially if making love during a period, you will find paper tissues very useful. Keep a box of tissues beside your bed so that you can easily and unobtrusively reach some to put against the woman's vulva and to wipe the man's penis after intercourse.

SMELLS, PERFUMES AND SCENTS

A few couples enjoy the smell of a special room perfumes, or joss sticks. This is a fairly minority pursuit in the West, but in the Orient smell plays an important part in lovemaking.

Certainly, a well-washed body in a man, and the fragrantly scented body of a woman, can be real turn-ons for most. But be careful not to so over-perfume yourself (whichever sex you are) that your natural body odours are masked.

The smell of a man's fresh sweat and a woman's vulva are designed to arouse the sexual appetites, but they cannot do so if commercial scents overwhelm them.

LOCK ON THE DOOR

One of the most vital pieces of bedroom equipment is some sort of lock on the door – unless there is no one in the household except the two of you. A simple bolt is best and serves to prevent unwelcome and unexpected visits, especially from children. Even parents have a right to their privacy at times: do not be hesitatant to ensure you get it.

PERSONAL HAVEN

A little attention to your bedroom will often pay dividends in your sex life and should greatly enhance your enjoyment of sex. Your bedrooms should reflect your sexual personalities and be a place where you feel at peace with the world, at one with each other and be a haven from the hurly-burly of life.

It is a personal room dedicated to you as a couple in which you have to make no concessions to the other occupants of the house. We all need personal space like this, and many couples lose out greatly if they do not have it.

CREATIVE FOREPLAY

For every couple, expanding and perfecting their sexual repertoire can pay dividends, and a good starting point is to experiment with arousal techniques

Considering the amount of time a couple spend making love – or the amount of time they could spend making love – there are probably very few partners who make use of their full potential for loving.

We are all capable of becoming expert lovers. It has nothing to do with size of sex organs, looks or breast size. Expert lovers are made, not born. And like everything else that we do successfully in life, it demands constant practice. All that are required are an open mind, a willingness to give sexually as well as to receive, and a sensitivity towards your partner's needs, both physical and emotional.

THE POWER OF LOVE
Some relationships can succeed on a sexual level alone, without emotion or caring. But for most people, men and women, a one-night stand is rarely a recipe for sexual contentment. This is because the experience of sex can be almost infinitely variable and the ability, and the incentive, to experiment and explore tends to exist more in a relationship where two people

love each other. Familiarity can be used to breed sexual fulfilment; although making love to someone for the first time can be exciting, advanced loving comes from an ability to anticipate your partner's needs.

FOREPLAY
Although for men in particular – and for most women – orgasm is the outcome of most sexual experiences, for the creative lover, it is only one feature of sex – it is an end rather than a means. For most of us, the quality of orgasms can vary with each sexual experience. By paying attention to foreplay – teasing and turning your partner on, exploring the potential of their bodies for sexual excitement – the quality of sex for both partners can improve almost beyond imagination.

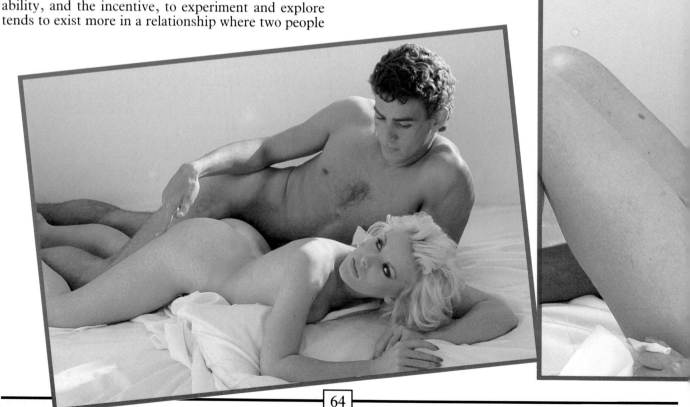

THE POWER OF SPEECH

It can sometimes be flattering for both sexes to be wanted purely for their body and nothing else – but only for a while. If you can make someone feel good about being loved, prized and cherished emotionally too, their own lovemaking becomes infinitely more responsive. Foreplay is not only about intimate caresses and kissing. It is also about things you say and how you say them. Saying 'I love you' and 'I want you' – assuming you mean it – can achieve more than the most advanced penile or vaginal control or advanced lovemaking techniques. A loving couple can show they care for each other in thousands of different ways.

WHAT WOMEN WANT

Women's sexuality tends to be more complicated than men's. One sexologist once said that a woman has only one erogonous zone – that of her own body. Yet no man knows what an individual woman most likes until she tells him or indicates her preferences during foreplay. A woman also has a greater capacity for orgasms than a man and her sexual potential is higher. It is sad that this sexual potential in so many women remains untapped by their partners.

A woman takes more time to become aroused biologically. She may be more receptive to sex at different times during her menstrual cycle than at others, and as a rule, her emotional and psychological expectations of sex tend to be higher than most men's are, which can tend to make her quite difficult to satisfy or fulfil.

In almost every extensive study on sexuality since Kinsey, the most widely voiced women's complaints about their partners in bed are that they do not show enough attention, they do not take enough time, they seem to be more concerned with their own pleasure than that of their partner and they are not tender enough.

For most men intent on improving the quality of their lovemaking the answer seems to be to take more time. Concentrate on pleasing her and by so doing you will please yourself.

WHAT MEN WANT

Sex manuals often describe men as uncomplicated sexually. Provided his penis is stimulated sufficiently, a man can achieve a satisfactory orgasm. Yet, although they are more genitally orientated than women, many men want to be loved and appreciated just as much as women.

This means that a man can be more simple to please in bed. Complications tend to arise because men are brought up to be so concerned about performance in bed. If a man can eliminate viewing the sexual arena as a contest and begin to see sex as a shared experience between two people, or if his partner can help him to see this – he can begin to realize his own unique potential for lovemaking. And this realization will make him a better lover.

EARLOBES

The ears are highly underrated erogenous zones either to touch or to kiss. For some people manipulation or kissing can be enough to trigger off orgasm. Heavy breathing into the ear can be a real turn-on, but for most men and women the point of the tongue run around the lobe before being pointed directly into the ear can be enough to drive them wild. Be careful though and only be tempted to blow gently – if at all.

EROTIC MASSAGE

The best foreplay is simple. Apart from that, there are few rules as to what one person should do to another. While in a loving relationship there is room for sex aids and sex toys, the greatest aid any lover has at his or her disposal is their own body. Before any genital contact, there are a number of exciting things you can try.

THE POWER TO EXCITE

Men are aroused more by visual stimuli than are women. The power of clothes to excite is a time honoured one and the loving woman should recognize the power of her own body, naked or partially clothed, to tease and arouse her partner. They key, as always to sexual enjoyment, is to use clothes, or the lack of them creatively. A woman's body is one of many reasons that her partner was attracted to her in the first place so it makes good sex sense for her to use it to the full. A little imagination can go a long way in pleasing your partner.

FOR BOTH SEXES

Arousal can be simple or complicated. One day it may take a few minutes, another day a few hours, and it can begin with a word, a touch or a glance. A couple may fancy leisurely unhurried sex or they may want to make love in a frenzy. There are no rules except to respond to what you sense your partner wants, and to make sure you both enjoy it.

Concentrate on the quality of your foreplay. If you feel that your partner wants something else, then try something new. Try not to think about technique – human beings are not robots – concentrate on being sensitive to the other's needs. Talk about what you want and ask about what they want. Decide first if the foreplay is to be mutual or whether one of you can lie back and enjoy the sensations. Use your whole body sensually and imaginatively to improve the experience for both of you.

THE SENSUAL TOUCH

Massage has the power to relax and excite. There is a wealth of techniques that a couple can use from the ancient and oriental to holistic and aromatic versions. Most of these techniques have been designed to relax. Where erotic massage parts company from most of the other versions is that it is designed purely to excite. It is best agreed beforehand who is to be massaged – then he or she can become the active partner next time. Because it is such a pleasurable experience, the couple's roles are probably best not reversed during a single bout of lovemaking.

PREPARATION

For erotic massage, it is best to use oil. There are a number of proprietary brands on the market which are available in sex shops, but generally baby oil or some sweet-smelling essence is equally good and much cheaper.

This massage is to be used as foreplay – intercourse will probably take place afterwards. However, there is no reason why orgasm should not take place as part of

he massage, either manually or orally – it is up to you. 't is probably best to have an idea of whether you ntend to make your partner come in this way, but it is is well to be flexible. Many lovemaking decisions are best on the spot.

FOR HER

Make sure that she is comfortable, lying down on the floor or the bed, and that the room is warm enough. Pour the oil into your hand and gently transfer it on to her back. Some 'experts' suggests this as the best and politest way of applying the oil but a good – if slightly surprising – alternative is to pour the oil direct from the bottle on to the skin.

Use delicate strokes on her back at first kneading the

Massage your partner's breasts – do it tenderly applying only very gentle pressure. Apply the oil and use your hands in a circular motion. Once the massage is complete, turn your attention to teasing her nipples

oil in. Pay special attention to the shoulders and shoulder blades and ease away any tension there. Increase the pressure and start to maintain a good regular rhythm. This is important. If the masseur chops and changes his style, it can be quite disconcerting for his partner as she can never totally relax.

When you have finished massaging her back, pour a liberal amount on to the backs of her legs. Again using firm strokes, massage each leg in turn up to the tops of the thighs. Part her legs slightly to do this but do not touch her buttocks yet.

When her legs are finished, pour a small amount of oil on to her buttocks, and into the cleft between them. Press quite hard and, using both hands, rub the oil in before delicately using a finger to massage the oil into the cleft. By now, she may be becoming sexually aroused. If you sense that this is so, you can gently turn her over and start on her front.

If you have decided to pour the oil directly from the bottle on to her skin, the principle should be already established. Pour some oil on to her upper chest and stomach and again, using firm, regular strokes knead the oil in. Avoid her breasts at this stage. Remember, the stomach can be highly sensitive when aroused so if you sense that you are tickling, leave her stomach and massage the fronts of her legs.

To maintain continuity, the imaginative lover should be able to use one hand to massage her thighs and the other to massage her chest. The secret of this particular technique is to start ever so slowly with the hands far apart and then to increase the pressure slightly as you bring them towards each other.

BREAST PLAY

Next, pour small amounts of oil on to each breast and gently, using both hands, rub the oil in. Circle the nipples without touching them and slightly increase the pressure. Tenderly knead her breasts and then slowly rub the oil into each nipple. Tease and tantalize using your hands in a circular motion. Then, when the time is right, you can turn your attention to her vulva.

FOR HIM

The rules of massage for the man are nearly the same as for the woman except that because most men are

When massaging your partner's bottom, press quite hard using both hands to push her buttocks together. Use a finer touch when applying and rubbing in oil into the cleft. She will find this highly arousing

more genitally orientated, it is best to spend less time on his less erogonous zones and move more quickly towards his buttocks and penis.

But do not hurry it too much. You will know how readily your partner becomes aroused and should be guided by his needs.

Provided the room temperature is warm enough, opt for pouring the oil directly from the bottle on to the skin. Make sure he is lying comfortably on his front and firmly rub the oil into his back. Apply some more to the backs of his legs and, using long firm strokes, rub it in from his ankles to the tops of his thighs.

Now pour a liberal amount on to his buttocks and into the cleft between and, again using firm strokes, rub the bodies of each buttock towards each other – do this quite vigorously as most men's buttocks and anus are highly sensitive. Even if you notice an erection at this stage, do not touch his penis yet. Use a finger to run along the cleft between his buttocks, teasing and tantalizing him. Use as much or as little pressure as you know he likes.

Now, turn him over and massage his front. Apply oil on to the fronts of his legs, his chest and stomach and rub it in. Circle round his penis, getting closer all the time without actually touching it. An almost unbearable method for most men is to massage his upper thighs with one hand while massaging his lower stom-

Massage your partner's thighs with one hand and his lower stomach with the other. Do not use your hands on his penis, rather increase the excitement by playing your breath across it

SKIN

Skin is our largest sexual organ and for anyone who doubts it, try this simple test. Ask your partner to blindfold you – or if you do not like the idea, just close your eyes – and ask him or her to touch you wherever they want but as lightly as a feather. The sensations should be exquisite.

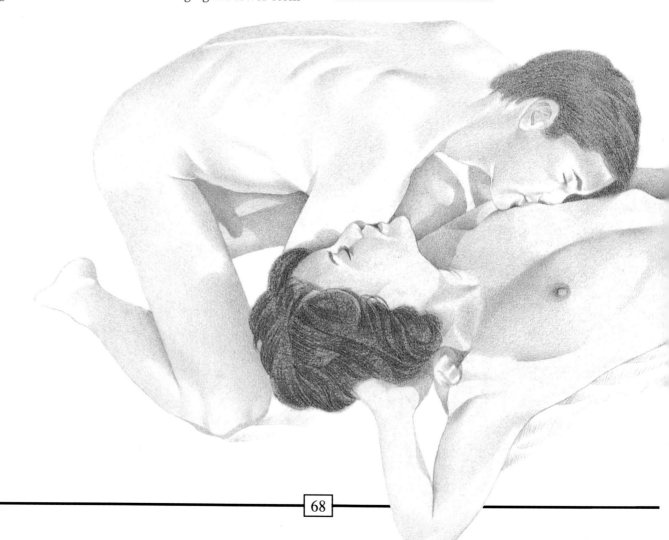

ach with the other. To tantalize him still further, lean your head over his penis so that he can feel your breath on it. By now you will know whether to bring him to orgasm.

SENSUAL KISSING

It is tempting for many lovers only to use the lips for direct mouth to mouth contact. Yet, kissing is a truly sensuous experience in itself and there are a host of variations that are worth trying. And the mouth is only one part of your lover's body to which your lips can be directed.

MOUTH TO MOUTH
Take your lover's face between your hands and trace a path with your tongue around their lips. Then run your tongue around inside their mouth teasing their tongue with yours. Use your fingers to caress your lover's scalp and nibble their ears and body with your lips and teeth. Take your time and vary what you are doing. A hundred little kisses can act as an erotic build-up to a full mouth-to-mouth attack. Use your hands to close their eyes as your tongue descends further into their mouth. Vary the times you do this as well: all this can be equally exciting fully clothed.

ANOTHER POSITION
Try kissing back to front. Lie your lover down – on the floor or bed – and kneel with their head almost

As your partner lies relaxed, use your lips to caress her nipples. Trace a path around their circumference with your tongue and kiss or suck them tenderly

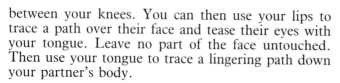

between your knees. You can then use your lips to trace a path over their face and tease their eyes with your tongue. Leave no part of the face untouched. Then use your tongue to trace a lingering path down your partner's body.

KISSING HER

For the man, try tracing a path around her breasts but even if you notice her nipples rising in anticipation, leave them for a while. Kiss her navel and, passing her vulva, move down her legs and kiss her calves and thighs and the backs of her knees. Take a toe into your mouth and gently suck it, avoiding the instep if she is ticklish. Concentrate on making the kissing almost a complete experience in itself. There may be occasions when you will want to move directly on to oral sex and breast play but, for the time being, concentrate on the less erogenous zones. Remember sex, good sex,

is about anticipation as much as it is about fulfilment.

Turn her over and repeat this unique tongue bath down her back. Go up the backs of her legs, stop and nibble her buttocks, tracing a path between them, and move up her back. Spend as long as is pleasurable for her.

KISSING HIM

The same use of the mouth can be equally pleasing for the man. Trace the path down his chest and stomach, carefully skirting his penis and ignoring for the moment any pleas he may make to you to take it in your mouth. Use your tongue but use the rest of your body as well. Use your breasts to hover over his face – let him take one in his mouth if he wants to. Kiss his feet, his calves and thighs and then turn him over and tease his buttocks. Forget intercourse at this state – concentrate on his experience.

WINE AND FOOD

Wine and food can be used to wonderful effect during foreplay. Not only can they help to set the mood – a small drink before lovemaking relaxes both partners, and good food can act as a real aphrodisiac to most couples – they can also be used as sex aids.

Food can be eaten directly from each other's bodies. Try placing soft fruit, honey – or wine – on your partner's genitals or breasts and licking it off. Not only is it delightful for the recipient and the giver – it is also a delightfully decadent feeling for both.

USING EROTICA

Although there is no substitute for your own body as a means of arousing your partner, erotica has its place in any relationship. It can come in many forms, – books, magazines, films, art and so on. A couple do not need to spend vast amounts of money on purchasing or hiring these items. A visit to a cinema, a passage in a novel, a sexy-looking picture can all provide the erotic stimulus to encourage a couple to make love. The key is to understand the stimulus and do something about it rather than to let it rest until it disappears into the subconscious.

VERBAL FOREPLAY

The accomplished seducer – of either sex – recognizes the value of compliments and flattery. It is not so much what is said, although pleasantries about oneself are always good to hear, but the fact that someone we are attracted to has bothered to make an agreeable comment.

If someone tells you that we look good or sexy, we are not going to disbelieve them. Add to that the odd present and the attentiveness that the seducer has as part of his or her armoury and the value of words as a means of arousal becomes only too clear.

In actual loveplay, it pays to keep the words as frank and earthy as possible. If most of us are delighted to hear how attractive we are to our partner, we are even more pleased to be complimented by them on our sexual attractiveness. For a woman to hear from her lover that she is uniquely desirable, or for a man to know that his lovemaking technique is unparalleled is

worth considerably more than any amount of sexual prowess or athleticism.

It is also a good idea to keep the words simple. If you want to say something earthy to your partner, it often helps to use explicit language rather than politely skirting round what you wanted to say: the basic nature of such words, used in the right context, can be a powerful turn-on for both sexes.

SEX GAMES

The inventive couple may use sex games as part of foreplay from time to time. These can vary from board games to more tantalizing games that a couple already know they both enjoy. Whatever the game – from dressing-up games where each partner takes on a role, to danger-of-discovery games or medical and seduction games – its purpose is generally simple. Games act as a highly-charged means of arousal and soon slot in the mind of each partner what is to come – before they even touch each other.

FANTASY

Fantasy can act as a powerful feature of arousal. But the nature of a person's erotic fantasies is such that sharing them demands careful judgement. Certainly, if your particular fantasy is for your partner to dress as a whore or act as a doctor in a doctor/nurse's game, then little harm can come from it. If, however, your fantasy involves another person, perhaps even a close friend, disclosing it to your partner could raise feelings of distrust or jealousy, so if this is the case, it is best kept to yourself.

Your partner's buttocks and her perineum are both highly sensitive areas – use your tongue and your lips to kiss and caress them

FOR HER

Almost anything can be used to arouse a woman if her partner and the atmosphere are right. Equally, the most skilled foreplay can leave the most sensuous woman cold and unsatisfied if the mood is wrong.

Given that her orgasm is primary and your own secondary, what follows is a list of suggestions for getting your woman in the mood for love and ensuring that her orgasm, or orgasms, are highly satisfying. Each is open to variations and can be adapted to suit your individual needs as a couple, but none should be rushed.

SHOWER TOGETHER

Conscientious personal hygiene is an essential requirement for good sex, and a shower is particularly suitable for setting the mood for love. Pour your partner a small drink and start the shower for her. Make removing her clothes part of the ritual – take them off slowly and kiss and caress her as you do so.

Use shower gel or soap to wash her thoroughly. Do her back first and her neck, all the time with the shower spraying water over her. If your shower is in a bath, sit down on the edge and take each leg in turn into your lap and soap it thoroughly. Stand up again and lather her breasts. Apply generous quantities to her buttocks and then use a small amount – too much soap can sting

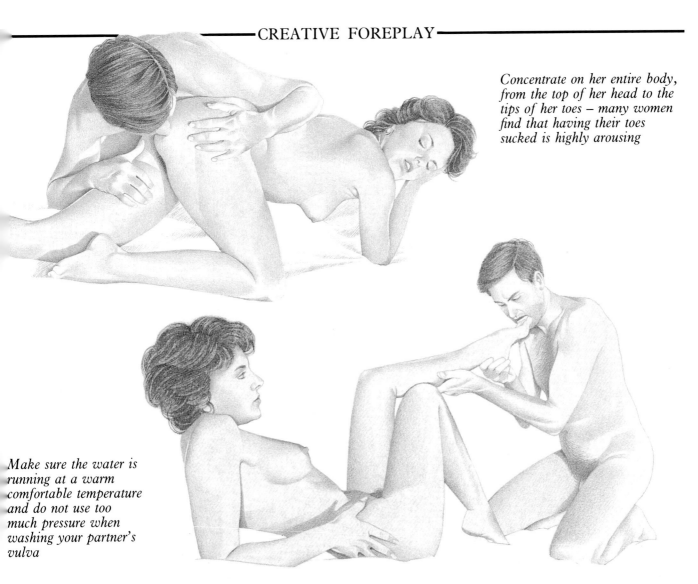

Concentrate on her entire body, from the top of her head to the tips of her toes – many women find that having their toes sucked is highly arousing

Make sure the water is running at a warm comfortable temperature and do not use too much pressure when washing your partner's vulva

– to lingeringly wash her vulval area thoroughly.

When you have finished, detach the shower spray and rinse her. Applying the nozzle very close to her skin use the jets of warm water to tease and tantalize her. Pay special attention to her breasts, spending as much time on this as necessary – the French recognize this as a healthy way of maintaining skin tone and shape as well as being undeniably erotic. Kiss her wet body, all the time keeping a regular spray going.

Finally, save the rinsing of her vulva until last, holding the shower attachment as you do this, but do not spray too powerfully. Use your free hand to rinse her vulva thoroughly and exaggerate how long this needs to take. Then when you have finished, rub her down with a warm towel, lovingly ensuring that every part of her skin is dry.

USE YOUR PENIS
Massage with the hands and a tongue bath can be highly erotic but a man has other means of exciting a woman in foreplay. Use other parts of your body to tease and excite. Lie your partner down and use eyelashes or hair to trace a carpet of sensation over her body.

Ice, fur and feathers can be used equally success-fully, but be careful not to tickle. Follow the rules of massage you know she likes, always leaving her most erogenous zones until last.

Your penis can also be used to good effect on her body. Use it to trace a small path around her lips and then move down to her breasts and rub it into them paying special attention to her nipples. Use it to tease her buttocks and perineum. Above all, use your imagination. If you both like a little mild bondage these sensations can be exaggerated if she is restrained slightly.

BREAST PLAY
Many women's breasts are highly sensitive during arousal. The imaginative lover can find all sorts of ways to caress and tease them.

Ice can have a wonderfully shocking value if it is placed in the palms of the hands and used to run a circular path around each nipple. The woman can be asked to go on all fours and dangle her breasts in her lover's face as he kisses them. Depending on how your partner likes them treated, they can be rubbed gently or more powerfully. Alternate between using the palm of your hand and your fingertips. Wine, yoghurt or even ice cream can be placed on them while an attentive lover licks them off. Use your chest – perhaps

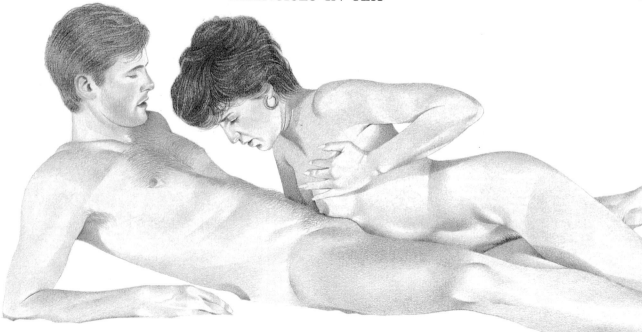

slightly oiled –to rub slowly against hers. Your penis – again sightly oiled – can be used to trace a path around each nipple.

And some women like semen over their breasts. If you masturbate yourself to the verge of orgasm, or she does it for you, you can then direct the fluid on to her breasts and rub it in for her.

BUTTOCK PLAY

A woman's buttocks are highly erogenous. If this is the case, there are a number of things you can do to excite and arouse her. For some women, the perineum – the skin between the vagina and the anus – is delightfully sensitive and is often totally ignored.

After her shower, lay your partner on the bed, with a couple of cushions under her bottom. You can then find out how sensitive her perineum is by licking and kissing it. Better still, if she has a vibrator, gently massage the perineum with the vibration turned to quite a slow speed.

Alternatively, some women like having their buttocks lightly spanked. Provided this does not get out of hand, and there is trust between both partners, it can act as a skin-tingling prelude to lovemaking. If the woman drapes herself over her partner's knee and raises her buttocks, he can use the flat of his hand to spank or fondle each buttock.

FOR HIM

If the mood is highly charged, most men can be brought to orgasm in seconds. Yet, if the foreplay is skilful and prolonged, his orgasm can be delayed almost indefinitely. The sensitive woman can up the tempo and bring it down always remaining one step ahead of her partner – and the orgasm will improve dramatically.

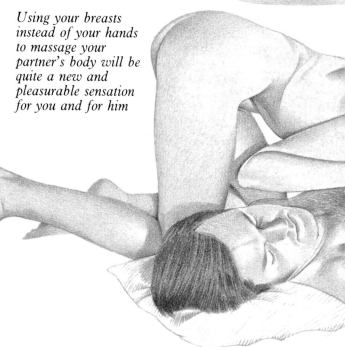

Using your breasts instead of your hands to massage your partner's body will be quite a new and pleasurable sensation for you and for him

YOUR BODY

Your body is probably the most exciting part – sexually – about you for your partner. If he has fantasies about you dressed in a particular way, it makes sense to indulge him once in a while. It does not devalue you in his eyes as a person, it is merely a means of his expressing his love for you by becoming aroused. Wear clothes he likes on the occasions you want to arouse him to a peak.

Many men find a semi-clothed women sexier than a naked one anyway. And if, for example, he wants you to look like a whore for him, why not do so and play the part to the hilt? Women often find that dressing up in an exaggeratedly sexual way is just as much a turn-on for them as it is for their man.

FOREPLAY – DO'S AND DON'TS

☐Don't go to bed with bad breath
☐Dress, if you are going to dress for bed, to look sexy
☐If you are not bathing together, make sure that

you are fresh and clean
☐Keep your nails short, particularly men – long nails can scratch the woman's vaginal wall, and even the fear of this happening can be off-putting

When giving your partner a tongue bath, if you drink some iced water or wine before you do this the chill of your tongue will add extra sensation

BATHING

Giving a man a bath can be an exciting way to bring him to the verge of orgasm. Run the bath for him, perhaps putting some essence in the water, and undress him. Soap his front down gently, avoiding his penis, using long strokes to relax him at first. Then ask him to turn over and wash the backs of his legs. Get him to raise his buttocks as high as he can and use a finger to wash his perineum. Use featherlight strokes to do this, keeping up a slow, but persistent pressure. Now, turn him over again and wash his penis and testicles. Make a ritual out of this, perhaps washing and rinsing the penis twice. Pull back his foreskin and, using the slipperiness of the soap, simulate masturbation – but only for a short while. After you have fin-

ished – ignore any pleas at this stage to bring him to orgasm with hands or mouth – dry him down with a warm towel and take him to another room.

Of course, it may suit both of you to bring him to orgasm then and there in which case you can always climb into the bath and make love.

BREAST PLAY – FOR HIM

Your breasts can be used on their own or with the rest of your body to provide exquisite sensations for your partner. To give him the full benefit, it is best to lie him back naked on the bed or floor or wherever is most appropriate at the time. Lean over him and use your breasts to trace a path over him from top to toes. Use one breast to trace a path around his penis and alternate between that and pressing it firmly down so that the penis is almost enveloped.

You can do the same to his back by turning him over. Run a complete path from head to toe and when your nipples are erect, run one of them along his perineum.

Do not forget his face either. Run your breasts over his eyes and his ears and allow him to take your nipples into his mouth if he wants to.

Apply a little oil to your breasts and dangle them over his penis. Lean forward and flatten them over it, taking the penis in between them. With slow rhythmic movements, this can be a tantalizing way to bring him to the verge of orgasm. Experiment with the position and choose one that feels most comfortable to you.

USE YOUR LIPS

Apart from kissing his mouth, use your lips to kiss him all over, paying special attention to his genital area, but without taking his penis into your mouth – that can always come later. Kiss his feet, perhaps taking his toes into your mouth. Do this facing him so he can see what you are doing. Work your way up his leg, by-pass his genitals and kiss his nipples if he likes this. Then descend slowly towards his penis, breathing close to his skin as you do so. Lift up his testicles and take them into your mouth one by one. Remember, though, that they are particularly sensitive so go as gently as you can. Too much pressure can be counter-productive – as well as extremely painful.

USING YOUR VAGINA

Perhaps the most intimate form of kissing is for a woman to use her vaginal lips instead of her mouth. If your vagina is already moist, there is no need to moisten it any further – otherwise apply a small amount of oil or KY jelly to it. Then, give him a genital version of a tongue bath, starting from his feet and working your way up to his face. The scent of your vagina as well as the unique intimacy of this form of kissing should excite both of you. Linger over each part of his body, but finish off hovering over his face before finally descending onto it and giving him a full genital kiss on the mouth, moving your buttocks from side to side and rubbing your vaginal lips firmly against him.

POSITIONS FOR LOVERS

Cosy, erotic, athletic and bizarre – all these words can be used to describe the wide variety of positions available to imaginative lovers

In most relationships, a couple will try out a number of positions for lovemaking early on, and then settle for the three or four that they find suit them best. There is absolutely nothing wrong with this – if the couple are happy with them, they are well served by what they like best. Yet, lovemaking takes place under so many varying conditions, and in so many moods, that it makes sense to explore all the options open to you.

The advanced couple can reject, accept – or more likely, modify – any of the positions that they favour and, if they want, introduce a host of new variations. There are never any hard and fast rules.

HOW MANY ARE THERE?

'Experts' have differed over the centuries as to how many positions a couple might use to make love – one researcher reckoned that there were as many as 10,000. This would range from the missionary position to the unorthodox, athletic and bizarre. And within each basic position, there would be so many variations – subtle and sometimes not so subtle – to bring the count up – for those who were counting.

In reality, there are five basic positions for lovemaking. The man-on-top position known as the missionary position, the woman-on-top position, rear entry, side entry and positions where both partners are standing.

The missionary positions are probably the most popular of all positions for lovemaking. They allow the man to take the lead, and they are romantic in that the couple can see each other at all times. Even if a couple do not use it for a while, they will return to it again and again.

Woman-on-top positions have a number of advantages as well. Here – with all the variations – the woman takes control. Her hands are free to kiss and caress her partner or to help bring herself to orgasm. She can either face him as they make love, or she can face away from him.

Rear entry or 'doggie-style' lovemaking is far more

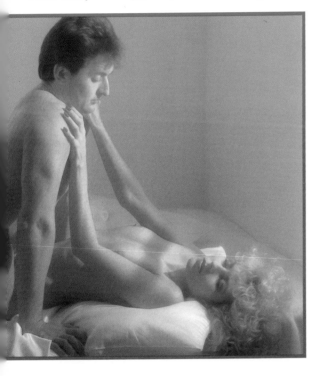

urgent, aggressive lovemaking. The man is free to thrust more powerfully than in any other position and some lovers find that this brings an animal-like quality to their lovemaking, which they may welcome from time to time. The woman can respond as much or as little as she likes. Its only disadvantage is that the woman cannot see what her partner is doing.

Side entry is relaxing and satisfying with the man taking the woman from the side rather than the rear. It is relaxing because it can only be performed lying down and, because the man wraps his body around the woman, body contact is at a maximum.

Standing positions are probably best left for the times when a couple fancy a quickie or they are feeling more athletic than usual, although there is no doubt, given that the time, the setting and the mood are right, that these positions have a rare charm all their own.

WHEN TO USE THEM
Often the key to a memorable bout of lovemaking is not to use a favourite position but to change positions as you make love. This style of lovemaking lends itself particularly to the couple who know each other's pet likes and dislikes. If the man has good penile control and can sense when the tempo needs to be increased, or the mood softened, the positions can be changed, not just once, but several times. Equally, the woman may suddenly wish to change from a passive to a more active role.

So, what started off as a fairly slow romantic session may well become more frenzied as passion takes over. A man-on-top position can readily be turned into a woman-on-top, a side entry position can become a more aggressive rear entry position and so on. And for the man who can hold his ejaculation back until his partner has had one orgasm and she wants more, he can stay inside her vagina, maintaining his erection before renewing the session in another position.

VARY THE PLACE
Of course the wise lover recognizes that it is not just a good position that makes for advanced lovemaking. A new place or a different time of day can turn even an old favourite into something new and memorable. And for those who really do not want to make a major change from what they like best, they can always try a subtle switch of position as they make love.

The sensations of both partners in a man-on-top position, for example, can become quite novel if the woman raises her legs and clasps them around her partner's waist – or places them over his shoulders. A rear entry position where the woman is lying face downwards on the bed can change dramatically if she raises her buttocks and offers them up to her partner.

And both positions can become completely different if the couple tries them out on the floor, or perhaps out in the open – weather and decency permitting.

FOREPLAY
No position, however, is going to achieve much for either partner – particularly the woman – if insufficient detail is paid to foreplay. So, unless the couple is planning to have 'quickie' sex, the use of creative arousal is essential – for both partners.

MOVEMENT
The scope for movement – other than just thrusting – in some positions is greater than in others. If the man's lower body is free to thrust, then the chances are that he has the option to experiment with greater sideways movement.

Moving his hips while holding his penis still – while rubbing his lower belly against his partner's clitoris – will achieve as much for her as any amount of determined thrusting. And the woman, when the couple are using a position where unlimited movement is possible, can use her lower body in the most tantalizing way to provide unique sensations for her partner. Also, in most positions, she should be able to experiment by contracting the muscles around her vaginal opening to grip her partner's penis. If she does this, her

partner's penis moves inwards and if the muscles are relaxed it moves outwards. This gives great pleasure, not only to the man but to the woman as well.

BACK TO BASICS

Some variations of the basic positions are so minute that they barely differ from the originals. Others are worth trying for differing sensations they provide for one – or both – partners.

MAN-ON-TOP
The basic man-on-top position has both partners lying down with the man entering the woman with his legs between hers, her legs drawn up and her feet resting on the bed. Interesting alternatives are:
☐The woman straightens her legs and keeps them spread wide on the bed rather than raising them. The man enters her in the same way but, because her vulva is now pointing straight ahead rather than upwards and towards her partner, the angle is subtly different. The man's penis is naturally pointing upwards and he is therefore able to stimulate her G spot – the sensitive spot on the front vaginal wall – to greater effect. The sensations for him will be slightly different as well
☐The man lies with his legs outside the woman's. Now, he can use his thighs to squeeze hers together

and her thighs will, in turn, compress his penis. If the woman expands and contracts her pelvic muscles while they are making love, she can provide markedly different sensations for the man. This variation is particularly recommended for women after childbirth where their vagina may have been slightly slackened
☐A pillow or two can be placed under the woman's bottom. Sensations in any of the man-on-top positions will become different as penetration will be deeper. The angle of the man's penis will be slightly different as well.

WOMAN-ON-TOP
The basic woman-on-top position is used by the majority of couples when the woman wants to take control of their lovemaking. She sits with her back erect, her knees resting on the bed by the side of the man. There are, however, a number of variations.

For the imaginative couple, lovemaking need never become stale – they will choose a position to suit their mood or inclination

☐The woman places the soles of her feet on the upper surfaces of her partner's feet and both of them spread their legs wide apart with their knees bent

☐The woman-on-top facing away is almost as well known as the basic position, but novel sensations during intercourse can be created for both partners if the woman turns right round from one position to the other

☐The woman squats over the man's penis but, instead of kneeling, she straightens her legs and rests them on his shoulders. She can then move up and down at her own pace. Of all the woman-on-top positions, this one allows the woman to turn right round without much risk of injury to the man. It also enables the man's penis to stimulate her at every possible angle. All he is required to do is maintain his erection and control the time that he climaxes.

REAR ENTRY

The most popular rear entry position is with the woman lying face down on the bed with her buttocks raised. The man kneels and enters her. Either partner can steer the man's penis into the woman's vagina. Variations are many, but here are some of the most popular.

☐Instead of kneeling, the woman lies flat on her face on the bed with her legs as wide apart as is comfortable for her. This makes entry a little more complicated but it provides the man with a different angle and is more restful for the woman, although movement for her is limited

☐Instead of kneeling between the woman's legs, the man can place his knees on either side of her. In this way he can ease forward until he is virtually sitting astride her back. The sensation is as close to 'riding' the woman as any other of the rear entry positions. Lovemaking in this position should not be hurried and is unlikely to succeed if the woman has not been stimulated earlier with some creative foreplay.

SIX VARIATIONS

For the fit and athletic, there are endless variations. What follows are six of the more exotic positions which can be considerable fun to try out for both partners.

THE RUTTING DEER

This is a variation of the man-on-top position that allows deep penetration and determined thrusting from the man. The top of the woman's body need not move but she can contribute to their lovemaking by determined pelvic movement with the lower half of her body – both up and down and rotating from side to side.

The woman lies back on the bed with the upper half of her body on the bed and her legs resting on the floor. Ideally, her buttocks should be resting on the bed. The man approaches her and, as he enters her, she bends her knees back towards her stomach while he supports himself on his hands and thrusts forwards.

To make penetration still deeper, the woman can bring her knees further back and rest them on her partner's shoulders. The elastic and athletic woman may even be able to cross them behind his neck.

PARTING OF THE WAVES

Although movement by both partners is limited, this position allows a unique angle of penetration.

The main problem lies in taking up the position. To do this, the woman should lie back near the edge of the bed and raise her legs in the air. The man kneels by her side facing towards her feet and should then be able to enter her. Then, as he slowly leans forward, the woman lies back. The man takes his weight on his hands on the floor while the woman uses her hands on his buttocks to assist his thrusting.

REACH FOR THE SKY

Perhaps not one of the most romantic positions; nevertheless, this one offers a unique angle of penetration for the man and therefore very different sensations for the woman. The woman lies on her back as comfortably as she can and parts her legs, raising them skywards. To start off with the man should kneel over her thighs while facing towards her feet. Then, as she raises her legs, he can enter her. The angle of his penis means that he will be hitting the back wall of her vagina

so this is no good for G spot stimulation, but he is free to thrust as hard as the couple likes and the position also allows for considerable sideways movement from the man.

For the couple who enjoy fantasizing as they make love, this position offers unique possibilities as – unless the man contorts his neck to look behind – neither partner can see the other.

WILD GEESE

The strength of this position is that it allows unique access for the man to use his hands on the woman's clitoris to control the pace of her orgasm – and it is more comfortable than it looks for the woman. It should only be attempted if there is a long rug or thick carpet on the floor next to the bed.

The woman rests her buttocks on the bed and straightens her back on the floor until she is comfortable – she can use the man's feet to support her head if need be. The man then sits on the bed between her legs and draws her towards him.

Because potential for pelvic movement from both partners is limited, this is a particularly suitable position if the man feels that he is in danger of coming too quickly. The woman can hold his penis inside her, perhaps contracting her pelvic muscles to grip him. If the couple wish to increase the pace, it is then a simple matter of the man drawing the woman up so that she is squatting over him. The initiative and the lead can then come from her.

THE LOVERS' EMBRACE

This position can be attempted on the floor but is probably best left to the bed. It demands poise and, above all, balance if it is to work properly – not only from the man, who will have to carry the weight of his partner, but also from the woman. It is best regarded as a position for fun – the throes of orgasm can lead to

THE LOVERS' EMBRACE
An intimate position which allows unique closeness

he couple collapsing on the bed or the floor and, unless they are careful, they can end up all over the place. Yet, for those who are capable of it, it offers a unique closeness and the chance for the woman to move relatively freely up and down – almost bouncing off her partner's penis.

It is best to start off with the couple standing. The man picks up the woman and puts his hands under her buttocks while she clasps her legs around him. He then – and this is the tricky part – bends his knees and lowers himself to a squatting position with her on top of him and she rests her legs over his thighs.

She should use her hands to direct his penis inside her at this stage, although the adventurous couple might like to try this when they are still standing: this provides a similar sensation and is less strenuous.

For the fainthearted, the man can assume a kneeling position and the woman can impale herself on him, if they are agile enough.

THE BANK OF THE NILE

For the woman, this is one of the most sedate-looking positions, although this is deceptive for it enables her to have almost unparalleled scope for movement. And for the man, it offers a rather unusual position and, therefore, unique sensations. The angle of his penis,

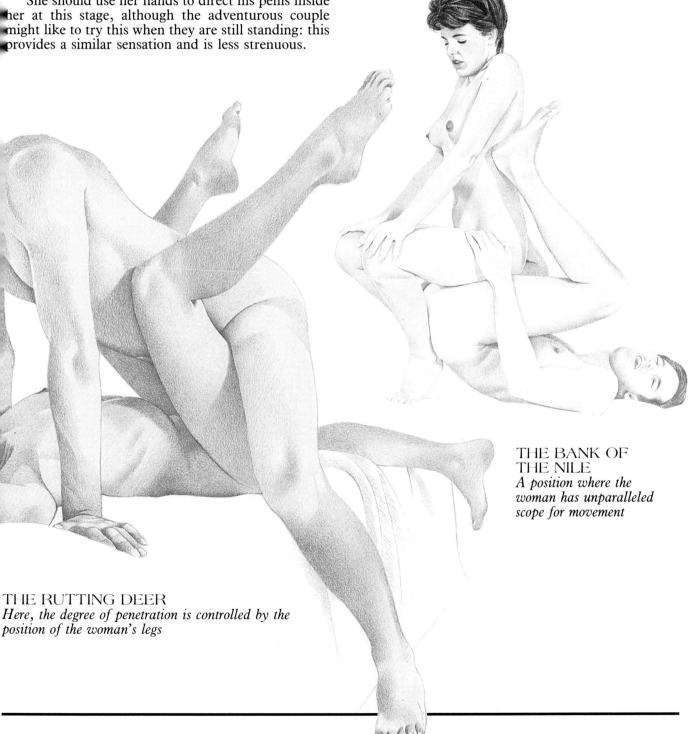

THE BANK OF
THE NILE
*A position where the
woman has unparalleled
scope for movement*

THE RUTTING DEER
*Here, the degree of penetration is controlled by the
position of the woman's legs*

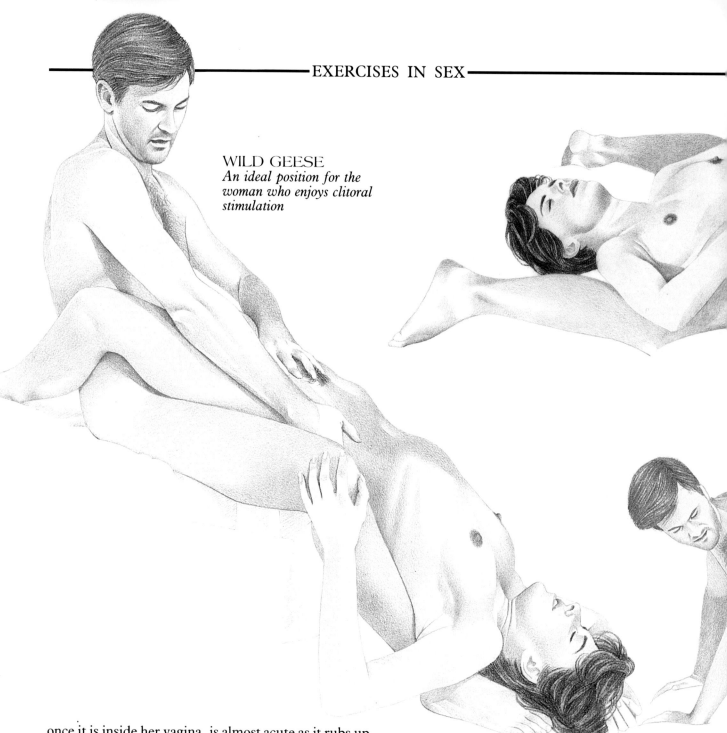

WILD GEESE
An ideal position for the woman who enjoys clitoral stimulation

once it is inside her vagina, is almost acute as it rubs up against the back wall of her vagina – something not normally achieved in intercourse.

The position is simple for both partners to take up. The man lies back on the bed and brings his knees back towards his chest. The woman then sits half-way up his thighs. Either partner can direct the man's penis inside the woman's vagina although it is probably easier for the woman to look down and use both hands to guide it in.

From this point on, the scope of the man to thrust or move is limited but, for the woman, it is immense. She can bounce up and down, or swivel sideways, always supported on the balls of her feet and on the man's thighs. Once the man's penis is inside her, she can use both hands on her clitoris to bring herself to orgasm. For the woman who enjoys fantasizing, it can be an ideal – as well as extremely comfortable – position.

ADVANCED POSITIONS

Advanced positions should be taken for what they are – a periodical excursion into differing sensations for both partners. But what should not be ignored is that they provide a couple with a novel and exciting way to enjoy each other – and an opportunity to have fun. And at no time is the ability to have fun greater than when a couple experiment with side-by-side positions or those where both partners remain standing.

HOW TO USE POSITIONS
Positions other than the well-known ones often look as if they have a bizarre or contortionist quality about them and, certainly, some require a degree of fitness,

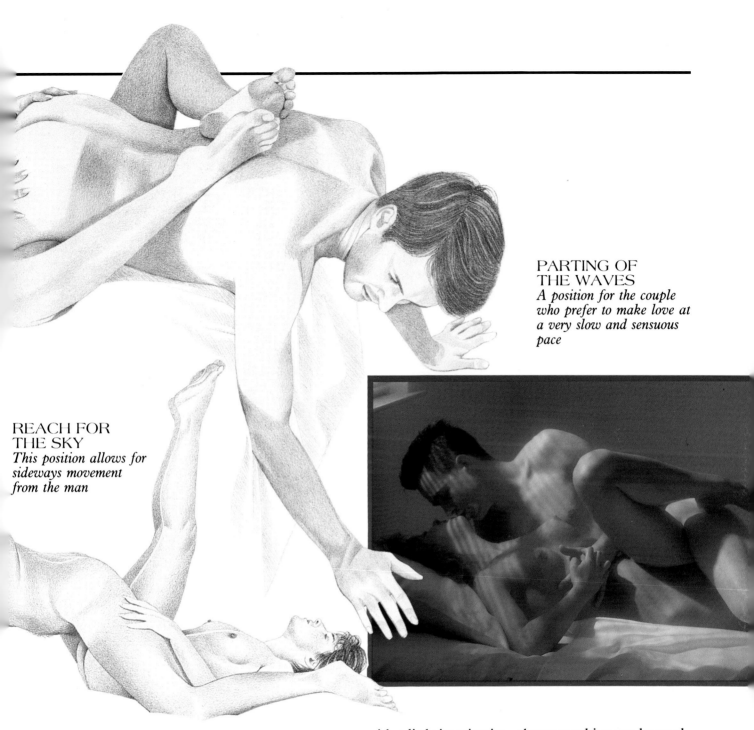

PARTING OF
THE WAVES
*A position for the couple
who prefer to make love at
a very slow and sensuous
pace*

REACH FOR
THE SKY
*This position allows for
sideways movement
from the man*

suppleness and athleticism which only a few lovers possess. Yet almost every position can be adapted by an inventive couple to fit their own unique needs.

And any one position does not have to be used for the full period of intercourse. There is no reason why a couple should not change positions several times during any one bout of lovemaking. A position that looks impossible can be used for a limited period of time before the couple convert to something more comfortable. Lovemaking, used like this, is fun.

USING PROPS
Props have a place in any advanced lover's repertoire, but they do not have to be complicated or expensive. Furniture and other objects around the house have the great advantage that they are always available and,

with a little imagination, almost anything can be used.

☐ **Chairs** Either on their own or placed strategically near the bed, chairs are probably the most versatile lovemaking prop of all. A couple can sit on them, they can use them for support – one partner can even stand on a chair. Used in the bedroom, chairs can be placed next to the bed to provide support in any variety of positions for either a person's feet or their head

☐ **Tables** For rear-entry sex, a table can prove to be an almost indispensable prop. The woman can lean over it as her partner enters her from behind, or a couple can lie on it – always provided it is strong enough

☐ **Baths** An excellent prop, a bath is probably more useful for foreplay than actual lovemaking – the average-sized bath is not comfortable for a couple to make love in. Like a table, however, baths can be especially useful for rear-entry sex – all the woman has to do is bend

western houses, which offers unique lovemaking possibilities to any couple, is a hammock. The couple become suspended in mid-air together and even the most basic positions can take on a novelty value.

SPLIT-LEVEL POSITIONS

The bed is by far the most popular place to make love. But many couples fail to recognize its unique value as a sexual prop when it is used in conjunction with the floor. Used this way, split-level positions become a real possibility both for conventional intercourse and oral sex. The idea is that one partner – usually the man – remains kneeling. The possibilities are endless but here are a few adaptations of the basic positions:

☐ **Man-on-top** The woman lies on the bed – across it rather than along it – with her feet resting on the floor. The man kneels before her to enter her. This may slightly restrict his thrusting movements but the angle of his penis, which will point towards her G spot, means that the position offers different sensations from the usual missionary position

☐ **Woman-on-top** The man lies across the bed with his feet on the floor as the woman climbs on top of him. She can either face him and control the lovemaking or face away. The latter position is more novel for both partners because she can lean forward as far as she is able – even using her hands to support herself on the floor if she is supple enough

☐ **Rear entry** The woman kneels on the floor and rests her chest and head on the bed as her partner, also kneeling, enters her from behind. Used in this way, the rear entry position offers even deeper penetration than if the position is practised on the bed.

A couple should experiment to see what suits them best. But almost any lying-down position can be used in this way.

VARIATIONS ON A THEME

There are a number of side-by-side positions that a couple can use although they tend to be a variation on a theme. Interestingly, though, these variations can provide a change of sensations for either partner, so it is worth experimenting with them to experience these novel movements and feelings.

SIDE-BY-SIDE

The basic side-by-side position is for the woman to lie flat on her back with her knees bent. Her partner lies on his side with the lower part of his body curled under her bottom so that her legs are across his thighs. This position, sometimes called the left lateral, is particularly relaxing and, because of this, is considered suitable for a couple to use when the woman is pregnant. Interesting variations include:

☐ The woman lies down on her side on the bed or

over the side as her lover enters her from behind

☐ **Showers** For both foreplay and intercourse, the shower offers a practical and novel place for making love. It provides support for the woman for a standing position and the shower spray can be used in a variety of creative ways

☐ **Stairs** Many couples do not use the stairs in their homes to full advantage when making love. Their main advantage – it helps if they are carpeted – is that they make up for any height discrepancy between a couple. The shorter partner – usually the woman – stands on the step above her lover. They can be a highly erotic venue for oral sex as well.

One other piece of furniture, not found in most

floor, but full length with her legs straight. The man lies facing her back and moulds his body to hers as he enters her. Body contact is kept at a maximum and the position is conducive to slow relaxing lovemaking. Thrusting comes from the man while the woman can use her pelvic muscles to grip his penis. Any other movement, however, tends to be limited

☐ The woman lies down on her side, as in the previous position, but instead of keeping her legs straight and together, she parts them as wide as she can. This will leave one leg straight on the bed with the other pointing upwards – rather like a dancer's exercise. The man then enters her, keeping his legs between her. As he is thrusting, he can bring his hand round and use it to stimulate her clitoris

☐ The spoons, where the man curls up to the woman and enters her from the rear while both partners are lying on their sides, is a particularly popular and relaxing position. But the penetration and degree of passion can be increased if the woman brings her knees up to her chest. The man then moulds himself into her as both partners take up what can only be described as foetal positions.

STANDING POSITIONS

Standing positions have a unique charm all of their own, but are best attempted when both partners are feeling energetic or when they want 'quickie' sex. Most can be used as intercourse positions in their own right but can also be converted to a floor or bed position where the couple can then reach orgasm more comfortably – always assuming that they want to. For the couple who have a marked height difference, standing positions are still possible. Stairs will allow for most discrepancies in height, as will a pile of telephone directories or similar large books which are not likely to collapse under the movement of lovemaking.

Probably, the standing position most people are familiar with is the front entry where the man stands in front of the woman with her back supported against the wall. Interesting variations of this basic position which are worth trying include:

☐ The woman stands against the wall and the man enters her from the front. At the same time, he lifts her up and supports her by placing his hands underneath her buttocks and then bounces her up and down on his penis. The couple have the option of using the wall as support or, if the man is strong enough, of carrying the woman around the room while still keeping the momentum going – although he will probably not be able to do this for long

☐ The man enters the woman from behind as she bends towards a wall and presses hard against it. This is a particularly good position for 'quickie' sex and the man can thrust hard while the woman uses her buttocks to move back and forth or rotate. This position has a raw urgency, like most of the standing positions, and this feeling can be heightened if the couple remain partially clothed.

ADVENTUROUS POSITIONS

For the couple who want to try some really adventurous positions using simply a chair as a prop, or who would like to try some of the more advanced standing positions for quickies, here are three of each to try. Be careful though. Some of them demand a high degree of suppleness, so if you take up a position and either of you feels any discomfort, stop and try a simpler position.

RIDE-A-COCK HORSE

Aptly named, this position is quite simple for the man and should not be too strenuous for the woman provided she is capable of taking some weight on her arms. The man sits down on the chair and his partner goes on all fours in front of him. He then gently pulls her towards him and lifts her legs while she supports herself on her hands. The man then wraps her legs around his waist as he guides his penis inside her. Using his hands on her buttocks, he controls her movement on him as his own tends to be somewhat restricted.

For the woman, the position can actually be quite comfortable although it might appear rather passive for her. For him, it can be highly stimulating, particularly visually, as he controls her movements and he has an intimate view of her buttocks and anus. As such, it is recommended as an occasional position for lovemaking or one to start off with before using a position that gives the woman more direct stimulation.

SQUAT THRUST

This position also requires the couple to use a chair and the couple should take care – particularly as orgasm approaches. This is because the woman is balanced on the chair and too much thrusting from the man, or pelvic movement from the woman, during the throes of climax could result in the chair toppling over with disastrous results.

Yet, the position has a lot going for it, especially for the woman who likes a G spot-induced orgasm, as the man's penis is rubbing directly up against the front wall of her vagina.

The woman should first stand on the chair and then get into a squatting position while supporting herself on the back of the chair. Provided her partner is supporting her at this stage – he could use one leg to secure the chair in position – she should be perfectly safe. The man next places his hands on her waist or the tops of her thighs and gently enters her. He should then be able to thrust quite gently and she should be able to respond by sensually moving her buttocks from side to side.

For the woman who enjoys fantasizing while she makes love, this position can offer quite unique sensations as she feels her partner's penis come inside almost from underneath her. At the moment of orgasm, the man should make a determined effort to control his thrusting.

REMEMBRANCE OF THINGS PAST

Although it can be difficult for the man to enter the woman from this position, once he has done so, it can be delightfully sensual for both partners – particularly the woman who lies back and lets everything happen to her. The chair is used to support her head and she can also use her hands to steady herself by holding on to the chair back. For the woman who fantasizes about bondage, she can image that she is tied up as her lover has his way with her. For him, this contact is solely

THE SQUAT THRUST
For the woman who enjoys a G spot orgasm, this position is excellent, but the man must take care to control his thrusting

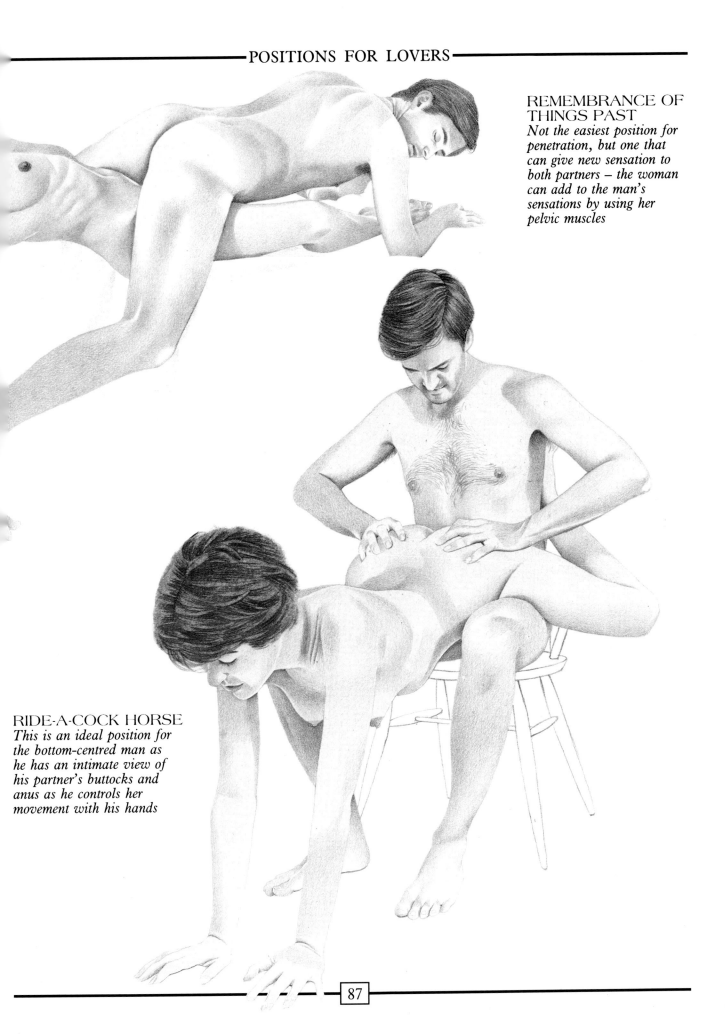

REMEMBRANCE OF THINGS PAST
Not the easiest position for penetration, but one that can give new sensation to both partners – the woman can add to the man's sensations by using her pelvic muscles

RIDE-A-COCK HORSE
This is an ideal position for the bottom-centred man as he has an intimate view of his partner's buttocks and anus as he controls her movement with his hands

AUTUMN LEAVES
One of the few positions where you can make love on the move, but the woman needs to have strong arms to support herself

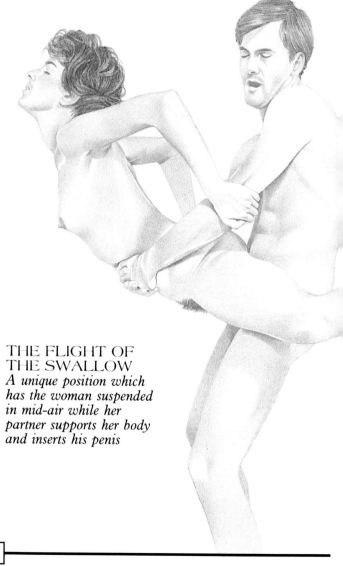

THE FLIGHT OF THE SWALLOW
A unique position which has the woman suspended in mid-air while her partner supports her body and inserts his penis

with the bottom half of her body which gives him the ideal opportunity to indulge in fantasy. He is in an ideal position to nibble her feet or stroke her legs. Also, he can use his testicles to stimulate her clitoris and bring her towards orgasm.

To take up the position, the man gets the woman to lie on the bed and then he pulls her backwards so that her head is supported on the chair. He brings his leg over, with his back to her and gets astride her before attempting to enter her. This may require some adjustment on the woman's part, as she brings her legs back. Once he is inside her, she can then bring her legs down. Her own movement is limited but she can use her pelvic muscles to grip his penis. The man is free to thrust as much as he likes and bring both of them to a powerful orgasm.

An interesting variation of this position is for the woman to support herself on the floor using her hands rather than the chair. Provided she has a supple back, this can provide highly erotic sensations for her as she 'abandons' herself to her partner.

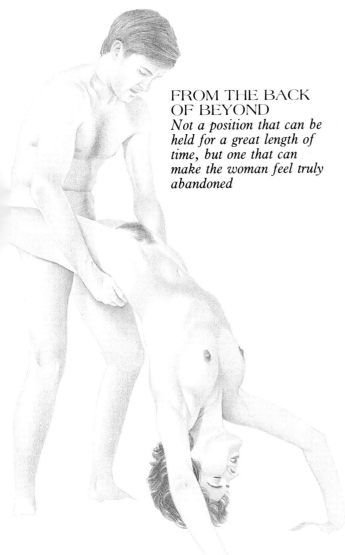

FROM THE BACK OF BEYOND

Not a position that can be held for a great length of time, but one that can make the woman feel truly abandoned

AUTUMN LEAVES

This position has a fun value all of its own and can instantly convert into another position if the couple want to enjoy a more leisurely orgasm – that of conventional rear entry – by them dropping to the floor.

The position is easily taken up. The woman goes on all fours and the man lifts her up to penetrate her. She supports herself on her hands while he takes the rest of her body weight by placing his hands on the tops of her thighs. The woman can clasp her legs behind her around his waist or place her heels on his back.

This wheelbarrow-like position really is one of the few where it is possible to make love, and have orgasms, 'on the move'. There are potential problems, however – if the woman moves too quickly, the man's penis can slip out of her. With this in mind, it is probably best left to the man to control the speed at which they move.

THE FLIGHT OF THE SWALLOW

This is a position that should only be attempted by the strong and athletic. From the man it not only requires strong arms to support his partner, but strong legs as well. And the woman needs to have complete trust in the man before she attempts this as at no time does she have any contact with the ground. Indeed, the only contact she has as she is held in space is with her partner's arms, which she holds onto for support, and his penis. Yet, for those who are capable of it, this position offers unique and varied sensations for both partners.

The position is best taken up with the woman on all fours in front of the man, who remains standing. She then arches her back and lifts her buttocks towards him as he places his hands under her waist and lifts her up in the air. If the man is appreciably taller than the woman, he may need to kneel for this first stage – after that, everything else is balance. The man rises and, placing his hands under waist, lifts her up. The angle at which he holds her will be dictated by the level at which he can comfortably direct his penis inside her. If a couple encounter difficulties with the man entering her, he can go inside her while she is still on the floor before lifting her up.

The position is best used as an occasional experience and should be used in conjunction with another simpler position for orgasm. To achieve this, it should be simple for the man to lower the woman – either on to the floor or the bed – and then use one of the more conventional rear entry positions.

FROM THE BACK OF BEYOND

Of all the positions shown, this one demands exceptional strength and athleticism – particularly from the woman. If she is capable of this, however, it enables both partners to experience the flavour of what feels like a really new position.

The woman starts off by doing a handstand with the man standing in front of her waiting to catch her. Because she will be taking her weight on her arms, a good alternative for those whose arms are not strong enough is to start off with a headstand so that she can support her body weight on her head as well.

Whichever method they choose, the man catches the woman and then brings her body right over so that she is literally offering her vulva to him. He then transfers his hands to her buttocks so that he can support her from there and directs her vulva towards him and then enters her. If he drops into a kneeling position, the woman can bring her legs right down and he can penetrate her from there.

The man controls the tempo by using the woman's body and bringing it alternately towards him and away from him using a sensual rhythmic motion. If the woman has exceptional balance, the man can support her under her buttocks and use his other hand to stimulate her clitoris. If the man drops to his knees, this readily converts into a position where he can perform oral sex on his partner.

For the woman, the principal sensation will be one of abandonment as she offers herself up to her partner. This position is not recommended for any great length of time, however.

PLEASING A WOMAN

The female sexual experience is very different from the male one. Understanding her likes and dislikes can do wonders for your lovemaking. But what gives a woman pleasure?

Probably the greatest single complaint that women have about men sexually, is that they do not give enough time to them.

A man is comparatively easy to please in bed. The focal point of his sexuality is his penis and the surrounding area, and direct stimulation is usually enough to bring him to his prime sexual goal – his own orgasm.

But women are much more variable in their approach to sex and what turns them on.

RANGE OF EXPERIENCES

For a woman, sex is not something that is concerned solely with her genitals. It encompasses a whole range of experiences and sensations all of which are expressed differently at various points in her life, from puberty through pregnancy to the menopause and beyond.

Sex can be basic or sophisticated, passionate or humorous. A woman's climax may be intense or it can come as a welcome relief – sometimes it may not be necessary at all. And for every woman, it can be all or some of these things at different points in her life. Little wonder, perhaps, that a man who hurries through intercourse as if he had a train to catch leaves a woman discontented and unfulfilled. A man may feel that it is impossible to please a woman sexually. It is not impossible: it is simply different.

A WOMAN'S BODY

Since women conceive and bear children, they tend to be more careful and selective sexually than men – if only because biologically they have to be wary about the type and quality of the man who fathers their children.

And even with efficient birth control, a woman knows subconsciously that any act of intercourse could mean a pregnancy with the resultant responsibility of looking after the child.

A man can have sex with a woman and know, biologically anyway, that this is the end of his responsibility. This means that men can be less discriminatory about their sexual partners than women.

As sexual beings women are far superior to men. Large areas of their bodies are sexually responsive, and many types of stimulation can be sexually arousing, and can bring them to one or more orgasms.

In addition, women can achieve a form of sexual pleasure outside their relationships with men – from pregnancy, breastfeeding and even from giving birth.

Men, by contrast, have a much smaller sexual repertoire. They have fewer erogenous zones and the vast majority are capable of only one orgasm at a time – after which they tire.

Given the variable nature of a woman's sexuality, it is understandable that many men fail to explore and exploit their woman's particular sexual needs.

TAKING TIME

The promise of a beautiful body is usually sufficient – initially – to arouse a man to want to have sex with a woman. This is why 'men's magazines' are full of pictures of naked women, and why pornographic films and videos are so popular with men.

This is not to say that men do not want to fall in love or be romantically treated by their partner, but the initial pull is often a physical one towards the woman's body and her physical sexuality.

Women, too, are initially attracted to what a man looks like but they are usually less specific about this physical appeal.

They certainly tend to put greater emphasis on feelings, emotions, intuition and personality and are less able, or inclined, to detach their physical feelings from their emotional ones.

This does not mean that some women are not interested in casual sex, but they tend to be less preoccupied with it than men.

Whereas a man is sexually aroused quite simply and quickly – after he achieves an erection, he wants to move towards orgasm as swiftly as possible – there are physiological reasons why it takes longer for a woman. In her unaroused state the vagina remains tightly

closed. Only after she has been caressed and cuddled and given an adequate amount of love play do the muscles of the vagina open and its walls start to pour out lubricating fluid. Only then does intercourse become easy and pleasant.

PLEASING THE WHOLE PERSON
Pleasing a woman is not simply a matter of sexual technique. Few women are turned on in bed if they have bad feelings or emotions about a man – however devastating he may be betweeen the sheets.

He should understand and respond to what his partner wants, not because he feels that this is what is required, but because he is sensitive to her needs. He needs to be attentive, tender and loving, he should ask what his partner wants and listen to what she says.

He should forget his preconceptions about what a man should or should not do. By putting her needs above his own he will reap the ultimate reward of not only pleasing her but improving his own sex life as well.

Just because something worked the first time, or was a success with a different partner, it does not always follow that it is the right thing to do. Men can sometimes be incredibly lazy and unimaginative about a woman's needs and desires during lovemaking and can lose out on their own enjoyment.

TALK AND TOUCH

These steps assume you are with one partner and that you love her. They are not a seduction guide on how to get a woman into bed with you. The most perfect sexual technique in the world counts for little unless it is joined with loving and understanding.

The first step towards pleasing a woman is to take a

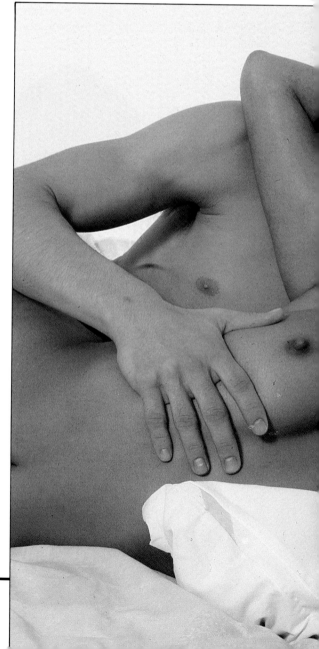

Some women like their whole breasts licked, others prefer their lovers to concentrate on the nipples

look at yourself and how you already treat her and try and improve on it. Then take every opportunity to show your love for her.

Give her presents for no reason, increase your physical closeness, kiss and cuddle, go out and treat her as if you were on an early date, be courteous and sympathetic without being patronizing.

See how you could improve on your personal appearance and behaviour and try behaving as you would if you had just started to go out with one another.

TALK AND LISTEN

A man can only really please a woman if he understands her unique, sexual needs. He can do this in one of three ways:

☐ He can learn – by trial and error – over a period of time what she likes best

☐ He can bring his own experiences of other women to the relationship

☐ He can encourage her to say exactly what she wants.

Obviously the ideal way is to talk about what she likes and dislikes but if she is reluctant to reveal her needs, fantasies and desires, try some gentle coaxing.

To do this it is essential to get the mood right. Kiss and cuddle a lot and get her physically aroused and relaxed. Sensual massage is a good ice breaker but a little alcohol or looking at a sexy book or film together can often trigger off a valuable revelation.

Some couples find that writing a sexy short story or 'filmscript' outline for an X-rated film helps. Going away often works best because once you are away from the cares and responsibilities of home and work you will both be able to relax.

It should not, of course, be just the woman who reveals her innermost needs in this way.

Ensure that the person revealing things is taken seriously and not judged or condemned for their revelations. And be realistic. If a person does not want to reveal their innermost fantasies, do not push them. A truly loving couple may be able to accept almost anything that surfaces but any desire for privacy should be respected.

Because a woman knows what she likes best, it is better that she tells you what she wants. Often, however, even with great sensitivity, care and time, many men cannot get their women to reveal much about their sexual likes and dislikes – even after many years of marriage.

There are a number of reasons for this but it is mainly that western culture used to, and still does in some quarters, believe that a man instinctively knows what a woman wants.

Not only does this put real pressure on a man but some women still believe this to some extent and become annoyed when their partner does not know, as if by telepathy, what they want.

As a result many couples never get to the stage of being able to share their real desires honestly and openly.

If your partner is unable, or simply does not want, to

reveal what pleases her best, the next step is to learn yourself what pleases women and then to apply the lessons to your own relationship.

WHAT PLEASES WOMEN GENERALLY

While the information contained in these steps has been gleaned through clinical experience, what pleases one woman may not necessarily please another. So be guided by your partner.

☐ Spend a lot of time in foreplay. Most women greatly enjoy kissing and cuddling and most need to feel loved before they can begin to enjoy themselves sexually

☐ Undress her slowly, praising her body as you do so. Shower or bath together if this turns her on. In any event make sure you wash your own genitals. Few women enjoy having any form of contact with a man whose personal hygiene is poor

☐ Take the telephone off the hook and make the surroundings as relaxing as possible. Most women find it difficult to relax and feel sexy if they feel they are likely to be interrupted

☐ Dim the lights, but do not turn them off because being able to see each other's bodies is a turn-on itself

☐ Above all, talk. Say how much you love her. Praise her body and say how sexy it is. Be gentle, tender and affectionate. Kiss her fat tummy, appendix scar or any part of her body that she is sensitive about, showing that all her body is special for you

☐ Take your time and do not touch her sex organs until she is ready. Because women generally take

A woman enjoys having her whole body stimulated during the course of lovemaking

A caring and sensitive man will make his partner feel that her whole body is special and unique for him

onger to become aroused than men, this opening
oreplay should be gentle and slow. Allow half an hour
t least to really please her but be guided if she wants
he pace to quicken.

DO WHAT SHE LIKES BEST

Because all women are so different in what best excites
hem you must always be aware of your partner's
pecial needs. Anything you may have learned through
our experiences with other women is helpful but may
not necessarily be what this woman wants. Be guided
by her to reveal her personal needs if she does not do
o spontaneously.

Watch and listen closely. The smallest grunt or
moan of approval, the shift of her body so that you can
do something better, a smile and a readiness to open

her legs wider are all signals to the sensitive man
☐ Kiss and caress her body furthest away from her breasts and sex organs and work your way towards them over several minutes. The feet, earlobes, behind the knees, the shoulders and the insides of the thighs are very exciting for many women but are often overlooked by men

While the woman stimulates her clitoris during intercourse, her partner can kiss or caress her calves

☐ Caress the more erotic areas such as her mouth and bottom, still keeping away from her genitals
☐ Now kiss her breasts gently. Some women complain that their man goes for them too soon and too roughly. Find what she likes and do it. Some women like their whole breasts sucked, others like the nipples sucked hard, or the whole breast teased with the tip of the tongue. Learn for yourself what is nicest for her
☐ By now she should be quite aroused and you can turn your attention to her clitoris. Use fluid from the vagina to moisten the whole area or you can use your own saliva. Again, be guided by what she likes best. Pay attention to the length of stroke you apply, the speed and type of movements she likes, the area to which it is applied and the amount of pressure you use. Keep up other activity elsewhere. Many women like to kiss and have their breasts caressed or kissed along with their clitoris
☐ Most women enjoy having a finger or two in their vagina when they masturbate. If she likes this, get into a position in which you can put fingers in her vagina and still carry on with clitoral stimulation
☐ Bring her to a climax if she wants you to – not forgetting to stimulate her elsewhere at the same time. Keep both hands and your mouth busy all the time pleasing her. Once she has had an orgasm she may want to have intercourse with you. Give her the chance to choose.

A PLEASURE SHARED

A couple who love and talk to each other may spend many hours learning exactly how the other masturbates by careful observation over several sessions. This personalized information is more valuable than any sex book when it comes to your own partner.

Unfortunately, some people are too shy to be able to do this so here are a few tips about variations that many

A pillow placed under the woman's hips raises the vagina to an angle that makes penetration by her partner easier. If he rests on his hands and knees he can more easily keep to the steady rhythm and continuous stimulation of the clitoris that is so conducive to orgasm, and his tongue is free to explore her mouth, neck and breasts

When the woman's hips are raised with a pillow and her legs are clasped around her partner, his pubic bone can be held against her vulva and pressed firmly onto her clitoris. Short rhythmic thrusts will then bring her to orgasm

women greatly enjoy but might be too shy to ask for even in long-standing relationships.

SOME SPECIAL VARIATIONS

Do not force any of these on your partner. Your aim is to please her and not to make her embarrassed or uncomfortable.

☐ Use a vibrator on her vulva or clitoris if she likes it

☐ Use the vibrator in her vagina while you caress her clitoris

☐ Use the vibrator on her anus while you put your fingers in her vagina and caress her clitoris with your tongue

☐ Stimulate her anus with your fingertip

☐ Use several fingers inside her vagina and do what she most enjoys. Some women like just two fingers kept still just inside their vagina while others enjoy three or four fingers being used to stretch their vaginal opening quite widely – especially when they climax

☐ Your partner may enjoy her cervix being played with – you will feel this as a knob rather like the end of your nose, deep in the vagina. She may be aroused if you stimulate the front wall of her vagina with either a vibrator or your fingers. This is the G spot area and can bring some women to a climax even without clitoral stimulation

☐ Indulge in sex games that turn her on. These can take many forms including dressing up for each other,

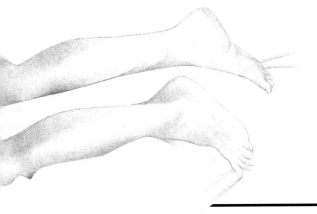

games that involve tying up – be very careful – taking different roles and many others.

INTERCOURSE

The overall aim of a man who wants to bring his partner to a climax during intercourse should be to slow his response down to her rhythm. The position that a couple uses is much less important than what they actually do.

☐ Do not rush. The chances are you will come too soon if you do. Contrary to what many men – and women – think, volent thrusting is not sufficient in itself to bring most women to orgasm

☐ Stimulate the clitoris. Some positions with the man on top allow him to rub his pubic area against the woman's and bring her to orgasm this way. Alternatively you can continue rubbing her clitoris with your fingers. Some women prefer to do this themselves

☐ Pay attention to the rest of her. Remember to stroke the rest of her body. Try patting or gently slapping her bottom, if she likes this. Do not forget her breasts. This is obviously easier if you are making love to her from behind or the side

☐ Be appreciative. Be responsive to what she says and does or any noises that she makes

☐ Cuddle up to her afterwards. A common complaint from women is that after intercourse the man turns away or even goes to sleep. Hold her close and savour the feelings you both have.

HER PLEASURE IS YOUR PLEASURE

Once you are familiar with your woman's likes and dislikes it is sensible on most occasions to stick to what she enjoys most.

Your partner's pleasure brings you pleasure, but you should be open to her advances so that she can enjoy your body and your sexuality too. Some women are most turned on by taking the lead sexually and greatly enjoy stimulating their partner. Pleasing her is not only a matter of what you do, it is also what you are happy and relaxed enough to let her do to you.

PLEASING A MAN

The woman who wants and learns to love her man in an exciting, inventive way will not only turn him on – she will reap rich benefits too

Modern man has a lot to live up to. Films and TV depict the ideal lover as a rampant male with an ever-ready erection who knows how to please a woman and who takes pleasure at the same time himself.

He shows few emotions yet he is understanding and strong with an almost infinite capacity to bring his woman to one – or usually more – orgasms. Women find him devastating and know instinctively how to please him.

Not surprisingly, however, most men are hardly sex machines. They are not always ready for sex and many suffer in today's performance-orientated society.

In some respects this is grossly unfair on a man. He may be easier to arouse than a woman but sex is only fulfilling as a two-way affair – something a couple do together, rather than individually. The woman who knows how to please her man learns how to please herself as well, and for many women their biggest turn-on comes from the reactions they can create in their partner.

A MAN'S NEEDS

Like women, men have their own unique sexuality. During the course of their lives their needs can vary from an insatiable desire for sex – usually in youth – where they are able to achieve orgasm several times a day, to a more regulated desire as they become older.

While their approach to sex is generally more basic than a woman's, men suffer uncertainties and pressures just as often which can all affect their love lives. In the 1970s, a research study by Shere Hite found a high proportion of men complaining about the quality of their sex lives, saying that they were always the initiators and that their women were too passive. Others complained about the predictability of their sex lives.

Studies and clinical experience show that most men are turned on by a willing woman, not just one who goes along with what is demanded of her or even 'forced on her'. When asked what single thing a woman could do to make them more excited, the overwhelming majority of a wide-ranging sample of 4,000 American men answered, 'be more active during sex'.

Even today, in our 'permissive' age, many women are still very shy about declaring their feelings for sex with their partner for fear that he may think them 'cheap'. It appears that some women, even if they are aware of this need and feel it strongly, even if they do recognize just how flattering and reassuring this simple change of direction could be, are still reluctant to show their willingness, to initiate lovemaking and take the lead in sex.

The world is a highly competitive place and men can feel easily threatened at work, at home – and in bed. Men who have to 'make things happen' both in and out of bed all the time often complain in research studies that sex is just another area where they feel they have to perform in order to come up to society's expectations of them.

Against this background a woman who comes half-way or more to meet her partner helps show him not only that he is still 'fancied' and loved sexually, but also that he is wanted and secure in a broader sense in this vital area of his life.

A MAN'S ULTMATE GOAL

In purely physical terms the act of intercourse is a relatively straightforward business for a man. Erection follows arousal, which is then followed by penetration. Ejaculation usually takes place a short time afterwards.

His body is arousable in a number of areas but his most sensitive and important area is on or around his genitals.

When a man makes love to a woman he has one principal goal – that of his own orgasm. Of course, he may want to please his partner as well – but his needs are considerably less variable than those of a woman, and usually more easily achieved.

But while a man's approach to sex may be more basic and less romantic than a woman's, he still craves love and attention and tenderness as much – if perhaps in a different way.

LOVE IN ACTION

To please a man you do not need any exotic skills or specialist knowledge. If you are to give him a really special time there are a number of preparations you can make.

□ Set the scene. Perhaps cook him a special meal or have a glass or two of his favourite drink

□ Be sexy for him. Men are very visual in their approach to love play. Wear something sexy that you know he likes

□ Take a bath or shower together. Many couples, once slighly aroused after kissing and cuddling, like to bathe each other. Your willingness to stroke him and to take the lead will greatly arouse your partner. Soap him all over, including his genitals. Make him have an erection and then let it go down as a tease for what is to come. Some couples prefer to prepare themselves separately and then present themselves 'ready for action' in the bedroom. It is up to you to do what is nicest for you as a couple

□ Decide whether you intend to bring him to climax with, or without, full intercourse. This can be a surprise for him but be clear in your own mind of exactly what you intend to do

□ Take responsibility for contraception. There can be fewer bigger turn-offs for a man than worrying if the woman he is about to have sex with is likely to become pregnant.

CARESS AND KISS HIM

Surveys show that most men enjoy kissing and cuddling. This may come as a surprise to those women who imagine that men only kiss and cuddle to please them.

Fortunately most women need few instructions on how to kiss and cuddle in that they tend to have a better instinct for caresses of the face and body than men.

As well as his mouth, kiss his ears – put your tongue inside and wiggle it around – eyes, neck, anywhere on his body (except, initially, his genitals). Massage him if he enjoys this or just stroke him in the places he likes best. Most men like their backs stroked, some like their feet massaged and almost all like their woman to run her body over theirs, especially if she runs her nipples lightly over him as she does so.

Bear in mind, though, that he is probably more genitally orientated than you are. While most women are contented to have their body stroked or massaged

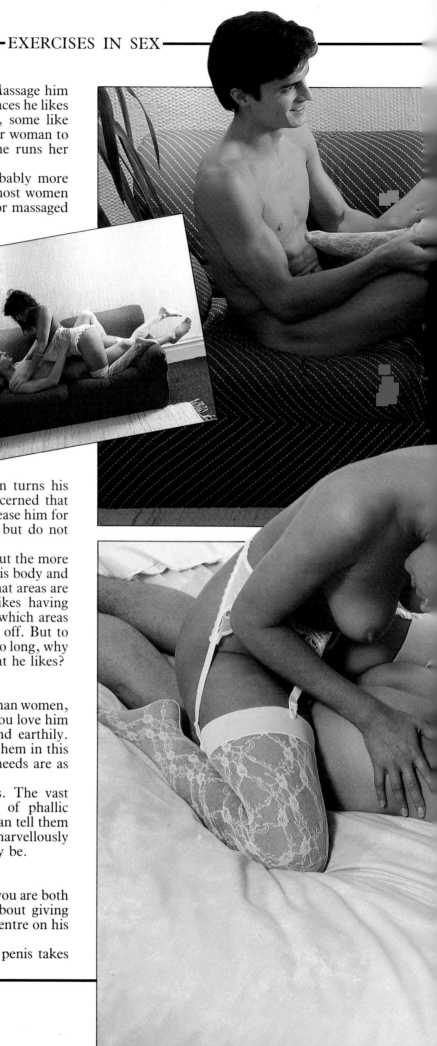

Dressing in underwear you know your man finds sexy, and letting him do the undressing, is one way of heightening his anticipation of what is to come

for a long period of time before the man turns his attention to their genitals, he will be concerned that you go to his penis rather more quickly. Tease him for a little while on other areas of his body, but do not spend too long over this.

This is a learning process, of course. But the more you take the initiative in sex and explore his body and reactions, the quicker you will discover what areas are the most sensitive and what he really likes having done. At the same time you will find out which areas to avoid and what (if anything) turns him off. But to avoid this period of trial-and-error being too long, why not simply ask him to whisper to you what he likes?

TALK TO HIM
Men are often more susceptible to flattery than women, so compliment him. Tell him how much you love him and how desirable he is. Talk frankly and earthily. Most men enjoy hearing a woman talk to them in this way, because it proves to them that her needs are as basic as theirs.

Tell him how wonderful his penis is. The vast majority of men harbour some vestige of phallic inferiority complex, and having their woman tell them it is beautiful, large or hard can be marvellously reassuring – however sophisticated he may be.

INCREASE HIS PLEASURE
Once you are actually in bed together and you are both becoming aroused you will want to set about giving him the most pleasure. For him this will centre on his penis and genital area.

Learning how best to handle a man's penis takes

time. The best source of information is your partner, so ask him what he likes and then do what he says.

You might also watch him masturbate and note his hand position, the speed at which he moves it, whether he stops and then starts, how firmly he grips his penis and so on. By so doing you should be able to become an expert and be able to stimulate it as well as – if not better than – he does.

Sadly, some women think that they can do just about anything to a man's penis and he will ejaculate. They are right to some extent in that some men can and do reach orgasm very quickly. What is important, however, is that the quality of a man's orgasm can vary enormously from occasion to occasion. Learning how to stimulate his penis properly can turn an ordinary lovemaking session into a memorable one.

The mistakes that women most commonly make are that they do not hold firmly enough, they use too slow a rhythm, or use an awkward grip. The most basic grips may be obvious, but there are other ways of using your hands. You could try using both hands and rolling the penis to and fro or stroke the tip with your fingers. Be guided by what the man likes. Alternatively use your body to caress the penis.

Another vital point to bear in mind is that, as with most aspects of lovemaking, different moods and various stages of the proceedings should dictate different and various approaches and techniques. There are no hard and fast rules – it is simply a case of learning when and how to adjust.

Soon, of course, the more adventurous and 'forward' woman will not only get to sense and know when to go fast or slow, when to be gentle or rough and so on – but she may well dictate things herself by creating and controlling the very mood of the lovemaking from the start.

SQUEEZE HIM

Some men like having their testes played with – others do not. If your partner does like it there are several pleasant techniques you can use.

Scratching the scrotum is a good start – run your nails up and down. Start near the anus and then scratch up along the 'root' of the penis to the scrotum.

Next, cup his scrotum in your hand, perhaps while you do something sensuous to his penis or his body with your other hand or with your mouth.

Using your hair to brush lightly along your lover's skin is an incredibly sensual way to stimulate him

Now try squeezing the testes themselves. Take one in between your thumb and several fingers – you will find that it is very slippery and takes some skill to anchor it between your fingers to squeeze it. Most men enjoy increasing pressure until they ejaculate, but it can be very effective and highly exciting to 'pop' the testes between fingers and thumb. As the man becomes excited his testes will swell considerably and become tender so be careful that you do not squeeze too much. Your partner will be able to tell you if and when to ease up.

ORAL CARESSES

Many men agree that either as part of foreplay or as complete intercourse in itself they find oral stimulation the most enjoyable part of lovemaking: in fact, it would probably be very difficult to find a man who was not highly aroused by his partner making love to him orally.

You can expand on the normal oral sex technique by lying astride your partner in the 69 position and using your vulva as your mouth to kiss him full on his lips. Move slowly from side to side sucking and kissing his penis as you do so. If you do not want him to climax in your mouth you can either bring him off by hand or let him come between your breasts.

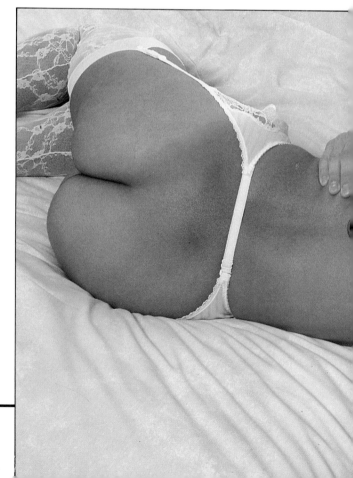

USING OILS

There is something very sensuous about having your skin rubbed with oil or cream – baby oil is cheap and just as good as the more expensive brands found in sex shops.

Put the oil into your hand to warm it up first and apply it lavishly over the man's body. Do not spend too long on this stage, but tease him by leaving his penis and balls until last.

Work your way round your man's body with the oil before applying some to his penis and testicles. Encircle the base of his penis with one hand then stroke it with the other, rubbing the oil in gently. At each stroke draw the head of the penis away from the hand encircling the base. Start gently and increase the pace – his responses should indicate how fast to go.

To make the experience even more sensual for him rub your body over his body allowing the oil to soak into yours. Alternatively let him rub the oil over your body or make him wait as you annoint your breasts. It is probably best to bring him to orgasm like this as few men will be able to hold out very long under such attentions.

OTHER TECHNIQUES

The anus is a very sensitive area for many men yet some feel ashamed to talk about it for fear of being thought homosexual by their partner. If you feel at home with the idea your man should find the following extremely arousing – but do be careful.

The anus may be a high pleasure zone but it can also be painful and there are real hygiene dangers unless scrupulous cleanliness is observed.

Your finger should be well lubricated with KY jelly or grease of some kind (saliva is rarely enough) before it is inserted into the man's anus. Once inside there are several things that men like the finger to do. Most like it kept still as you caress him elsewhere, but a few enjoy the woman pushing it deep inside them to massage the prostrate gland. This can be felt on the front wall of the rectum as a walnut-sized lump which is firm to the touch. Massaging this gland produces sexual sensa-

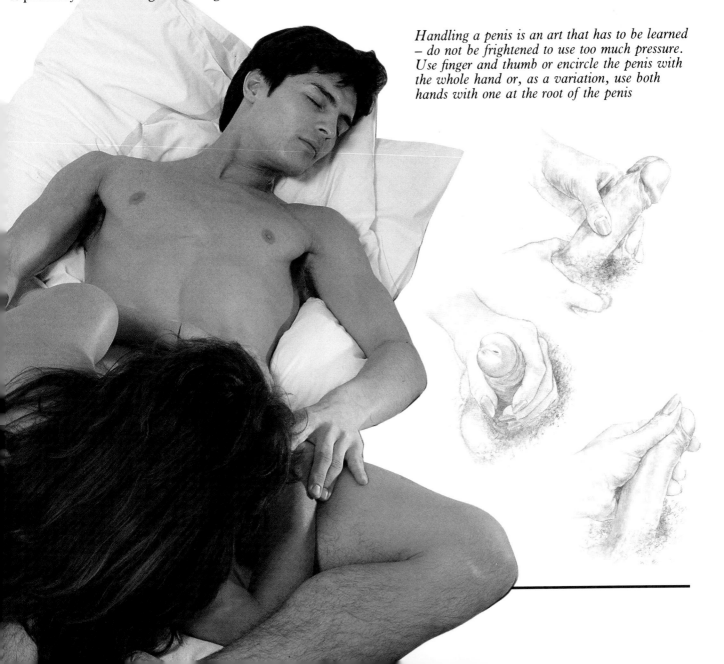

Handling a penis is an art that has to be learned – do not be frightened to use too much pressure. Use finger and thumb or encircle the penis with the whole hand or, as a variation, use both hands with one at the root of the penis

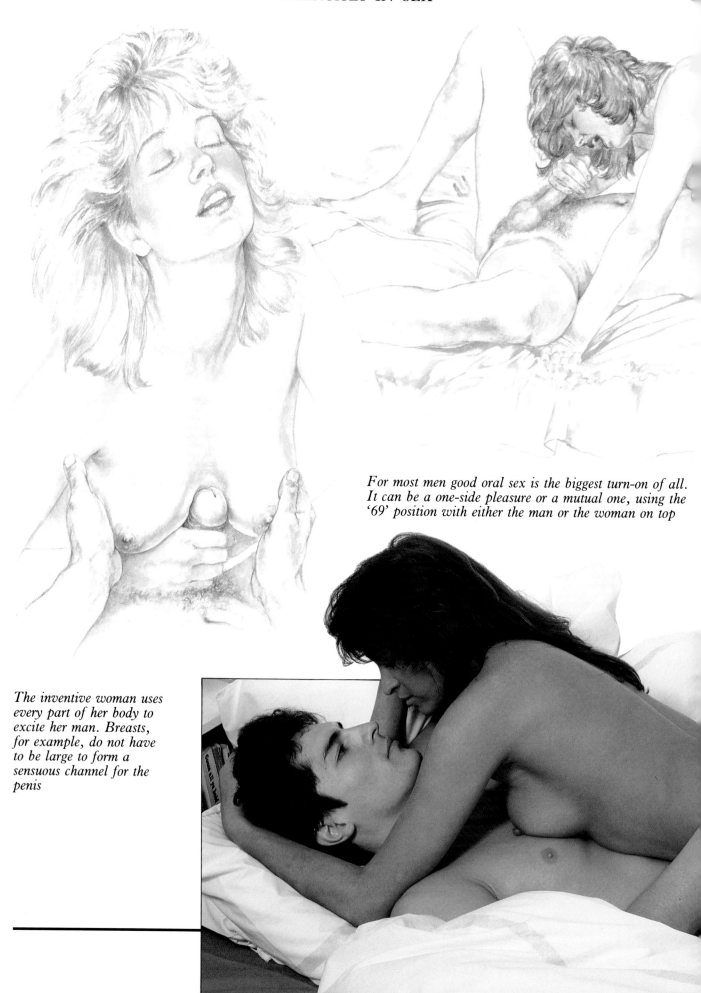

For most men good oral sex is the biggest turn-on of all. It can be a one-side pleasure or a mutual one, using the '69' position with either the man or the woman on top

The inventive woman uses every part of her body to excite her man. Breasts, for example, do not have to be large to form a sensuous channel for the penis

tions in nearly all men and can make some men ejaculate even without having an erection.

SEX GAMES

Many men, partly because they are so visually arousable compared with women, greatly enjoy sex games of various kinds.

These can take the form of mother-baby games, restraint games, dressing-up games, doctor-nurse games, indulging fantasy games and many others.

The woman's body is often the greatest single turn-on in the run up to sex itself, so any sensible woman uses this knowledge to excite her man and so increase

the quality of the act for him. It is only when the furs, the dress or the place become essential for enjoyable sex that a couple need become concerned. The vast majority of such games are played by couples simply as enhancers to make things better or to get the party going.

BEING INVENTIVE

There are few things that turn men on more than an inventive woman in bed. If the man is usually the one to initiate sex it comes as a delight to have the woman take the initiative because it shows him that she has needs herself and that she is prepared to 'use' his body to satisfy herself. This can have a powerful effect on most men.

Try new intercourse positions. Several studies, and clinical experience, show that men want more variety in the mechanics of intercourse. Try a new position every month or two just to keep the momentum going – surprise him with it; do not tell him in advance. Masturbate yourself in front of him – most men enjoy this. Use your vibrator on yourself and use a dildo too if it turns him – or you – on. Surprise him by asking for, or demanding, sex in unlikely places. Making sexual advances to him on a picnic, in the back of a car, in the bath or shower can all be great turn-ons. (Remember, though, that intercourse in a public place is against the law.)

Involve him in the choice of your clothes, especially your underwear and swimwear. Spending a morning buying underwear or bikinis with you will set him up beautifully for good sex later. Go through mail order catalogues together and get him to tell you which underwear he thinks is most sexy. Make a show of trying it on when you get it. Do a little fashion show for him – perhaps even doing a real striptease (pp 122–127 give more guidance on this).

CHANGING POSITIONS

The most popular position for intercourse is the missionary position – with the woman on her back and the man lying between her legs.

This is mostly chosen by women, though, because they see it as 'romantic' – the man is in control and there is obviously more intimate face-to-face contact. Men, however, often have other ideas which vary according to their particular sexual needs, and these should be taken into consideration when deciding how best to please him.

A man who greatly fancies his woman's bottom, for example, will enjoy making love in rear-entry positions. A breast man will like to have intercourse with his woman's breasts from time to time with her grasping his penis between her breasts or with him ejaculating over them and rubbing the semen into her nipples with the tip of his penis.

The variations are endless and a thoughtful and inventive woman will use her body to arouse her man in the most rewarding ways – for herself as well as her partner.

AFTERPLAY

For some couples, falling asleep in each other's arms after lovemaking is ideal, but for others a little gentle afterplay is the perfect ending

We hear a good deal about foreplay, the prelude to intercourse, but little is said about afterplay. Most experts, however, have claimed that some sort of afterplay is essential if a lovemaking session is to be complete. Van de Velde, author of the successful 1920s sex book, *Ideal Marriage*, said that in afterplay 'a man proves whether he is an erotically civilized adult'. Although few people today would go that far, many would agree that a man who simply sees sex as something to satisfy himself in a 'wham-bam, thank you Ma'am' sort of way is uncaring and selfish.

Some relationships work perfectly well along these lines, of course, with the woman masturbating afterwards – through the man or by herself – or not needing to do so at all. Surprisingly large numbers of women appear to be fully satisfied with quite rough, hurried intercourse and they do not need, cannot cope with, or

For him *Caressing his bottom and the area at the base of his spine will prove to be a gentle turn-on. Do not push the pace – his mind will turn to lovemaking in time*

For her *As she lies stretched out and relaxed after orgasm, lightly kiss her all over. Start at her feet and slowly, very slowly, work your way up her legs. Do not rush – keep the pace slow and relaxed*

even do not want much in the way of foreplay – let alone afterplay.

IS AFTERPLAY NECESSARY?

In practice it is a little confusing for most couples to think of afterplay as a special or even separate part of lovemaking. There should simply be loveplay – which occurs before, during and after lovemaking sessions.

Loveplay begins with the first caress and ends when both partners are totally satisfied, asleep or not. We say asleep because the majority of couples make love in bed in the evening and so use sex as a relaxing prelude to sleep. And what could be nicer than cuddling each other and falling asleep together? For many this is the best way to end the day. Any 'afterplay' then would seem not only inappropriate, but positively distracting. A woman who is satisfied, and not necessarily by having orgasms, is often happy to cuddle up to her man to relax or even to fall asleep.

However, the majority of sexual encounters do not end up with the couple falling asleep in this way, and they may well indulge in one or another form of afterplay.

WHAT IS AFTERPLAY?

The popular image of afterplay with a couple discussing art or the meaning of life is one that few couples live up to – or would even want to. For most of us it merely takes the form of a relaxing activity together – talking or cuddling each other or re-stimulation in preparation for a further bout of lovemaking.

Given that intercourse is an intimate experience, involving sharing and caring behaviour, it is hardly surprising that many couples feel exceptionally close after sex. Some do not, of course – at least not always. We all have off-days, worries, concerns and stresses. If we are upset or worried about something, sex will not necessarily make it go away, and we can easily go straight back to worrying about it once the immediate pleasures and distractions of intercourse are over. All too quickly the real world can intrude with all its problems.

For many people sex itself is unsatisfactory, at least on some occasions, and sexual failures and disappointments are common in most marriages. It is fairytale fantasy to expect the average couple who have made love hundreds or perhaps thousands of times to be 'lovey-dovey' every time after sex – if only because any one episode may leave one or the other feeling bad rather than good.

Because it makes us aroused and is a promise of what is to come, foreplay is bound to be more important and valued by the average couple than afterplay because, as with so many things in life, the preparation and anticipation is often as good or even the best part. There will never be the same excitement and drive to

To turn your partner's mind to another bout of lovemaking, leisurely kisses on her back will both relax then arouse her after a time

indulge in afterplay as there is to enjoy foreplay, and this is especially likely to be true for men who, on average, build up and resolve their sexual excitement more quickly than women.

ANXIETY AND AFTERPLAY

There are a large number of women who, either consistently or inconsistently, do not reach orgasm during lovemaking. Some find themselves left high and dry when their partner has finished, because they feel it is somehow aggressive or wrong to tell their partner exactly what they like, where they like it and for how long.

Some women have found various means to deal with their resulting frustration. Some find an excuse to go to the bathroom, where they masturbate themselves to orgasm in solitary silence. Others may try to persuade their partner to continue lovemaking, and if he will not, resentfully steel themselves to endure the frustration. Some women resort to faking orgasm to bolster their partner's ego and stop him 'feeling vulnerable'.

Yet many of these women might find, were they to tell their partner at the very moment of frustration, that he would be only too eager to bring them to orgasm orally or manually – he might well be turned on by the prospect. Far from making the man feel vulnerable by admitting that his penis alone does not make her climax, a woman can add another dimension to sex by inviting her partner into her most intimate sexual life.

Many men also experience anxieties, which they may try to hide by getting sex over with as fast as possible. Some men will turn away after making love instead of using these post-lovemaking moments. It is a sad comment about the so-called 'joy' of sex that many men and women often feel they have to resort to such patterns of behaviour.

THE FACE OF SEX

To many women, sex is an affirmation of their love for their partner – indeed intercourse often tends to have more emotional overtones for women than for men. This means that it will take longer for the average woman to 'wind herself up' emotionally for sex – and correspondingly longer to let 'let herself down' afterwards.

To totally relax your partner, massage her from top to toe. If you position yourself correctly, you can work on her legs, gently applying fingertip pressure to her calves and massage her back at the same time with your other hand

After orgasm, concentrate on areas other than the genitals – nibbling your partner's ear is one way of showing gentle affection in a mildly erotic way

This pattern does not apply to all women, of course. Many, especially younger, women are easily aroused and quickly lose their sexual arousal after intercourse, just as men do.

For those women who see sex as part of the way they show their love for their man, rather than simply a form of sexual release, it can be offensive to have a partner who seems to want them only for what is to come, as this appears to be uncaring afterwards. The responsibility for afterplay here lies firmly with the man.

AFTERPLAY AS FOREPLAY

Given that a lovemaking session is pleasant, or even very good, most people enjoy relaxing together afterwards. A drink, listening to music, talking or having a cigarette are common afterplay pastimes as the couple relax in the after-glow of the sexual encounter.

RELAXING AFTERPLAY
None of this needs to be prolonged and formalized. The direction and nature of what happens is bound to be linked to the time of day, the mood, and the situation in which they are making love.

Clearly, early morning sex hardly lends itself to prolonged lying around afterwards because most people have to get up to run the family or go to work. On holiday, however, early morning sex can be prolonged and enjoyed in a totally different way, perhaps even used as a prelude to going back to sleep.

Relaxing afterplay can act as a reinforcement of a couple's love bond. This is a good time to compliment each other with ego-boosting remarks which are all too often left unsaid.

Every lovemaking experience should leave the couple satisfied, but not satiated. Ideally, we should all be so delighted with what we have experienced that we are

For him *Kissing or licking his nipples is a sensuous and gentle form of teasing. Caress his body at the same time and this will increase his level of excitement*

For her *Concentrate on the legs and feet. Start at the toes and work your way up her legs. Keep clear of the genitals at this time – just build up the suspense*

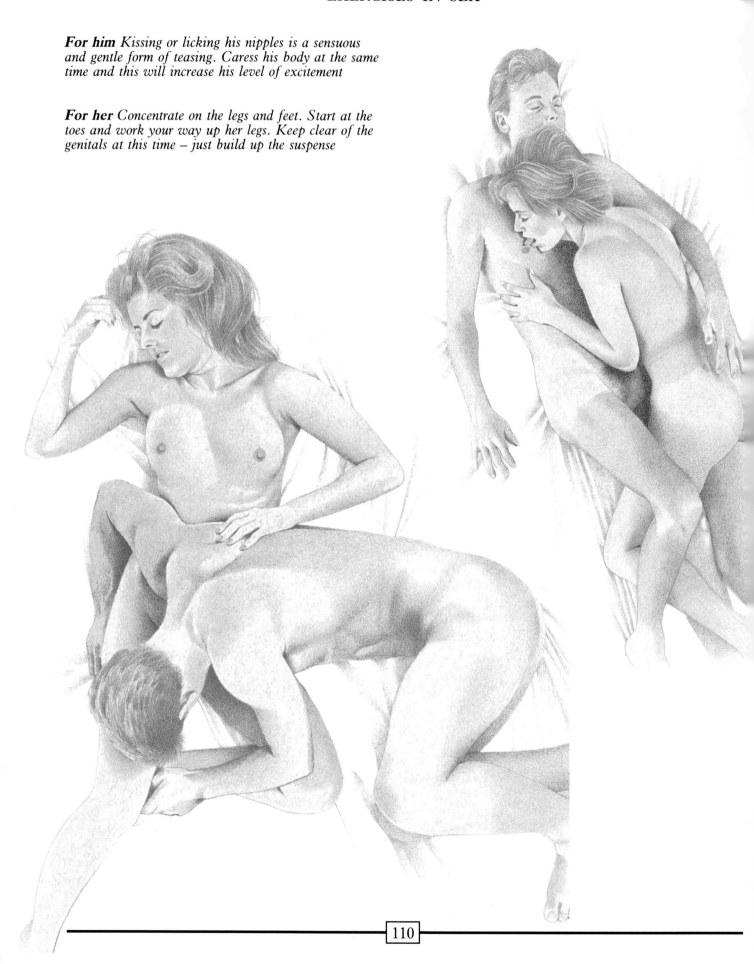

looking forward to the next time with eager anticipation.

Sweet nothings and praising remarks are, in this context, a part of afterplay for this time – yet foreplay for the next time. It does not really matter if it is an hour later – or a week. It serves the same purpose.

We all take our partner for granted much of the time, but a few words of praise or genuine thanks for a lovely experience works wonders for a relationship, especially if one or other feels low or sexually insecure. For the woman who feels she is losing her looks or who is menopausal, or for the man who is plagued with worries about sexual inadequacy, such praise during afterplay encourages further sexual activity and boosts their morale.

It is important to stress relaxing afterplay because the vast majority of people find sex a release of tensions and a promoter of relaxation. As a result, many dislike further physical stimulation – unless they are unsatisfied during intercourse itself – and some find it a positive turn-off. It is probably best to leave each other's genitals and other erogenous zones alone after sex – unless, of course, you intend to re-arouse each other.

RESTIMULATING THE WOMAN
For some couples, however, a sexual episode need not end after one act of intercourse. They want to restimulate each other or, more often, bring the woman to orgasm to satisfy her.

Unfortunately, many a woman who has one orgasm during sex and who is still edgy after her partner has come, fails to make her needs known and as a result ends up feeling cheated, unfulfilled, or ignored. But the man cannot be a mind-reader, and such a woman will have to spell things out or guide him into restimulating her other than with his penis. There are many

alternatives he can try, all of which work well.
□ Oral stimulation is highly effective provided the man has no scruples about licking and kissing a vulva that can have his own semen over it
□ Stimulation with the fingers, either the woman's own or her man's, is a more common form of restimulation. What can be very nice is if the man in this post-coital relaxation stage cuddles into his woman's breasts, kissing or sucking them and cuddling her as she masturbates
□ A vibrator or dildo can restimulate some women, and can be especially useful for those who want a vaginal orgasm but have not reached it during intercourse.

For many women, however, such 'artificial' aids can seem cold and practical at the best of times, but particularly in the warm glow after sex.

DO WHAT SHE LIKES
Many a man finds that doing these things re-arouses him, and before he knows it he is making love to his partner again. Some women like to be made love to once as a form of foreplay towards the next time, when it can often be better for them.

They let their man make love to them quickly, possibly even roughly, and then start real foreplay with a view to having orgasms both before and during sex.

This can be a particularly good way of coping with the man who comes too quickly. The couple make love so that the man is not so 'trigger-happy'. He then spends time stimulating her and bringing her to orgasm while he is building up to his next erection –

By the time both partners have given and received so much attention, they should be ready to make love once more

which can often be much harder and longer-lasting than before. This way of running things can work well even for the man who does not come too quickly, especially at the start of the day when he is fresh and full of energy.

The golden rule in all of these restimulation ideas is to do exactly what the woman most enjoys. This should be all the easier if the man has already come. He will have relieved his urgent need and can then concentrate entirely on the woman and her needs – and be totally unselfish in his lovemaking.

The selfishness of men is a common complaint that women make, especially of the man who simply goes for his own pleasure and ignores her needs. 'All he wants me for is physical satisfaction – I sometimes feel I might as well be anyone', is the kind of thought that is often expressed in various ways. Many men still do use their partners simply to satisfy their needs, although this kind of behaviour and attitude is, thankfully, fast disappearing.

RESTIMULATING THE MAN

All these restimulation techniques enable a woman who needs or likes to have several orgasms to do so and so be totally satisfied at any one lovemaking session.

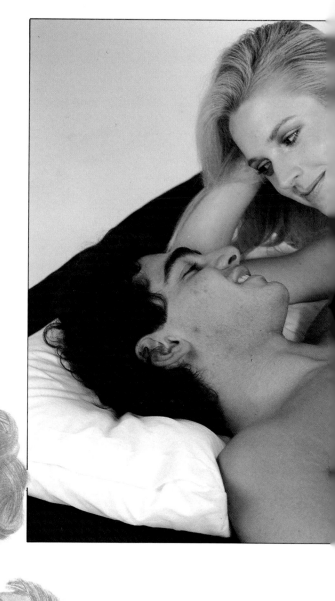

While your partner lies on his stomach relaxing, try a little sensual massage. Apply gentle pressure to his back and move over the whole area. Starting at the back of the neck, move over the shoulders, down the back to the base of the spine

Caress your partner's body with your own. Gently stroking him with your nipples, particularly if they are erect, will act as a turn-on. Sit astride him and lower your body on to his – nothing is more erotic than skin to skin contact. At this point let him take the passive role and you can take control of the situation

The tender touch – slowing drawing your finger over your partner's chest will relax – or excite – him

But some women only have orgasms with penis-in-vagina sex and so need, or want, their man to become erect again. And many men, especially younger ones, want to have intercourse more than once at one session. Here are some ways to restimulate your man.
☐ Use any method you know works first time around. This should produce the desired result in younger men; men much over forty may need something more
☐ Oral sex is the best and surest way of ensuring that a man comes up to scratch second time around. If you are still aroused, yet unsatisfied, you will probably be even more willing than usual to fellate your partner to encourage him to perform. Go gently though, especially if has just come – let him subside for a few minutes. Some men need ten minutes or more before they welcome any powerful stimulation. Try to remember that, unlike you, he is over the top of the orgasmic hill and will need to be re-aroused slowly and lovingly if he is to perform again to your satisfaction. Cuddle him and use your body to turn him on, and once he shows signs of being on the move again spend some time caressing his penis with your mouth and lips. Few men can resist the soft, moist approach for long, and he will soon be ready to make love again
☐ Most men need more powerful stimulation second time around so it is a matter of experimenting with things you know he likes or might like. Doing things to yourself can work wonders and stimulating him with oral caressing, anal play, 'dirty' talk, an erotic magazine or book, a sexy video or whatever may do the trick
☐ Some couples use their favourite sex games as a turn-on for second-time sex and almost anything that a shy or inhibited couple finds difficult or anxiety-producing in normal love-play can often be indulged in happily after a bout of lovemaking has relaxed them
☐ Use food as a turn-on. Find a snack that can be eaten with the hands – asparagus or bananas are ideal as they can be fed sensually and slowly to your partner
☐ If you have made love during the day, suggest you and your partner bathe together. A change of venue may well rekindle his interests in lovemaking. Let him lie in a warm foam bath and soap him all over
☐ If your partner is a 'romantic' at heart, music may well do the trick. Put on a favourite romantic record, preferably one that reminds you and him of some previous lovemaking occasion.

IMAGINATION & INVENTION

Predictability may be valued in certain areas of life but, when it comes to sex, experimenting with new techniques is always a bonus

Lovemaking may be infinitely variable, according to the 'experts', but for most couples there comes a time in their sex lives together when they crave for something a little novel. And however satisfactory their orgasms may be, they long for a way to perk them up and make that one session of lovemaking particularly memorable. Exploring variations of lovemaking techniques they both are familiar with can open up new options and provide new sensations.

WHY IS VARIETY NECESSARY?

Sex can be mundane or satisfactory – it can also be relaxed, slow and sensual, quick and explosive, athletic and exciting – even bizarre. It is up to us to decide which sort of sex we want at any particular time. The advanced lover knows his or her – and their partner's – limitations and weaknesses and exploits them in their sexual lives together.

There is a time to be selfish and a time to give. Introducing variety into one's sex life means that, sexually, all things are possible. And by knowing what

A simple cushioned chair can provide a number of exciting possibilities for the imaginative couple

s available, a couple has the option to accept or reject a particular lovemaking technique – or perhaps adapt it to their own individual needs and preferences. If a couple always approach sex with an open and willing mind, they will never become bored.

THE MALE RESPONSE

The male sexual response is much more physical and therefore more rapid than the woman's. A man can become aroused and ejaculate within minutes – some within seconds – if the level of arousal is strong enough. If a woman's clothes, body, smell and touch arouse him to a sufficient degree, it is even pos-sible that he may have an orgasm almost immediately.

For unlike a woman, a man's sexuality – centred as it is on his penis – needs 'positive sex'. Most men cannot be passively made love to in the sense that they must have an erection. Yet, there can be times for any man when his bank of sexual experience needs a little modifying.

The woman who understands this will be prepared to experiment with her man's erotic arousal. By so doing, she will enable him to exploit and take his own sexuality to the limits. His imagination and her inventive use of it can be the most valuable sex aid of all for the couple who are in tune with each other.

Even a frequently-used position can become a novel experience by making love in the living room, for instance, instead of the bedroom

THE WOMAN'S RESPONSE

The woman's response is much more varied than the man's and is therefore open to considerably more variation. Because the potential is so vast, it comes as no surprise that so many women find that their sexual resources, to a large extent, remain untapped by their partners.

The golden rule for men is to see their woman's sexual needs as individual and unique – which they are – and to introduce variations during foreplay and intercourse as often and as creatively as possible. And if her response is negative, then all is not lost. Because the brain and the emotions are such powerful sexual triggers, what may be unsuccessful in one arena may become highly sensual in another.

So to avoid trial and error, the wise lover listens and learns. And for the expert male lover, the key to truly satisfying his woman is sensitivity to her needs. And for both, the key requisite for a varied and fulfilling sex life is an open mind.

NOVELTY

When it comes to actually finding new ways for both partners to use their imagination to enjoy sex to the full, the possibilities are endless. Even for the couple who like a strong element of predictability in their sex lives, a favourite position or technique can take on new dimensions if it is practised in a different venue or in a slightly different way. What follows are suggestions to perk up a couple's existing sexual favourites. Even if the missionary position were a couple's only form of sexual expression, transferring it

outdoors or to the living room floor from the bedroom could give it a novelty value.

USING CLOTHES
Almost everyone finds clothes exciting sexually if only from time to time, although men are more easily aroused visually than women. So, for men particularly, their partner dressing sexily can have a dramatic effect on their arousal and the intensity of their orgasms.

Just something as simple as wearing suspenders and stockings and encouraging her partner to use 'quickie' rear entry sex can turn the whole routine nature of a

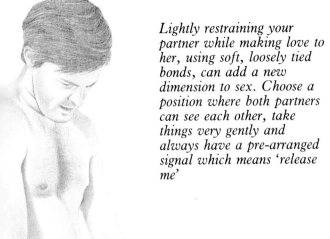

Lightly restraining your partner while making love to her, using soft, loosely tied bonds, can add a new dimension to sex. Choose a position where both partners can see each other, take things very gently and always have a pre-arranged signal which means 'release me'

favoured position into something new. Perhaps clothes offer some sort of restraint which may go some way to explaining their sexual appeal. Certainly oral sex for both partners can be much more arousing for some couples if one of them is partially clothed.

BONDAGE

Bondage is the gentle art of tying up your lover – or being tied up by them. The idea is not to make your partner do something that they would not do if they were not restrained. It is to enable one partner to tease the other until they almost beg to be brought to orgasm. So, the sex repertoire of the advanced couple can be greatly enhanced if they choose to make re-straint part of their love-play from time to time.

There are dangers, however. The advanced couple should have agreed on a set of ground rules before-hand, the principal one being a signal that really does mean 'release me'. Knots should never be too tight, nothing should ever be tied round the neck and gags – if they must be worn – should also be quick-release.

The dangers for the couple who truly trust each other and know each other's pet sexual likes and dislikes, however, are minimal.

BLINDFOLDS

Provided a blindfold is not tied too tight, it can provide unique sensations from even the most tried and tested lovemaking techniques. This is because if we do not use our eyes – or any one of our other senses – the remaining ones tend to be magnified to compensate. And so it is, if the ability to watch what one's partner is doing sexually is taken away temporarily. Masturba-tion and receiving oral sex, as well as a full-blown erotic massage, can take on new dimensions.

DIFFERENT TIMES OF THE DAY

Sex can be fun whenever a couple choose to make love, but so often they neglect the options of making love other than late at night – and usually in bed. Inevitably, practicalities dictate the times when couples can have sex, but it is always worth looking at the possibilities of making love at different times of the day and in different places.

And it does not always have to be full intercourse. A caress, oral sex or even quickie sex can all be highly arousing and need not take much time. The couple who are in tune with each other's own unique needs always find the time and the place to make love.

EROTIC VIDEOS

Erotic videos can have their place in a couple's sex lives, if only to add a little variety occasionally. Apart from making your own video, one exciting way to use videos is to watch them together and mimic what is happening on the screen. So, if the man is performing cunnilingus on the woman, so too can the man watching do it to his partner. And if the woman is fellating the man on the video, the video can even be put on hold while she takes his penis into her mouth.

Do not take the imitation too seriously, though, as there may be sexual practices shown that neither partner wants to become involved with.

MASSAGE

Sensual massage will always be part of foreplay for the advanced couple. It is a tried and tested means of arousal – for both men and women. But there are variations that advanced lovers can find exciting and stimulating.

☐ **Feathers** The use of feathers on either a man's or a woman's body as a means of bringing them towards orgasm can be a tantalizing experience. Use them as you would use your hands doing a conventional sensual massage, leaving the genitals until last. A paintbrush can be almost as exciting if creatively used

☐ **Ice** Ice has a curiously shocking value which some lovers find highly stimulating. The only rule is to let it melt down so that there are no square corners – ice straight from the freezer could damage the skin. Use it to trace a path all over the body – paying special attention to the breasts, buttocks and genitals. Some couples can find a small piece of rounded ice popped into the anus just prior to orgasm intensely erotic

☐ **Wear gloves** For some men particularly, the sensation of their partner using rubber household gloves to masturbate them to orgasm can be quite unique. For those who do not fancy that, leather or fur gloves can provide a variety of novel sensations for both partners.

SENSUAL GAMES

For the couple who want to increase their erotic repertoire, here are a few sensual games that they may like to play. If they do not appeal for one specific reason – restraint is not to everyone's taste – think how they might be adapted. They are designed only as starting points before adapting them to a couple's own unique and individual style.

DELAYED ORGASM

This technique can dramatically increase the sensations if the passive partner is restrained, but this is only optional. If one or both of you do not like the idea of restraint, ignore it.

HIM – FOR HER

Get your partner to lie back on the bed and make herself as comfortable as she can. Use dressing gown cord or something similar to tie her feet gently together and then do the same to her hands. Use oil on her body to give her an erotic massage, paying attention to every area of her body, legs, buttocks, breasts and so on without touching her genitals. Use your penis to excite her as well, perhaps by tracing a path along her body. If you like oral sex, allow her to kiss your penis and take it into her mouth. But remember, it is the quality of her orgasm you are after – not your own.

Now, facing towards her feet, place your knees on either side of her and use your tongue on her clitoris, using gentle but rhythmic strokes. As she becomes more aroused, insert one or more fingers inside her, perhaps trying to find her G spot. Keep using your hands and mouth, building up the tempo until her orgasm approaches. When this happens, stop and reduce the pace until her desire to come subsides. How often you do this is up to you, but the whole idea is to make her restraint work for her and turn it into one of the most memorable orgasms she has had. You can either complete the experience for her using your hands and mouth, or you can turn round and enter her in whatever positions seem most suitable.

For some couples, mild spanking adds extra fun to lovemaking – take care not to use too much force and never let the situation get out of hand

Watching sexy videos can greatly increase your level of arousal – mimic the actors performing oral sex but do not force your partner to try out anything he or she does not want to try

HER – FOR HIM

The principle of this restraint game is much the same. Get your partner to lie back while you tie his feet together and then his hands. Massage him, ignoring his genitals and then when he is aroused and has a firm erection, face away from him and kneel so that your vulva is close to his face and your mouth to his penis. Lightly brush your vulva against his lips and take his penis into your mouth. Grasp the root of his penis with your hands and build up a slow rhythm, licking and stroking and all the time increasing the pressure on his lips as you move your body from side to side.

As his orgasm approaches, stop fellating him and concentrate on using your body to excite him, keeping the pressure on his lips from your vulva and perhaps using your breasts to tease and tantalize him. Then, when you sense that the time is right, take his penis into your mouth and start again, increasing the pace and the pressure. Judge how often you should repeat this stage. Then, when he can finally take no more, raise the tempo. Suck hard on his penis as you take it into your mouth as deeply as you can and move your head up and down, at the same time using your hand to masturbate him. Move your vulva across his mouth until he comes.

SPANKING

Men seem to enjoy spanking more than women, although there is no denying that it plays a part in some couples' sensual repertoire. Like bondage, it should never be allowed to get out of hand which is why, if advanced lovers recognize this and use it as part of their own love-play, it can provide different sensations and lend a new degree of urgency to their lovemaking.

For the man to spank the woman, it is probably the best done when she is draped over his knee as he gently smacks her buttocks. For the woman who likes this, the man can keep his other hand busy, perhaps stroking her clitoris or even inserting his finger inside her vulva.

For the man who knows the finger and thumb technique – inserting one or more fingers inside her vagina, perhaps stroking her G spot as he uses his thumb on her clitoris – the extra dimension of smacking her raised buttocks can be highly erotic and memorable for both partners.

Equally for the man, having his buttocks spanked is more erotic if his buttocks are raised as he offers them to his partner. The advanced lover who recognizes this preference in her partner can dramatically increase the intensity of sensations for him by alternating between squeezing and parting his buttocks and smacking them while masturbating him with her other hand. It is probably best if the man lies down on the bed and just raises his buttocks rather than lying over her knee, but that is up to the couple concerned.

POSTILLIONAGE

For both sexes, postillionage, inserting a finger in the other's anus, can be highly erotic. The only danger is that bacteria lurk inside the anus so a man should never transfer his fingers from the anus to the vulva. Equally, a woman is best advised not to use postillionage on her partner and then masturbate him for much the same reason.

The position is all important. For truly sensual sensations, it is probably best that the recipient goes on all fours. For the man, this means that access to his

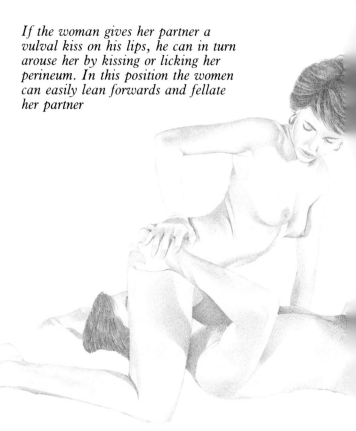

If the woman gives her partner a vulval kiss on his lips, he can in turn arouse her by kissing or licking her perineum. In this position the women can easily lean forwards and fellate her partner

prostate – his own G spot – is possible and the woman can use her finger to give him this type of orgasm alone. Alternatively, she can use her other hand on his penis to masturbate him and give him a truly memorable orgasm. For her, postillionage is best used in conjunction with intercourse – probably from a man-on-top position. If she raises her legs and clasps them around his waist – or better still his neck – the man can choose his moment and, as orgasm approaches, insert a finger inside her bottom.

For both sexes, KY jelly should be used on the finger to make the entry to the anus as gentle and as comfortable as possible.

KISSING THE PERINEUM

For men and women, the perineum is delightfully sensitive both to the light touch of a finger or tongue and mouth. For those who like the idea, unique sensations can be provided by the giver running their tongue along the crevice in between their partner's buttocks. It is best if the receiver takes up a position lying on their stomach on the bed, perhaps with a couple of pillows placed underneath their stomach for more comfort.

FEMORAL INTERCOURSE

This is another way to orgasm for the man that can be used occasionally. Originally employed as a method of birth control or a means of preserving virginity, the man presses his penis between his partner's closed thighs and ejaculates between them. The penis should be placed near the top of the thighs so that the shaft goes between her labia and she in turn presses down hard on it. Some women say that it can give a keener sensation than actual penetration. Almost any position can be used for this method of intercourse — provided the woman can press her thighs together around the man's penis.

The kissing and licking of the perineum can be independent or can be used in conjunction with masturbation. It is probably best not to indulge in oral sex immediately afterwards. And it is a good idea for the giver to wash their mouth out with a mouthwash afterwards especially if he or she has popped the tip of their tongue into the other's anus.

CREATIVE USE OF THE VIBRATOR

For the woman who uses a vibrator on herself, or gets her partner to, a delightful variation from conventional techniques is simply to vary her position and mix vibrator use with creative use of her partner's hands and mouth. So, if the woman goes on all fours, the man can get underneath her, and use his tongue on her clitoris while inserting the vibrator inside her.

Another variation is for the man to enter her from behind while the woman uses the vibrator herself on her clitoris. The permutations are almost endless. And for the bottom-orientated woman, there are dual vibrating devices on the market that she or her partner can insert into her anus and her vulva.

Pamper your partner – let him lie back relaxed while you bring him to a climax. Use your hands to arouse him and then, when you think the time is right, use your mouth to give him a memorable orgasm

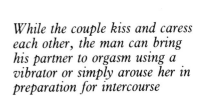

While the couple kiss and caress each other, the man can bring his partner to orgasm using a vibrator or simply arouse her in preparation for intercourse

STRIPTEASE

Watching a bored stripper take her clothes off may not turn your partner on, but watching you go through the same routine could be quite a different matter. Try it and see what happens

Striptease, as the name suggests, involves two parts: stripping off one's clothes and, in so doing, teasing one's audience. Anyone can undress in front of their partner, unless they are very inhibited, but few people fully realize the erotic potential of striptease, whether as a bit of fun or as a prelude to lovemaking.

FEMALE PRESERVE?

Generally, stripping has been seen as a thing that women do for men – whether in public in a striptease entertainment, or in private.

But now that sex roles are less rigidly defined, and women are more open about their expressions of sexuality and their desires and needs, it is becoming apparent that they enjoy seeing naked men or men in varying degrees of undress.

Today, in a number of countries, the male stripper has become a popular form of entertainment for many women.

A SHARED EXPERIENCE

The vast majority of couples, however, see striptease in terms of the woman doing it for her man. This need not just be a one-way affair, though, with the woman doing something to turn on her man. The man will certainly enjoy it, but the woman can also become aroused by her own sexually explicit behaviour as well as by the effect she sees it having.

UNDRESSING FOR FUN

If you have never removed your clothes in front of a man except to 'undress', you will probably find stripping somewhat embarrassing the first time.

One way around this, as with many things in life, is to get some professional guidance. You could go to a strip club with your partner and see how the professionals do it. This in itself will help to reduce your inhibitions and will show you that stripping can be a clever and titillating performance.

An alternative for those who do not wish to make an excursion into a club is to hire a video and watch a professional stripper in the comfort of your own home.

GETTING STARTED

Having gained some ideas from watching a video or a live stripper, prepare the scene and yourself beforehand to ensure the best possible outcome.

You could have a small drink to loosen up, then make sure the lighting is good and that you are going to be uninterrupted. Choose suitable music – the record or tape should last longer than the average three or four minutes, so that you have plenty of time to complete your strip.

HER FOR HIM

The basic principle of stripping is to reveal the obvious first and to save the best bits – the tease – until last.

☐ Make up and do your hair, paint your nails, have a bath and so on. The bath is particularly important if you are going to go straight from the strip into lovemaking

☐ Choose your clothes carefully. Avoid fiddly fastenings – everything must come undone very easily and you should be able to undo everything yourself, unaided. Wear only a very few clothes and only those that can be easily removed. Wear a dress (or blouse and skirt), bra and pants, stockings and suspenders, high-heeled shoes and perhaps some body jewellery

☐ Put on the music and settle your partner down in a chair or on the bed. Kiss and stroke him a little to get him excited and interested. After this you are not going to touch him, nor let him touch you, until the whole strip is over and you make love

☐ Start by dancing around to the music as if you were dancing at a disco. When moving, emphasize your breasts, legs, and bottom. Run your hands down the outsides of your hips and thighs, over your arms, and over your breasts. Run your fingers through your hair and generally cover your body with strokes as though it were your man doing it

☐ Slowly undo your blouse in a teasing way to reveal more of your breasts, and when all the buttons are undone, turn around with your back to him and tease

down the top of your blouse and remove it. Cover your breasts with it and turn around so that, apart from your bra straps, it looks as though your top is naked beneath the crumpled blouse. Never remove any garment like this over your head – it rarely looks elegant and ruins your hair style. Now throw the blouse over to him to reveal your top half

☐ Undo the waistband of your skirt and wriggle out of it, letting it fall to the ground. Step out of it and kick it over to him. Do the wriggling out bit very slowly and seductively, teasing him as it slips down your hips to reveal your panties and suspender belt. This can all be greatly enhanced by turning around and revealing your bottom as it emerges from the skirt. Next, take off your shoes slowly and sexily

☐ Sit on a high stool or chair and slowly undo your stockings from the suspenders one at a time. Roll down one stocking at a time to the toe and remove it sexily. Once you have removed your stockings, put your shoes back on – this can be very sexy from the man's point of view. Caress your legs and thighs to the music as you sit down. Now you are wearing only bra, knickers and shoes

☐ Stand up and dance some more to the music. Now emphasize your breasts, because they are to be the next centre of attraction. Remove first one bra strap and then the other, and with your back to your man undo the clip behind. Hold the bra to your chest with your hands over both breasts and turn around to face him. Now, to the music, do a 'peep-bo' with first one breast and then the other and finally, when you sense this has gone on long enough, toss the bra to him

☐ Dance around more, now wiggling your breasts to the music, and go over to him and tease him by hanging your breasts very close to his face but without letting him touch you anywhere. If he tries, leap away and do not let him do so. The secret of a good striptease is 'look, don't touch'

☐ Now go back to your dance position out of his reach and slowly and sexily remove your panties. Turn with your back to him and edge them down ever so gently in time to the music. Let them fall to the ground when you are facing towards or away from him, whichever you know he prefers. Kick them over to him or pick them up and drape them over him

☐ Dance around now to the rhythm and then remove your suspender belt or G-string and display yourself really well and stroke and caress yourself to the music all over your body

☐ Lie down on the floor and writhe around to the music. Facing him, open your legs and stroke your vulva. Lie on your tummy and then get on all fours and caress your bottom so that you are totally open to his view. When lying on your back caress your breasts and nipples. Wet a finger or two and moisten your nipples and then caress your clitoral area, if only in a teasing sort of way. From here on, it is likely that your partner will want to join in the proceedings as he will have been teased quite enough.

HIM FOR HER

Preparing to strip is much the same for men as it is for women. Most men find stripping more difficult than do their partners, and men's clothes are not intrinsically as sexy and so look less attractive when being removed.

But some men can be really sexy when they strip and greatly excite their women. There is only one rule – remove your socks early on. Anything else looks ridiculous and greatly detracts from the sexiness of the event.

☐ Start by dancing around slowly to the music. Now remove your tie slowly and sexily, if you are wearing one. This can be draped around the woman's neck or somewhere else if you like

☐ Undo your shirt buttons slowly from the top to show your chest. Reveal one nipple at a time and then re-cover it

☐ Remove your shirt by letting it fall to your feet – do not pull it over your head. Kick it to one side

☐ Loosen your waistband or belt and remove your socks. Undo your flies, or get your partner to do so, but forbid her to touch anywhere else, and slowly edge your trousers down, perhaps with your back turned to your woman so that she can enjoy your bottom being revealed. Once your trousers are off, dance about sexily to the beat. Stick out your pelvis and rotate it to the music

☐ Put your hand inside your pants and stimulate your penis

☐ Turn your back to your partner and slowly tease down your pants, one side at a time, to reveal one buttock at a time. Pull them completely down and let them fall to the floor and then kick them over to the woman

☐ Move enticingly to the music and flick your penis outwards towards her, perhaps right in front of her, but do not allow her to touch it

To add an extra bit of spice to the proceedings, turn your striptease into a double act with your partner. You can either remove a few items of clothing yourself and then let him help you finish the job off, or else let him undress you bit by bit, stringing the action out to increase the anticipation

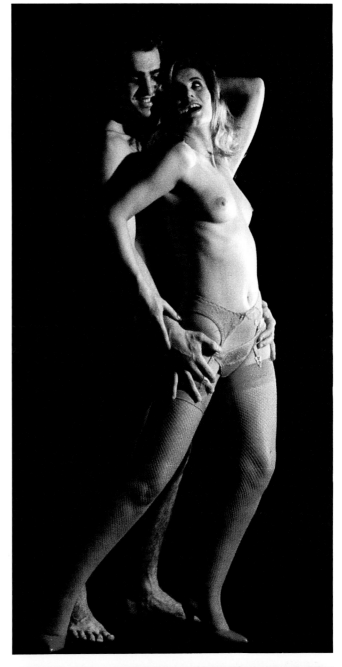

☐ Caress your balls and penis and stroke all over your chest and tummy. By now you will probably have a strong erection, and the rest is up to the woman.

INFORMAL STRIPTEASE

Lovers who are tuned in to each other's sexuality can go in for all kinds of other subtle forms of striptease – and, with a little imagination, they need not be confined to their own home.

When going out somewhere formal, perhaps to a disco, dinner or party, just as you are about to go in, remove the woman's panties while you are in the car. For the more bashful who do not like taking chances in public places, this can be done at home before you leave.

In the summer the woman can go out somewhere formal and public with simply a dress and shoes on and nothing on underneath.

Similar pre-stripping routines for men are not usually practicable on the grounds of comfort and public decency.

Any or all of the above hints can be a real tease for the couple who share the secret. There is a build-up of sexual tension and expectation, which means that the couple will be ready for making love later when they are alone.

GAMES TO PLAY

A woman who is pre-stripped under her clothes can drive her man wild with anticipation. When dancing, she can press her bra-less breasts against him, or she can 'accidentally' brush her breasts against him, if that turns them both on.

When they are alone together, she can open her legs as she sits opposite him so that he can see up her skirt or get a full view of her panty-free vulva. Or she can put one foot out of the car on to the road while the other remains in the car to reveal her vulva as he opens the car door for her to get out – the possibilities are endless and a loving and inventive couple will get hours of fun out of such games.

Some couples are highly aroused by the woman exibiting herself in this way when other people are around. The turn-on is knowing that only they know that the woman is naked beneath her dress – the others are missing out.

EVERYDAY UNDRESSING

But you do not need to indulge in formal striptease or the playful strips to have fun. You can just as easily make everyday undressing a bit of a tease for your partner if you wish.

Just make a little effort to remove your bra sexily or to make a show of removing your panties. 'Accidentally' sit down opposite your man to remove your stockings, after having already taken your panties off. Men can, of course, do similar things.

All of this raises sexual expectation and, by increasing anticipation, heightens sexual excitement and makes for more stimulating and sensual lovemaking.

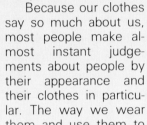

Like everything we do, clothes reveal, and are dictated by, our personalities. They say something about the way we really are.

Because our clothes say so much about us, most people make almost instant judgements about people by their appearance and their clothes in particular. The way we wear them and use them to enhance, or detract from, our sexuality also speaks volumes.

Many clothes styles, such as tight jeans in either sex, leave little to the imagination and reveal as much as they conceal. Frank nudity is not culturally acceptable in the western world, but many styles of dress enhance the sexiness of what is underneath,

rather than hiding it. So it is that a girl in a clinging T-shirt, no bra and tight jeans probably looks sexier than she would be going about her daily life completely naked.

Much of the pleasure we gain from looking at bodies comes from the promise of what is to come – not what is actually revealed. Many men say that a partly-clad woman is more sexually arousing than a naked one. And women, too, can be more turned on by

the sight of a handsome man in briefs than by a full-frontal view of male nakedness.

There is little doubt that there is something 'naughty' or prohibited about undressing other people. Socially this is forbidden. Between lovers, however, so used to seeing each other's bodies, slowly undressing each other can become an integral step in their sexual repertoire – a pleasurable part of the prelude to making love.

WHY STRIPTEASE?

We wear clothes as much for protection against the weather as we do to adorn our bodies, but there can be little doubt that clothes often enhance our attractiveness to the opposite sex.

SEX AND WATER

The feeling of weightlessness experienced in water can add a new dimension to a couple's lovemaking. And a bath or shower can provide an exciting venue for sex

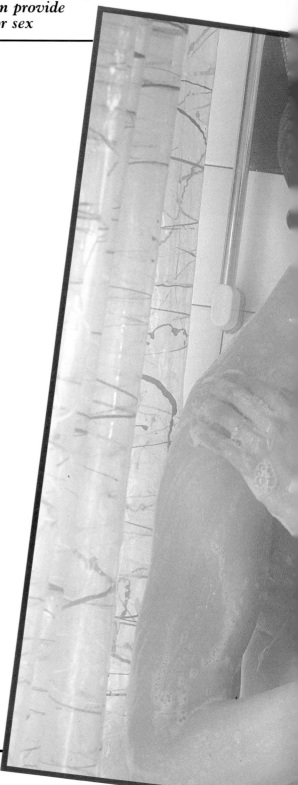

Water has long been considered to have relaxing and healing properties, and this – together with its potential for sensuality – has always made it a powerful force when combined with sex.

The human body is composed mainly of water and we start life in a watery environment – in our mother's womb – so water plays a central role in our lives from the very beginning. And the wetness associated with sexual arousal makes water an evocatively sexual element.

WATER GAMES – INDOORS

At home, there are many ways that water can be used to make lovemaking more exciting. Getting into the bath or shower together can be a tantalizing run-up to intercourse, a new place to have sex, or just a soothing way to relax together afterwards.

BATHING

The most common thing we do with water is to wash ourselves. The feel of water on the skin can be invigorating, or relaxing, depending on its temperature and how it is used.

Many people find that either sensation can enhance their enjoyment of a particular lovemaking episode. Applying soap and stroking your partner's body – or your own – can be a good excuse for intimate physical contact that might not otherwise occur.

Bathing can also make a couple feel sexy, because it unites them in a comforting 'back to the womb' way, as they share the same watery environment. This is where the otherwise restricting design of a bath can work in the intimate couple's favour.

Close physical contact becomes essential and continual with the constant intertwining of legs and the search for comfortable positions in which to caress or lather each other.

UNDERWATER SEX

Intercourse underwater is rather difficult to achieve even in a large bath, but the woman can kneel up in the water and be entered from behind, or the man can lift up her pelvis as he kneels in the water and enter her as she lies back supporting herself on her elbows on the bottom of the bath.

A shower together can be a long, warm and sensual experience – or you can make it stimulating and energising, with a hot shower followed by a brief cold one to make you both refreshed and tingling all over

A SENSUAL EXPERIENCE

If you want to make a real fuss of your partner in the bath, soap them down, and treat the experience as a version of a watery sensual massage.

Depending on the size of your bath you can do this as you kneel by the side of the bath, or in the bath with your partner, if size allows.

Use the soap to clean every nook and cranny leaving the genitals until last, and then rinse your partner down. Then turn sensual massage into a sexual caress, and bring them to orgasm.

For the more adventurous, you can get your partner to support their weight on their elbows, and allow the lower part of their body to float to the surface. Their relative weightlessness will make this quite comfort-able for them. Then you can bring them to orgasm with oral sex.

To finish off, allow them to lie back and wallow in the afterglow of orgasm and then – when they are ready – dry them down with a towel, taking as long as necessary to turn that into another sensual experience.

Most will content themselves with a bath or shower together (right). A hot tub (below) is an expensive luxury, but is ideally designed for relaxed lovemaking

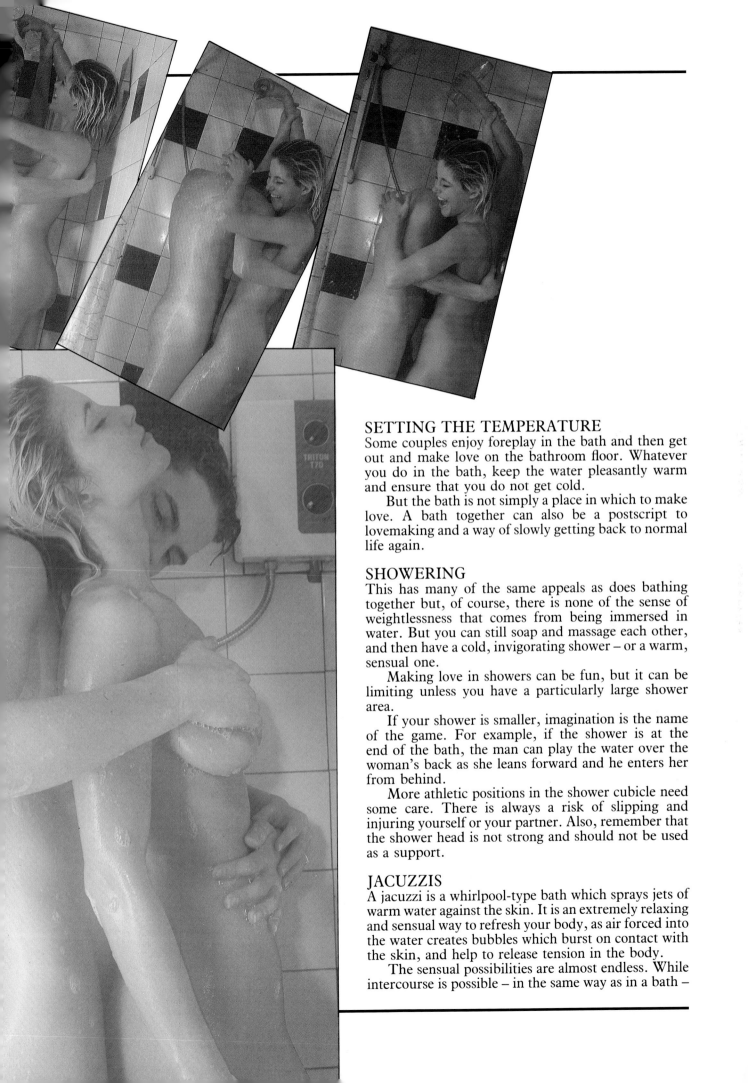

SETTING THE TEMPERATURE

Some couples enjoy foreplay in the bath and then get out and make love on the bathroom floor. Whatever you do in the bath, keep the water pleasantly warm and ensure that you do not get cold.

But the bath is not simply a place in which to make love. A bath together can also be a postscript to lovemaking and a way of slowly getting back to normal life again.

SHOWERING

This has many of the same appeals as does bathing together but, of course, there is none of the sense of weightlessness that comes from being immersed in water. But you can still soap and massage each other, and then have a cold, invigorating shower – or a warm, sensual one.

Making love in showers can be fun, but it can be limiting unless you have a particularly large shower area.

If your shower is smaller, imagination is the name of the game. For example, if the shower is at the end of the bath, the man can play the water over the woman's back as she leans forward and he enters her from behind.

More athletic positions in the shower cubicle need some care. There is always a risk of slipping and injuring yourself or your partner. Also, remember that the shower head is not strong and should not be used as a support.

JACUZZIS

A jacuzzi is a whirlpool-type bath which sprays jets of warm water against the skin. It is an extremely relaxing and sensual way to refresh your body, as air forced into the water creates bubbles which burst on contact with the skin, and help to release tension in the body.

The sensual possibilities are almost endless. While intercourse is possible – in the same way as in a bath –

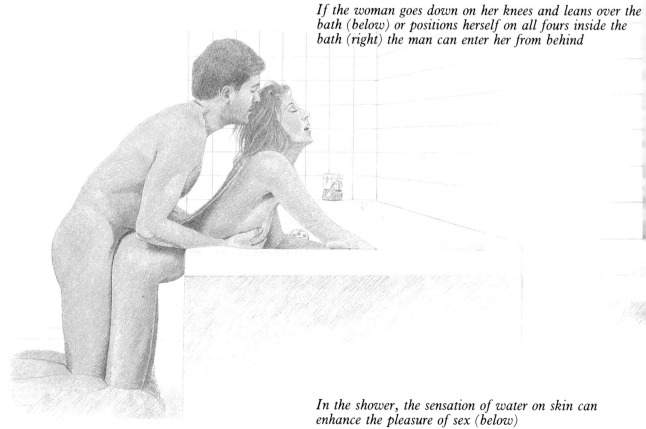

If the woman goes down on her knees and leans over the bath (below) or positions herself on all fours inside the bath (right) the man can enter her from behind

In the shower, the sensation of water on skin can enhance the pleasure of sex (below)

it is the flow and power of the water that can provide an almost complete experience in itself.

WATERBEDS
Fashionable in the 1960s, waterbeds consist of a large water-filled bag which forms the mattress of the bed. It can be as rigid or as flexible as you wish – depending upon how full you make it. Lying on the mattress (covered with a sheet in the normal way) gives an eerie sensation which some people like but which may make others feel slightly sea-sick. The bounce in such a bed makes intercourse interesting, as it allows the couple making love to experience unusual rippling sensations – as if they were making love at sea.

Also, as the couple move about, the bed seems to envelop their bodies, making for a unique experience.

WATER GAMES – OUTDOORS
Outdoors, an intimate encounter by the sea or in a swimming pool can be a highly erotic and sensual experience, although what you can do in public is restricted by the law. You should make sure that you are completely alone if you want to make love in a public place.

SWIMMING POOL
Making love in a swimming pool can be extremely arousing. Simply being in the warm water with your

While supporting the woman under her buttocks and lower back, the man can penetrate her. She weighs almost nothing like this, and can be positioned at many angles easily – making new penetration positions simple to achieve.

For those who do not have a pool of their own, similar fun can be had at the seaside – but as it is a public place, make sure you find somewhere deserted.

SEASHORE

Lying on the beach at the water's edge in a warm climate can be romantic and arousing, but the realities of sand and sex are a little more sobering.

As each sand-laden wave breaks, it makes for very considerable friction between penis and vagina, which can cause irritation. To avoid this, you could try getting into deeper water before starting to make love. If the shore line is covered with boulders, an encounter at the water's edge is possible without much hazard although it will probably be quite uncomfortable.

WET LOOK

A man or woman clad only in a wet and clinging cotton (or other thin material) shirt reveals their physique in a very tantalizing way as the water makes the now transparent cloth mould to their body. Both men and women say how sexy this is.

A wet body is sexy in itself. Advertisements for holiday resorts usually picture semi-clad people relaxing by the sea, with slicked-back hair, and limbs glistening wet, or shining with suntan oil. Here, the link between water and sexuality is quite obvious.

lover is stimulating enough, but you will need your own pool if you are to take the matter to its logical conclusion.

WEIGHTLESS SEX

In a swimming pool, the woman can float on her back in the water in the shallow end while the man walks backwards down the slope until his penis is floating horizontally on the surface of the water. Now penis and vagina are at the same level.

The man can rest on his elbows, while the woman sits astride him and lies back, using his knees for support

EXPLORING
FANTASY

*Sharing your private fantasies with your partner can add
an extra dimension to your sex life provided you
both view the revelations with care*

Sexual and marital therapists have found that an individual's fantasies say a lot about his or her unconscious sexual needs and wishes. They can thus be very useful tools in understanding what is really going on in a relationship, as opposed to what simply appears to be happening.

When a woman appears to be highly uninhibited or sexually aggressive, for example, but has fantasies that seem to belie this, such a revelation can shed light on why it is that she behaves the way she does, though everyone, perhaps even including her partner, thinks she is sexually 'together'. Dreams and fantasies, therefore, can provide useful windows through which to view the unconscious mind.

This knowledge can be used by the average couple too. You do not have to be a professional to learn more about each other's sexuality. But unlike telling a neutral professional about such things, there are pitfalls when it comes to sharing fantasies with your partner.

EXAMINE YOUR MOTIVES
First of all it is vital to be sure of your motives for wanting to share fantasies. The only valid motives revolve around using the information to understand each other better and to enrich your sex life.

When discussing fantasies, it makes sense to go very gently and lovingly, or your partner could see your interest as intruding on his or her private thoughts. The result could then be a shying away rather than a getting together on the subject. When handled carefully, however, the subject of fantasies usually gives pleasure to both and can help a partnership grow.

FEAR OF SHARING
For some individuals the idea of sharing fantasies is appealing in theory, but they are afraid that their partner will somehow put them down or ridicule them once they know what really turns them on. Many other people are actually ashamed of their innermost thoughts, mainly because they imagine that they are the only ones to have them. Yet others, of both sexes, fear that because their fantasy involves someone other than their partner, their lover will be offended.

If a man's major fantasy is about his secretary, for example, his partner could be forgiven for thinking that, given half a chance, the fantasy could become a reality, or indeed might already have done so. When it comes to this type of fantasy, however, it is vital to remember that most fantasies are not ways of satisfying unfulfilled desires. Indeed, many fantasies are attractive only in the mind. If they were to be offered to the individual in real life, they would often immediately back away.

WHEN NOT TO SHARE
The best rule about fantasies involving specific individuals you both know personally is, *do not* share them. Sharing a fantasy about a film star you have both seen is, of course, totally different because such a figure is no direct personal threat to your relationship.

Many women save their favourite fantasies for masturbation – a time when they are in total control of the action and can dictate the pace of their arousal using the techniques they know they enjoy the best

Restricting one of the senses during sex tends to heighten the remaining ones making you much more sensitive to your partner's touch. Blindfolded, a person can let their fantasies run free

Similar problems occur with those who have fantasies about their opposite sex parents. Quite a few women have fantasies about their fathers. Usually they are unconscious in origin and get pushed straight back into the unconscious as soon as they surface to consciousness. For some of these women, fantasy of any kind becomes impossible – they say that they never have them. In reality they do, but they are so unacceptable to their conscious mind that their unconscious policeman censors them. This means that they do not enjoy the beneficial effects that other people get from their sexual fantasies.

Therapy can help a woman such as this to bring her fantasy material to the surface, where it can be confronted and dealt with. This then clears the ground for her to enjoy fantasies that can add to her sexual pleasure rather than detract from it.

GOING EASY
When it comes to sharing fantasies, the watchword must be caution. Start by talking over your least threatening ones. Set the scene first, perhaps by having a small alcoholic drink to relax you. Choose the time and the setting and make sure that things are very loving and sexy. Preferably wait until you are both aroused a little and talking intimately.

If, at any time, you find your partner backing off from what you are saying stop and try again another day. People's abilities to tolerate knowledge about one another's intimate lives vary as time passes over the years, and it could be that what was unthinkable to share one month, becomes quite acceptable a few months later.

Exactly how you share your fantasies will, of course, be up to you but almost any method that reassures the other that whatever they say will be used positively within the relationship will work. At first this might seem strange to you, but if you do it in the context of sexual arousal you will probably soon find that the revelations greatly enhance your sex life.

A WATCHING BRIEF
A more subtle and less threatening method of finding out about your partner's fantasies is to watch closely what he or she finds sexy. A woman who enjoys romantic fiction will, for example, most probably enjoy romantic fantasies that do not involve sexual intercourse at all.

Being vigilant all the time will usually yield good results. Look out for what most turns your partner on at films, when reading magazines, when watching TV, and so on. Take these hints and use them to build interesting sexual events into your life.

If, for example, your lover always turns to the underwear pages of your mail order catalogue, then how about using this as a sexual adventure by going through them with him and choosing something you both fancy for you to wear. When it arrives, you can enjoy an evening of fun dressing up, perhaps even with him photographing you as if you were a model.

Clothes play a major part in some people's fantasies – for the woman who wants to play the 'whore', scanty underwear in 'tarty' colours can allow her to take her fantasies into her lovemaking

For the man who fantasizes about being dominated by his woman, woman-on-top positions are ideal, and when facing away from her partner the woman is free to fantasize, thus allowing her to increase her level of arousal

Oral sex features highly in the fantasies of both sexes and, nowadays, is also part of most couples' sexual repertoire, allowing them to make fantasy a reality

Look too for particular situations in life that seem to turn your partner on. Some totally 'sexless' things can be very arousing and can be used to enrich your love life.

USING MAGAZINES

Another good way of making things easier for you both when trying to communicate fantasies is to read sexy magazines together, especially those that have readers' letters. Particular themes and notions that seem to be of interest to one of you can be the trigger point for further discussion, and even the revelations of very intimate personal fantasies.

This makes things much easier than sitting down 'cold' to talk about fantasies. It makes it easy to say something like 'that sounds fun, why don't we try that sometime?' In most loving relationships it is simply shyness that prevents the couple from sharing more of their intimate sexual thoughts.

PUT IT IN WRITING

A plot that often works well is to write a sexy play or an outline for a sexy video, to be read by your partner.

In this, each partner writes a short outline making it as sexy as he or she wants it to be, knowing that it will be read by the other, perhaps in private. This reveals all kinds of interesting material about your partner, which you then have the option to do something about. It is simply another device for sharing thoughts that you might otherwise be bashful about.

Having said all this, there is no sense in sharing any fantasy that you feel unable to share, just for the sake of it. There is no law that says you have to and you should not be bullied by your partner into doing so.

A truly loving partner will respect your desire to keep some of your fantasies secret – though this does not necessarily mean that you will never be able to tell, when you think the time is right. Maybe unconsciously you do not trust your partner enough to use the knowledge to your benefit; this could change in time.

DOING SOMETHING ABOUT IT

So far we have assumed that one or both partners wants to get to know more about the sexually intimate thoughts of the other, but what does someone do when he or she has learned these things? How can the material be built into a couple's day-to-day sex lives to make things better for them both?

First, let it be said that even if someone shares a fantasy readily with their partner, this does not mean that they necessarily want to make it come to life.

Things can thus become very confusing for the non-fantasizing partner who understandably might think that, with enough encouragement, the fantasizing partner could overcome their shyness and act out what he or she enjoys in their fantasy.

TREAD WARILY

It is easy to see what a minefield fantasy is because although the man, for example, may be highly aroused

As women tend to need more stimulation than men to put them in the mood for sex, using fantasy as a part of foreplay while their partner caresses their body can greatly help to increase their level of arousal

by his partner's fantasy, and may even build it into his fantasy bank too, he will have to tread carefully to be sure that he does not deter her from revealing other fantasies that could be built into their sex lives.

Sometimes, the revelations of one partner's fantasy opens doors for the other partner. Just knowing that his wife has such sexy thoughts can often be a turn-on for a man. Suddenly she has an increased value to him because she comes down off her pedestal of 'virgin mother' and becomes more like the 'whore' he really wants.

USING KNOWLEDGE CONSTRUCTIVELY

Perhaps the best way to handle things is for the individual to say at the time of the revelation that they want the other to know about it but not to take it as a signal to do anything about it. This need not, however, be a cause for gloom and doom in the partner to whom it is revealed.

For example, in the case of the woman who has fantasies of anal sex but does not want to actually have

anal sex, it is possible to make use of the information in a constructive way. Her partner could ensure that they make love in rear-entry positions that encourage or enable the woman to fantasize about anal sex. Perhaps the man could, while making love to her vaginally, say sexy things about her bottom and talk about how much he wants to have anal sex with her. All of this heightens the sexual value of that episode to them both, yet it has not involved actual anal intercourse.

Other fantasies, such as those involving bondage or group sex, can be dealt with in similar ways – by pretending, rather than experiencing, the act.

A FEAR OF DEVALUATION

A fear that many people have is that having shared their fantasy, it will cease to be of value to them personally. This may occur but usually does not. On the contrary, a loving couple can use their knowledge of each other's fantasies to encourage each other during foreplay, to tease them kindly but sexily and to heighten the value of any given sexual episode.

Telling a fantasy in this way adds to, and does not reduce, its value to its 'owner'. It is simply another way of sharing the most intimate parts of your life that a truly loving and caring relationship does in other ways all the time.

ACTING OUT FANTASY

When it comes to agreeing to act out your fantasies there is a lot of fun to be had. Common sense will guide the average couple in the way that they do this but a few suggestions may not go amiss.

Remember that fantasy material is, almost by definition, difficult to reproduce in real life. The beauty of fantasies is that the individuals and situations involved are perfect for the purpose of sexual arousal.

This can mean that, when acting out a fantasy, the reality does not come up to your expectations. If this is so, it could be that the value of the fantasy is reduced for the future, in which case it probably makes sense to stop doing it and to turn to other material in your fantasy bank.

LOOKING OUTSIDE THE RELATIONSHIP

For many fantasies to become realities you will need to be fairly inventive about locations, clothing, what your partner will do and so on. This often calls for a compliant partner and many people do not, of course, have one. Looking outside the relationship to satisfy one's fantasies in real life can be hazardous, so beware. If you are taken in by the novelty and excitement of the whole situation and leave your partner, you could live to regret it.

If you do decide to do this, remember that it is your partner who supplies your daily needs in the real world and that another individual who is only good for indulging fantasy material is probably much less of a whole person to you. Be careful not to get carried away with the fact that acting out a fantasy is so arousing that you over-interpret the value of the whole relation-

If a man has fantasies about that well-known fantasy figure the 'bitch goddess', his partner can easily slip into that role from time to time, dressing for the part in a way she knows will turn him on the most

If sado-masochism features in your fantasy bank, you can introduce it into your sex life in a limited way – using props in your sex games can add a touch of spice, but take care things do not get out of hand

ship with that person. This happens in affairs quite commonly.

The other person will do things that you may have been fantasizing about for years, but which your partner will not do. This can be heady medicine which makes rational judgements about the true value of the newcomer almost impossible to make.

Try to stand back from the new relationship enough to be able to judge it as a whole.

BEING FAIR WITH YOUR PARTNER

Lastly, when acting out things be careful that your partner is put under no undue pressure to comply with your wishes. It is all too easy to make things difficult so that he or she feels emotionally black-mailed into doing things they really do not want to do.

Many individuals would greatly like to enrich their sexual and emotional lives but need more than a little nudge to make it actually happen. Such people are often the most vociferous when complaining about how boring their sex life is.

Others may really want to do something new and creative with their partner but will find it difficult or

even impossible unless their level of arousal is very high or they have had a small amount of alcohol to reduce their inhibitions. Once the spell has been broken, it is often a simple matter of repeating the circumstances once again so that it is less intimidating. After this things should go smoothly.

LIVING WITH FANTASY

For many people fantasies, especially their favourites, will always remain a secret. For the very open couple who share easily and are totally uninhibited with each other, however, such caution will seem strange and unnecessary.

Perhaps in an ideal world all couples would be in this position and the sharing of fantasies would be as neutral a subject as what happened at work that day. On the other hand, perhaps that would reduce the magic and power of this complex side of our sexuality. Whatever the case, men and women will continue to spend their time fantasizing and even if a couple never manage to share their intimate fantasies with each other, the fact that they do fantasize will benefit their sex life.

MAKING LOVE WITHOUT INTERCOURSE

A truly loving couple have a rich and varied sex life because they realize that sexual intercourse is only part of making love. For them, every day provides a fresh opportunity to arouse and excite each other

Our sexuality is so broad a part of our personalities that expressing it only through sexual intercourse leaves a large number of our resources untapped.

There are several advantages to knowing how to make love without having intercourse. Many, if not most, couples have times in their lives when they would rather not have intercourse, yet still want to show their love and affection for each other.

There may also be times when a couple might positively want to avoid intercourse and yet act lovingly towards each other – for example during pregnancy and childbirth, or later, around the menopause. Or it may be that a couple have a physical problem that makes intercourse difficult, or that one or other of them is recovering from a heart attack or a serious operation or illness.

For many loving couples making love without having intercourse plays an important role in their daily lives. There is a lot more to love than purely genital sexual activity, and there are many ways for a couple to enrich their time together and add more fun to their lives.

NON-GENITAL LOVEMAKING

Touch can be a valuable tool in any loving relationship. A couple can make love all day by touching a lot, but expecting no great sexual arousal or indeed any genital activity to follow.

Kissing and cuddling, as a part of everyday life – on leaving the house, on returning home, or simply for no reason at all – help keep a couple's feelings very much alive, make each feel wanted and say 'I love you' without using words. A little touch, a pat on the bottom or just running fingers through the other's hair can often convey more than words.

Sometimes, of course, such casual touching and petting can be more deliberately arousing, and this serves to heighten the expectation of intercourse which both partners know will follow.

THE 'ON' 'OFF' MODES

Far too many couples have only two modes of operating when it comes to sex – the 'on' and 'off' modes. Either they are having intercourse or they are sexually switched off from each other. There is nothing in between. So, many oportunities to express simple affection or to arouse each other remain almost completely unexplored. But the loving couple who are tuned in to each other are constantly demonstrating their fondness for each other in both sexual and non-sexual ways, so that when they do make love it is in the context of spontaneous loving feelings for each other and is likely to be more pleasurable and relaxed.

Many couples fall into patterns in their lives which prevent this kind of ongoing lovemaking from occuring. If you see each over a hasty breakfast and then one, or both, of you slumps into a chair when you return from work, only to be aroused to change the channel on the TV, it is not surprising that little lovemaking goes on.

You have to make time to be together, even if it means putting aside a few evenings a week which are exclusively yours. This is especially necessary during the learning phase of non-intercourse lovemaking. But you do not have to create situations artificially. An extension of everyday activities can be fun if you turn them into a part of your lovemaking.

A cuddle while you are gardening, or running your hands up a partner's thigh while he or she is up a ladder can turn even a boring chore into a part of lovemaking. Such things broaden the scope of what two people can do without having sex or indeed without even touching each other's genitals.

Sensual massage can also play a similar role in lovemaking. There is only one rule – that the partner receiving the massage remains completely passive and leaves all the decisions to the pleasure-giver. The goal for the massager is to devote himself – or herself – totally to giving their partner pleasure.

The massage is better in this context if the genitals are left alone since it is not a prelude to intercourse, although sometimes intercourse will follow naturally. The very fact that the couple end up pleasing each other, yet do not have to go on to intercourse, can be a wonderful token of affection and a boost to the morale.

A couple doing this several times a week are making time exclusively for each other, and by so doing they are showing that they care about each other's responses and feelings.

Any room in the house, and any household chore – however everyday – can provide an opportunity to show affection

GENITAL LOVEMAKING
WITHOUT INTERCOURSE

An extension of this non-genital kind of lovemaking is to start involving the genitals in one way or another. At the simplest and often highly-arousing level, one partner can stroke or gently fondle the genitals of the other while going about their everyday business at the same time. This is not taken as far as sexual arousal but is one step up from the normal kissing and cuddling that a loving couple may do.

This may lead on to various activities including

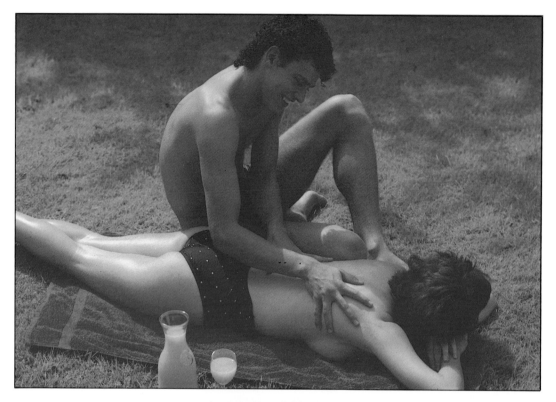

(Right) There is nothing like a relaxing morning for working up an appetite for lunch. On a sensual holiday make the food simple – or prepare it the night before

(Above) Applying suntan oil on to a warm skin can be a sensual experience in itself – whether you are applying or receiving it

(Right) On a warm summer's day playing water games outside can be more sensual than a shower indoors. They can be more fun as well

mutual masturbation and oral sex – forms of non-intercourse lovemaking that can be used when intercourse is forbidden or unwise for some reason. Many couples indulge in these sorts of lovemaking as a matter of course, but they can be especially useful for those couples who are unsure of their contraceptive safety or who simply want a change.

The couple who play like this rarely have trouble knowing when and if the other wants sex, and, if one of them does not, there are no bad feelings and moods. The trouble with couples who live in either the totally 'on' or 'off' sex mode all the time is that if, for whatever reason, intercourse does not happen, then either or both may become frustrated, resentful or start to feel unloved.

A 'SECRET' SEX LIFE

A really close couple is rather like a secret society of two. They have all kinds of ways of communicating with each other that do not involve speech, and when they do speak it can be in their own private language.

SECRET SIGNS
People in a longstanding relationship find that they instinctively know what the other is thinking and how they are reacting. With simply a glance or slight movement they are able to express this understanding. This is all part of being affectionately in tune.

A couple may also have secrets that they do not share with others, yet which bind them together and are even designed to turn each other on. Perhaps a good example of this is the woman who, just as she is entering a restaurant for a night out with her partner, reveals she has nothing on under her dress. This is usually enough to keep the whole evening going.

Because no one else realizes that such games are going on between the two they become all the more delicious.

Dancing and other situations in which close contact occurs can be used to whisper a little promise that will arouse interest in what is to follow later that evening. 'Accidentally' touching a particular part of your partner's body, or brushing against it in company, teases him or her because it cannot be remarked on, yet it still has the desired effect.

Many couples also have a private language which they use, even in front of others, to communicate their love for and anticipation of one another. The name of a particular food, for example, may be a codeword for sexual intercourse, or a person's name may be used to indicate a specific part of the body.

THE WELL-TUNED COUPLE
The couple who express their love all the time are more tuned in to each other and constantly have their value to each other reinforced.

Also they are less likely to have problems with jealousies, can flirt within the bounds they have both agreed on and do not necessarily see contacts with the opposite sex as threatening to their love bond because they are secure in their feelings for each other. More importantly their lives together are enriched and they have more fun, all of which serves to make them feel more wanted and more loved.

Such couples do not just copulate. They are always making love to each other – and this becomes a personalized, one-to-one, unique and enhancing experience of two well-attuned lovers.

BACK TO COURTSHIP
Many couples have never really had a courtship – they have rushed from a flirting interest in each other to bed, and then headlong into a full-blown sexual scene. This is a pity because it short-cuts so many of the learning phases of the development of a male-female relationship. So it is possible that for some people going back to the stage of early courtship may be a completely new experience.

Obviously, everyone's idea of what constitutes courtship varies, but there are some ideas that sexologists have found to work in practice.
☐ Take every opportunity to show your love for each other in non-genital ways
☐ Give each other unexpected presents, however small and inexpensive. It shows you are thinking of each other
☐ Increase your physical closeness short of genital contact
☐ Kiss more

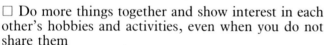

(Above) Sometimes words are not necessary. A soothing massage for your partner at the end of the day can say so much more

(Left) Helping a partner to dress – before going out – can be almost as tantalizing as removing their clothes later when you get home

(Right) What more perfect way for the sensual holiday to reach its climax than to cuddle up and make slow, sweet love?

□ Do more things together and show interest in each other's hobbies and activities, even when you do not share them

□ Phone up 'for no reason' just to tell your partner you love him or her

□ Leave little love notes in places around the house where you know they will be found as a delightful surprise by your partner

□ Go out with each other as if you were on an early date, taking care to be extra courteous, caring and sympathetic

□ Think about ways in which you could improve your personal appearance according to your own particular ways of pleasing each other.

GETTING THE MOOD RIGHT

People may be so shy that as much as they want to behave in less inhibited ways they simply cannot. Such individuals or couples need a little help to get off the ground. Here are some hints:

□ **Alcohol** A glass or two of your favourite drink can be relaxing and may help to start things going. But drink too much and nothing will happen. So take it easy. Alcohol lowers the inhibitions in just about everyone and if this makes one partner less shy or more accepting of the other's loving advances, it might be worth a try

□ **Place** Almost any room in the house can be sexy if the mood is right, and there is always an alternative to

the bedroom if you are both feeling sexy. If one partner has a fantasy about making love out of the house – in a field or the back of the car – the other might consider making use of it to please their partner

☐ **Dress** We all feel more attractive in certain clothes than others, and dress is a part of all social occasions whether they have any overt sexual purpose or not. Many men are turned on by the sight of their lover's bottom bending over to pick something up. An appreciative pat or stroke is worth a thousand words in such situations and can start the ball rolling

☐ **Erotica** Many couples fail to make sufficient use of erotica to arouse themselves. This can take the form of sexy clothes, erotic pictures in the bedroom, erotic books or videos, and can be extremely effective.

☐ **Acting** Fun and games between couples often arise out of acting in various situations. This can occur in the most spontaneous of ways, from the woman flirting with the man as she puts his food on the table, to him pulling her forcibly to him and playing Tarzan when they are out walking together. More formal games can involve the couple playing out any roles which they know will turn the other on.

A sensual holiday is an ideal way to devote yourselves to rediscovering intimacy. Be it a morning, a day, a weekend or longer, there are great pleasures to be gained from setting aside time just to be together and indulge in romantic behaviour and sensual games.

THE INNER AND OUTER SELF

It is important that the care of your body extends into your inner self in order to maintain a balance and feel truly 'at one' with yourself. By ensuring that diet, health and relationships are all getting the attention they need, you can be confident that any problems you may come across in your sexual life will be minor ones that are easy to resolve

BODY IMAGE

The pictures we have in our own minds of how we look can be vastly different from the reality. Why do we not see ourselves as others see us?

'Inside every fat person there is a thin one struggling to get out.' This sentiment highlights a number of important truths. One of these is that the 'outer' person (reflected by height, weight and body fat) and the 'inner' person (reflected in an individual's ideal body image) are two very different things. What we think we look like, and more importantly what we think we ought to look like, often bears no resemblance to how we actually are.

In one recent North American survey, it was found that as many as 34 per cent of men and 38 per cent of women were dissatisfied with their overall physical appearance. Moreover, when asked about their attitude to their current weight, 41 per cent of males and 55 per cent of females expressed dissatisfaction.

THE 'IDEAL' IMAGE
The vast majority of overweight and obese people in western society want to lose weight. This is understandable given the medical emphasis on the health

isks of too much fat. What is less easy to understand s the desire of many normal-weight and even under-weight people, particularly women, to lose weight.

The explanation commonly advanced for this phenomenon involves the emergence of the 'thin body' cult. Over the last twenty-five years, the female body shape that has come to be accepted as the ideal is a slender one. An extreme example of this ideal was represented by the skinny models in the 1960s.

One group of North American investigators has shown that it is possible to measure the change in the 'ideal' female body shape over the past twenty years. They did this simply by studying the vital statistics of female models appearing as centrefolds in Playboy magazine and those of contestants in the Miss America Pageant competition. Both centrefolds and pageant contestants have become thinner over this period. With smaller bust, larger waist and smaller hip measurements, the Playboy centrefolds have changed their shape to one which is more tubular and less 'rounded'.

WHY DOES PHYSICAL APPEARANCE MATTER?

Ask anyone in the street how important physical attractiveness is in determining an individual's personal worth and you will probably receive the socially accepted answer – what a person looks like on the outside (the 'outer' person) does not matter, it is what they are like on the inside (the 'inner' person) that counts. Although in a caring society this may be the ideal situation, in practice the reality is very different.

A series of studies, again in North America, have shown that physically attractive people are judged as having more positive personal qualities of all kinds than physically less attractive individuals. It has also been found that the physically attractive are more successful in both work and leisure pursuits.

In start contrast, lack of physical attractiveness has been found to generate negative attitudes in others. In one classic study, children were shown pictures of other children with various kinds of physical disfigurements and disabilities including a picture of an obese child. These pictures produced negative reactions from the children generally, yet the obese child was selected as being the least liked. It seems that how we look does make a considerable difference to the way we are treated by other people. And being markedly overweight or obese can produce notably strong negative reactions in others. It is not surprising therefore that overweight people should wish to reduce their weight while others strive to avoid being fat.

WHAT IS BODY IMAGE?

The term 'body image', as used in scientific and medical literature, is defined as the picture we have in our minds of our body and of our feelings towards it. In practice, we distinguish between our own view of the size and shape of our body – *body image distortion* – and any negative feelings towards it – *body dissatisfaction*.

Body image distortion is generally thought of as reflecting an error of judgement while body dissatisfaction is regarded as a statement of how we feel about our bodies.

SELF IMAGE

We have a number of images of ourselves which we carry around in our heads. As well as our body image, we have a self image, a social image and a sexual image. In fact, for all of those situations or events in which we regularly participate, we have a personal image of ourselves which changes with time and response to our various successes and failures. While it is of course

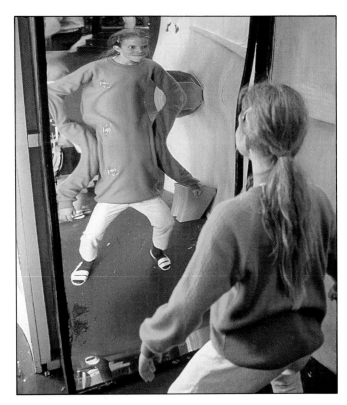

Just as fairground mirrors can create body image distortion, so can the mind, leaving an individual with an unreal opinion of their body size

possible for us to have widely differing images of ourselves at different times – for example a very favourable 'work' image combined with a poor 'social' image – in practice, poor images tend to go together.

Thus, a poor body image tends to accompany a poor social image and a poor sexual image. A person who has a distorted body image and a high level of body dissatisfaction tends to avoid social situations and in time can lose whatever social skills they previously had. If they have a sexual partner, a poor body image can substantially affect their sexual image of themselves and their sexual behaviour as well. They may avoid undressing in front of their partner or shy away from being touched on parts of their body which they consider less than physically acceptable.

HOW DO WE MEASURE BODY IMAGE?

Many different methods have been developed for measuring an individual's body image. Accuracy of body-size estimation has been assessed through simple paper-and-pencil tests – for example, by asking a person to draw an accurate picture of him- or herself – or by asking them to stand in front of a large sheet of paper pinned to a wall and to mark in their judgements of their body widths, face, waist, hips and so on.

Additionally, a variety of techniques using sophisticated equipment have been developed for measuring accuracy of body-size judgements. Such methods include movable lights, light beams, distorting photographs and, most recently, distorting video camera images. One method which has particular appeal is that involving the distorting mirror. Like fairground mirrors, this method uses a metal mirror which can be bent either horizontally or vertically or both, to distort the individual's image – their task is then to readjust the mirror to produce an image which appears correct.

By contrast with the assessment of accuracy of size and shape estimation, measurement of body dissatisfaction/disparagement has largely been achieved through paper-and-pencil tests. In these, individuals are usually asked about how satisfied they feel with their bodies in general and various parts of their bodies in particular. It is also possible to obtain measures of body dissatisfaction by using the more technologically-sophisticated types of equipment used to estimate body size.

For example, people can be asked to reset the distortion in the mirror twice – once to represent the way they think they are right now, and once to indicate how they would ideally like to be. The difference between their actual and their ideal judgements can then be used as a fairly reliable index of their current body dissatisfaction.

WHEN DO WE DEVELOP A DISTINCTIVE BODY IMAGE?

Before they reach adolescence, children may make major errors in assessing their body size and shape. This may be due to the fact that generally they show relatively little concern about the way they appear to others and in consequence they probably study their own bodies less fiercely. Concern about physical appearance begins in a major way during adolescence and this is when girls, in particular, first start to show an attitude of critical appraisal towards their own bodies – and often envy of other people's.

The evidence seems to suggest that as we get older so we become more accurate in assessing our body size

and shape, but so also do we become more accepting of the bodies we have. It is comforting to note that such acceptance of our own bodies is usually accompanied by increasing enjoyment and satisfaction in lovemaking, particularly among women.

DO MALES AND FEMALES HAVE DIFFERENT BODY IMAGES?
One consequence of the difference between the sexes in terms of ideal body build is that women tend to go in for dieting more than men while males tend to opt more for physical exercise. However, a significant proportion of both sexes now seem to be using a combination of both methods.

WHO HAS A DISTORTED BODY IMAGE?
Twenty years ago it was thought that, apart from amputees, neurological cases and patients with schizophrenia, the only people who had a distorted body image were patients suffering from anorexia nervosa. Since that time, it has become recognized that a distorted body image, in the form of over-estimation of body size, is found among many groups. Those with eating disorders, such as anorexics and bulimics (people with an abnormal craving for food, who 'binge' and then make themselves vomit), clearly show it.

GENERAL DISCONTENT
A likely explanation for the spread of body-image distortion from selected patient groups to the population at large has already been suggested. The 'thin body cult' has emerged over this time period as previ-

No matter what shape you are, or what image you see in the mirror, you are unique and special to your lover; and any inadequacies you may feel about your body image can be dispelled when your partner shows obvious delight in and desire for your body

When a person loses a great deal of weight their body shape changes rapidly, but it takes more time for the mind to readjust to the new image

ously described. Unfortunately, these cultural and social pressures towards 'thinness' have occurred during a period of time when better nutrition in western societies has produced a steady increase in average female weights. Thus while young females have been getting fatter and healthier they have been presented with an ever-increasing image of slimness. It is not surprising, therefore, that more people, particularly women, have become discontented with the natural shape of their bodies.

WHAT HAPPENS WHEN PEOPLE CHANGE IN WEIGHT?
People with anorexia nervosa who have lost a lot of weight see themselves in general as fat. When they gain weight, they often see themselves, paradoxically, as less fat. That is, weight gain is often accompanied by a more realistic set of judgements about body size and shape.

When people lose weight, however, the opposite does not necessarily ensue. Studies have been carried out on patients who lose weight as a consequence of some kind of counselling – either individual or group – or as a consequence of surgery. Results have shown that while all patients describe a positive change in how they feel about their bodies, only those on long-term counselling become more accurate in estimating their actual body sizes.

DIET

Are you getting enough vitamins, minerals and roughage in your diet, with the right combination of protein, fat and carbohydrate? If you feel there is room for improvement, take a close look at what you eat

Today, diet is far more than just a means of losing weight. In 1984, only 12 per cent of people polled in the United Kingdom said they chose food for its health value. Two years later, in a similar poll, over 50 per cent – and rising – put health considerations first.

FOOD FOR LOVERS

In the complex chemistry of the sexual body, male hormones such as testosterone and female hormones such as oestrogen depend on supplies of key vitamins and minerals for production. But fortunately there is no need to go textbook in hand to the food store in search of trace elements such as selenium (present in semen) or the longest list of vitamins on a cereal packet.

Food manufacturers are fighting off the 'threat' of the wholefood movement by listing specific chemical contents of their wares and making direct connections to the glossy hair, strong teeth and clear skin that result from adequate supplies of these key ingredients.

A BALANCED DIET

The truth is, however, that once you have established a well-balanced and varied healthy diet, you will be getting adequate amounts of all the vitamins, minerals and other special nutrients that your body requires.

For it to be balanced, a diet should contain sufficient amounts of carbohydrate for heat and energy. It should also contain enough protein to maintain the body tissues. Small amounts of fat are needed for their vitamin content, as well as for insulation. Fresh fruit, vegetables and cereals are essential – these provide vitamins, minerals and roughage.

Of course, people do suffer from special deficiencies at times – for example, additional iron may be of benefit during heavy menstruation. And some claims for the virtues of specific diet items are intriguing – the role of zinc in increasing sperm counts and developing 'super-babies' is one current dietetic enthusiasm.

But most experts believe that, if you are eating a varied diet, it is just about impossible to go short of proteins, vitamins or minerals.

CUTTING DOWN

Where most of us do go wrong, however, remains in getting too much, rather than too little. If you are beginning to share a new approach to diet with your partner, the benefits begin with understanding together the danger areas in diet today.

Since many couples nowadays share the shopping – and more and more share the cooking – a good partnership in diet begins at the supermarket shelf. The average couple in the West consumes, between them, one tonne (1000kg) of food a year.

As men and women seem to have specific weaknesses for foods that can seriously damage the waistline (his may be the pub lunch and hers the mid-morning snack), the couple that diets well together will point out each other's special risk areas.

OLD ENEMIES
The old enemies remain *too much sugar, too much fat, too much alcohol*. Average adults in most developed countries consume 43kg of sugar a year. That is the weight of a sack you could just about raise from the ground and enough calories to fuel you for a 3000 kilometre walk.

It is easy to see how the sugar tots up once you realize that a single glass of most soft drinks contains some five teaspoons of it. But remember, it comes at you in unexpected ways too – manufacturers lace savoury sauces with it, for example.

TOO MUCH SUGAR
Sugar's gift of instant energy is mostly unnecessary and the calories it provides are empty calories. That means no other nutrients come with them.

For well-fitting clothes – and teeth that do not need filling – aim to cut your sugar intake by half. Since it is much easier to do other people good than to help oneself, sugar cut-down is an area where partners can effectively help each other.

Buy low-calorie soft drinks to stock your fridge. Put one, not two, spoonfuls in coffee. Leave cans of fruit in syrup on the supermarket shelf. Grow out of added-sugar breakfast cereals. And when you have to say sorry, say it with flowers rather than chocolates.

HIDDEN FAT
Too much fat goes straight from the plate to the waistline – and lags your veins on the inside by depositing cholesterol. But although everyone knows by now that fat is a potential heart-stopper (heart disease is the biggest killer in the western world), there are still many ways in which fat can grease its way past the watchful shopper.

Even lean sirloin steak, for example, has 10 per cent fat. Cheddar cheese has a fat content of 34 per cent, against the 4 per cent of most cottage cheeses.

When you realize that the average adult needs no more than 80 grams of fat a day, it is easy to see how swiftly the total can be reached. One quarter-pound burger, at 20g of fat, takes up a quarter of your daily fat ration. One helping of double cream (which is 50 per cent fat) knocks out 13g.

SLIMLINE PRODUCTS
Why not take the opportunity to treat your partner to the new low-fat products available? The dairy industry – which until recently was busy persuading us to swallow more full-cream milk in the name of health – has now swung into production of a whole range of skimmed and semi-skimmed milk versions.

There is certainly a dramatic fat content difference at stake – 1g of fat in a pint of skimmed milk, as against 22g in ordinary milk.

ALCOHOL – EMPTY CALORIES
Alcohol is – very much more than milk – a drink that fuels trouble. Those who remain mystified by the speed with which the occasional drink adds weight should understand the way that most alcoholic drinks work as a body fuel.

Most alcoholic drinks are nutritionally poor but rich in calories – available in a form that the body grabs first and fast for its energy needs. When a proper meal comes along, the body will tend to 'bank' the surplus energy it contains – adding it straight to your fat layer.

A POSITIVE APPROACH
A good diet should mean a list of positives, once one has cut the trio of sugar, fat and alcohol down to size. For couples who see diet purely as a weight problem, the dinner table can rapidly become a tedious calorie-counting battleground.

A negative – even punitive – approach to diet remains common. And where only one partner is 'on a diet' in the traditional sense of a 'slimming diet' they can often be a depressing person to be around.

FIBRE GUIDE

Lack of fibre in our diet is a result of the advances in food technology this century. Modern food processing over-refines foods – removing the husks of wheat and producing more white sugar, for example.

Insufficient cereal and vegetable fibre in your diet can lead to disorders of the large intestine and may lead to conditions such as bowel cancer, heart disease, constipation and piles.

Whole foods are a better source of fibre than added bran. Remember:
□ one apple has one tenth of your daily needs
□ one jacket potato has two fifths
□ six slices of wholemeal bread have one half.

Usually, since fashion dictates it, it is the woman who gets locked into battle with a weight problem. Although almost as many men will fail a weight-height ratio test, it has been traditional to indulge excess male weight.

For too long, women have accepted that they are the 'guilty' partner where being overweight is concerned. Obediently, as a result, countless women have endured punishing diet regimes laid down by experts – who are quite often male.

FIBRE

Food with plenty of fibre, such as potatoes or bread, will satisfy without adding unwanted calories. Forget the notion that bread and potatoes are fattening. It is the butter you spread and the fat you fry in that does the damage. Cut your bread and chips thicker (matchstick-style chips are far more fattening than rough-cut ones).

Fibre does far more for the body than simply provide the 'roughage' which helps prevent constipation. Although fibre has no nutrient value in itself, many experts believe that too little fibre in the daily diet can add to the risk of developing diabetes and even heart disease.

Many popular 'high-fibre' diets work by adding bulk to the diet while cutting back on over-enriched dairy and meat foods. Most recommend that an intake of 50g of fibre a day is beneficial – and that is easily come by if you eat more wholemeal bread, breakfast cereals, pulses, fresh fruit and vegetables. Wholemeal bread has a fibre content of 9 per cent against the

almost negligible 3 per cent contained in white bread

It should not be necessary to add fibre as a supple ment to your meals. A sensible return to the kind o high-fibre diet our ancestors enjoyed for centuries wil quickly seem natural to you.

NEW TRENDS IN DIET

It is a return to natural habits that seems to characterize what is happening to many people's diets today. Since food is of great importance to everyone, there will always be bursts of enthusiasm for a new 'wonder diet' or a new scare that some familiar food item is a danger.

If trying an all raw food diet takes your fancy, give it a try. And if you have an immediate weight problem to tackle, you may well find a disciplined diet a benefit in the short term for quick weight loss.

What is happening throughout the western world in terms of normal daily diet, however, is a steady shift to less meat, and fewer dairy products, and to more fresh vegetables and cereals. There is a growing awareness of the damage that an over-refined and over-processed diet can do.

A SHARED DIET

Partners can share this journey of discovery and explore a healthier diet together. But risks arise when one partner is more enthusiastic about making a diet change than the other. People can swiftly become boring about heartfelt subjects such as vegetarianism or the dangers of additives.

Eating habits, remember, are formed very early in life. They are part of our earliest memories and closely linked with our first loved ones – our parents. That is why diets – national and local – persist so strongly.

When we make new partners in life, a shared understanding of little preferences and idiosyncracies at and around the dining table goes a long way to ensuring mutual harmony.

The secret of forming a new, healthy diet pattern may lie in not going over the top in extreme attitudes. If your partner has an occasional weakness for cream cakes or the kind of fried breakfast favoured in traditional British circles, forgive the lapse.

BACK TO NATURE

The new trend of health consciousness has led to a widespread fall from favour of so-called convenience foods.

Public enthusiasm for natural food is forcing manufacturers and farmers to rethink the way they stock our larders. Huge sums of money are at stake. Already there are signs that the old bad habits of encouraging over-consumption of dairy food and meat products are creeping back in the guise of offering health and strength through old-style 'square meals'.

But today's sensible partners are re-exploring old routes to health – the ones that the human race has known to work over hundreds of thousands of years – which stress the importance of a varied, balanced diet.

DIET TIPS

☐ Avoid late night heavy meals – they are the most fattening

☐ Cook vegetables briefly – just until crisply tender. Remember the basic rule: above-ground vegetables go into boiling water, below-ground start from cold

☐ Check cheese and yoghurts for their fat content. Some Greek yoghurts, for example, are comparatively high in fat

☐ Watch out for the fattening power of snacks. A can of cola, sausage roll and fruit yoghurt comes to 480 calories. A cooked meal of grilled fish, white sauce, carrots, beans and fruit to follow can come to only 280 calories

☐ Trim fat from meat. Grill rather than fry. Go for chicken and fish as often as possible

☐ Go for slow but steady weight loss if trying to slim, rather than opting for drastic weight loss as soon as possible

☐ Eat as many vegetables as possible – and the fresher the better

☐ Remember that the key word to ensure you are having a healthy diet is variety. A balanced mixture of fresh sources of carbohydrate, protein and fat will ensure that you live a healthier, longer life.

VITAMINS AND MINERALS

We only need minute amounts of vitamins and minerals, and eating a wide range of fresh foods means we will not need any supplementary pills

People who are concerned about eating in a healthier way are naturally interested in vitamins and minerals. Yet so much that is written about these nutrients only increases the mythology which surrounds them. Sometimes it seems that they are almost magical – perhaps this feeling is understandable because of the differences to health that such small quantities can make.

WHAT IS A VITAMIN?

The word 'vitamin' is used to describe a wide range of organic substances which differ greatly in their chemical structure and the way in which they affect the body. But they all have two features in common:

□ they are essential in small amounts

□ we cannot make them entirely ourselves, so they must be provided in another way, usually from food.

Far from being helpful, large doses of some vitamins can be dangerous, particularly the fat-soluble ones such as vitamins A and D which can build up in stores of body fat to toxic levels. Any excess of the water-soluble vitamins – the B group vitamins and vitamin C – is usually lost in urine. Evidence suggests, however, that high intakes of vitamin C may lead to kidney stones in some people and may interfere with absorption of vitamin B12.

'FASHIONABLE' MINERALS

As we learn more about the interaction between nutrients, there has also been growing concern among nutritionists that over-enthusiastic supplementation with some of the more 'fashionable' minerals may actually cause health problems. We should be able to get enough of the major minerals (see chart page 157) and trace minerals we need by eating a well-balanced, and mostly fresh-food, diet.

Interest has been growing in recent years in the 'trace minerals', so called because they are needed in such small amounts. One of these is chromium. It has only recently been recognized as an essential nutrient for humans, as it acts with insulin, the main hormone controlling the use of glucose in the body. But while chromium supplements cannot cure diabetes, they can sometimes help in milder blood-sugar disorders. Diets which are high in fats, sugar and refined starches contain less chromium and also make more demands on the body for insulin. So it has been suggested that modern eating habits may in fact be putting some people at risk of developing chromium deficiency.

Possible links between a lack of chromium and heart disease are also being investigated. At the present time it is hard to suggest a 'recommended intake' – but a sensible safeguard is to ensure that plenty of fresh vegetables and wholegrain cereals containing chromium are eaten.

COPPER

This is a trace element which is essential for growth in children. It plays a part in making healthy blood, bones and skin. When children do not get enough copper they develop anaemia, fragile bones and diarrhoea. However, concern has been growing that adults may also develop problems due to low intakes of copper if they rely too much on processed convenience foods which lack copper.

Some animal studies suggest a link between low intakes of copper, raised cholesterol and heart disease. But before you rush off to start taking copper supplements, remember that it can be toxic in large amounts, causing damage to the liver.

In fact, over-enthusiastic use of zinc supplements can interfere with copper in the body and lead to deficiency symptoms so that zinc, another mineral now much in vogue, must be used cautiously as a supplement.

ZINC

Zinc is necessary for growth, sexual development, wound healing and the perception of taste and smell. A severe deficiency which is seen in some parts of the world may lead to dwarfism and sexual immaturity. Such a severe deficiency is unlikely in Britain, but

VITAMINS

	Why it is needed	Good food source
Vitamin A (retinol)	For normal vision, maintaining healthy skin and other living tissues. May also be involved in taste and balance	Fat-soluble – found in margarine, butter, cheese, cod liver oil, liver
Vitamin B1 (thiamin)	Essential for normal functioning of nerves and muscles	Yeast, brown rice, wheat germ, Brazil nuts, pork
Vitamin B2 (riboflavin)	Healthy skin and eyes. Release of energy from food	Good sources are liver, kidney, cornflakes. Milk is an important source in the UK
Vitamin B6 (pyridoxine)	Essential for growth, blood formation, protection from infection, healthy skin and nerves	Yeast, liver, mackerel
Vitamin B12 (cyano-cobalamin)	Needed by rapidly dividing cells such as those in bone marrow which form blood. Also needed for healthy nerves and reproductive system	Widely available from animal foods. Almost entirely absent from plants. Vegans must take supplements
Other B vitamins Nicotinic acid	Involved in the process which releases energy within the cells	Foods rich in protein are usually rich in this vitamin – peanuts, liver, pork, beef
Folic acid	Essential for renewal of blood cells, skin and digestive tract	Raw, green vegetables are a good source – the vitamin is easily destroyed by cooking
Biotin	Essential for metabolism of fat	Yeast, liver, kidney, eggs
Pantothenic acid	Helps release energy from food	Found in all food except pure sugar and fats. Liver is an especially good source
Vitamin C (ascorbic acid)	Improves absorption of iron from food. Essential for keeping skin and cartilage healthy, and for healing wounds	Fruit and vegetables, particularly citrus fruit. In UK, potatoes are an important source
Vitamin D	Essential for absorption of calcium from food and hardening of bones along with calcium and phosphorus	Fat-soluble, found in oily fish, margarine. (Most obtained by action of sunlight on skin)
Vitamin E	Speculative. Important in maintaining functions of cells	Fat-soluble, found in vegetable oils and fatty foods, peanuts, olive oil
Vitamin K	Essential for formation of factors involved in blood clotting	Most vitamin K in the diet comes from vegetables. Broccoli, cabbage and lettuce are all good sources

milder disorders affecting taste and smell have been seen in American children. Lack of zinc may play a part in anorexia nervosa and supplements have helped some sufferers from this condition.

Over-supplementation with zinc, however, can affect not only copper in the body, but also the absorption of iron, leading to anaemia.

In the United States there are now official recommendations for intake of zinc and if you want to play safe, the sort of foods that will ensure that you are getting enough are meat, fish and milk. Although cereals and pulses appear to be rich in zinc, it is not absorbed well by the body in this form.

MANGANESE

Nuts, wholegrain cereals and green leafy vegetables contain large quantities of manganese, which is essen-

of processed foods. This ensures that there is no risk of taking toxic amounts or creating a problem by interfering with another nutrient.

RECENT DISCOVERIES

In recent years more insight has been gained into the role of vitamins in the maintenance of health with less emphasis on the avoidance of simple deficiency diseases which are unusual in the United Kingdom. For example:
□ The role of vitamin B6 (pyridoxine) in helping women to control pre-menstrual syndrome is clearly important, although not fully understood yet
□ Speculation about vitamin E continues and it may have a role in our growing understanding of heart disease. But claims that large doses will help with problems such as sterility and muscular dystrophy or

MAJOR MINERALS		
	Why it is needed	**Good food sources**
Calcium	Essential for formation of bones and teeth. Calcium in blood regulates activity of nerves and muscle	Milk, cheese, whole grains, leafy vegetables, egg yolks
Phosphorus	Essential for hardening of teeth and bones	Milk, cheese, lean meats
Iron	Essential for the formation of haemoglobin, the pigment that carries oxygen in blood	Liver, meat, eggs, whole or enriched grain, leafy vegetables, nuts, dried fruit
Iodine	Essential for production of thyroid hormone	Iodised salt, seafish, seaweed
Magnesium	Essential for proper bone formation and healthy nerves	Nuts, soy beans, cocoa, seafood, whole grains, beans and pulses

tial for the normal development of the skeleton in childhood. It may also play a part in cholesterol metabolism and healthy reproduction.

Certain types of sterility may be linked to low intakes of manganese. Although manganese is among the least toxic of the trace elements, in large quantities it may interfere with the absorption of iron into the blood from the small intestine.

SELENIUM

Another trace element which is currently attracting a lot of attention is selenium, because of suggestions that low intakes may be linked with cancer of the breast, cancer of the large bowel and heart disease. It is found in the largest quantities in foods which contain a lot of protein. Meats and seafood are rich sources. Selenium may also improve the absorption of vitamin E from food. Similarly, there is no doubt that vitamin C improves the uptake of iron.

Whenever we are thinking about vitamins and minerals it is important not to overlook the way that they interact with each other. This is one of the reasons why supplements are not advisable except where the doctor has a good reason for suggesting one. It is far better to improve the diet overall, by ensuring good variety and keeping down the amount

help the athlete's performance are not confirmed by scientific research
□ Evidence is accumulating which links low intakes of folic acid early in pregnancy with the birth of babies with spina bifida. Studies to assess the value of supplementation during pregnancy are being carried out.

Drinking alcohol, smoking, stress and the contraceptive pill can affect vitamin levels in the body and many medications can interfere with their absorption and use by the body.

VEGETARIAN DIETS

In many instances larger quantities of vitamins and minerals are found in vegetarian diets and vegetarians may well be healthier than other people. But it is important that meals are planned to provide from other sources the vitamins and minerals usually found in animal foods.

Vegans who exclude milk, cheese and eggs from their diet should take supplements of vitamin B12. Calcium may also need to be taken in this way. Both vegetarians and vegans need to make sure that they are getting enough iron. But perhaps, we would all benefit from paying a little more attention to this mineral – as iron-deficiency anaemia is the only really common mineral deficiency in the United Kingdom.

AROMATHERAPY

Why not experiment with the art of aromatherapy – using essential oils extracted from plants – to soothe, relax and heal your body?

There can be few therapies more pleasant than aromatherapy, especially when it combines carefully chosen scents with soothing massage or long, lazy baths. Aromatherapy involves the use of essential oils to treat a wide variety of physical, mental and emotional problems. It is also a therapy you can practise on your own or with your partner to relax, reduce stress or promote feelings of well-being. But you would be well advised to first consult an experienced aromatherapist who can guide you on the selection of oils most suited to your individual needs and in the various methods of using them.

PLANT SOURCES

Many flowers, leaves, seeds, barks, roots and even resins and the rinds of some fruits contain tiny droplets of essential oils. These aromatic essences are the naturally occurring chemicals that give that plant or part of the plant its characteristic smell.

Each essential oil is extremely complex, containing a number of different substances in varying combinations and concentrations. For example eucalyptus, which is extracted from the leaves of the eucalyptus tree, contains aound 250 different constituents.

Not only do essential oils vary from plant to plant; they may also vary according to the part of the plant from which they are extracted. For instance, we obtain myrrh and frankincense from gum resin, camomile from flowers, cardamon from seeds, patchouli from dried branches and sandalwood from the bark of the appropriate plants. And if we take the orange tree, for example, we find one type of essential oil in the flowers, termed neroli, another in the rind of the fruit, which is known as orange and a third in the leaves, called petitgrain. Each is put to a very different use in the practice of aromatherapy.

Essential oils will often be more concentrated in one part of the plant than another at different seasons and at different times of day. So it may be important not only to choose the right few weeks in which to gather the plant but also the right time. Moreover, the chemical constituents of the oil will also be affected by both soil and climate. That is why oils from certain countries may be considered to be of better quality than similar oils from elsewhere.

COST
Of course, essential oils do tend to be expensive. There are two reasons for this. One is that large quantities of a part of the plant are generally needed to produce small quantities of essential oil. It has been

Teas (far left) made by steeping certain fresh or dried herbs and plants in boiling water are known to be natural remedies for a wide range of ailments, for example insomnia, coughs and period pains. (Left) Rosehip tea, rich in vitamin C, is good to stave off colds

In many Eastern cultures, medicines made from plants and herbs are still widely available. This 'medicine man' selling his cures in a street market in Kathmandu, Nepal, is a common sight in most markets

calculated that 200kg of fresh lavender flowers are required to produce just 1kg of essential lavender oil. And in the case of rose petals, which contain very little essence, about 2000kg of petals are needed to produce about 1kg of rose oil.

The other reason for the high price is that careful methods of extraction are vital if the oils are to retain their individual properties and therefore their effectiveness in therapy.

EXTRACTION
One method of extraction is known as *enfleurage*. The best quality petals of a particular flower will be spread on trays of fat or vegetable oil and replaced at regular intervals until the fat becomes saturated with the scented molecules. This process could take as long as three months.

The essential oil is then separated from the fat and purified. Oils obtained in this way are usually of very high quality and more expensive than those obtained by other means.

The most common method, however, is distillation. The parts of the plant to be used are placed in a large container and steam is passed through it. The essential oils evaporate and when the steam cools they condense. As the oils are not soluble in water they are easily separated and collected.

Another method of extracting is by using a suitable solvent such as alcohol which will dissolve the essential oils. They are then distilled and extracted. Essential oils can also be squeezed from the rinds of fruits such as lemons and oranges by hand pressing.

Once extracted, essential oils can be adversely affected by exposure to heat, light, air or moisture, so they should be carefully stored in dark, airtight bottles in a cool dry place.

TRADITIONS
Modern aromatherapy draws on a number of ancient traditions from China, India, Egypt and other early civilizations. It also draws on European folk medicine dating back to the Middle Ages. In ancient Egypt the use of essential oils was perfected to a fine art. Aromatic oils were used for perfumes, medicines, inhalations, embalming, religious ceremonies and – not surprisingly – for cookery. They included myrrh, frankincense, origanum, bitter almond, juniper, coriander and calamus among others. Cedarwood oil was used in particular for embalming. The Jews used aromatic oils for anointing for religious purposes. Myrrh and frankincense are among those mentioned in the Bible.

For the Greeks, essential oils served both as perfumes and medicines. Wealthy Greeks would sometimes anoint different parts of their body with different oils, for example their chest with palm oil, knees and neck with thyme, arms with mint and eyebrows and hair with marjoram. And one famous perfume containing myrrh was also used to reduce inflammation and heal wounds.

The Romans were even more extravagant than the

Greeks in their use of scented oils. They perfumed themselves, their clothes, their beds and even their military flags. Large quantities of oils were also used in massage, both in the public baths and their own homes.

In medieval England, aromatic oils such as mint and rosemary were often mixed with strange ingredients such as flies and lizards – seemingly for medicinal purposes. Although the complaint may have been internal, the mixture was applied externally, often by massaging in front of and behind the affected part. This practice is still observed in aromatherapy today. Aromatic oils were also burned or carried as a form of protection against the plague. This is not as far-fetched as it might sound. Since many aromatic oils have strong antiseptic qualities they may indeed have offered some protection.

In the seventeenth and eighteenth centuries, essential oils were widely used in medicine and by the nineteenth century many essences were being tested reasonably scientifically. But even though their properties were in some cases upheld, their use gradually declined with the advent of chemical drugs.

Some essential oils have, however, remained in

One method of extracting the essential oils from rose petals is by distillation (below). Steam is passed through them, to evaporate and collect the oils. (Bottom) Herb gardens for studying herbal medicine have existed for centuries

general use for medicinal purposes. Clove oil, for example, is sometimes recommended to ease toothache, peppermint oil for indigestion, and eucalyptus oil is found helpful for respiratory problems. Lemon and orange oils are still used for natural flavourings and other essential oils are found in perfumes or even in toothpaste flavouring.

MODERN AROMATHERAPY
Modern interest in aromatherapy could be said to date from around 1928, the year when a French chemist, René Gattefossé, published a book on the subject and used the term for the first time. His curiosity had been aroused by his research in the cosmetics industry, which revealed just how powerful many essential oils were as antiseptics.

It was further stimulated by an accident. While working in the laboratory he burned his hand badly and without thinking immersed it in a bowl of lavender oil that stood nearby. To his amazement the burn healed extremely quickly and left no scar.

Further pioneering work in aromatherapy was carried out by another Frenchman, Dr Jean Valnet, who used aromatherapy in World War 2 to heal wounds and later to treat many other conditions. And it was a French biochemist, Mme Marguerite Maury, who explored and developed other applications for essential oils, particularly in the field of massage.

VISITING AN AROMATHERAPIST
The best way to find out about aromatherapy is to consult an aromatherapist – but make sure that you select someone who has a recognized training in massage. Your first visit will probably last about one and a half hours but it is always a good idea to check on this and the fee beforehand. You will begin by discussing the problems you want assistance with, for example tension, or difficulties in sleeping.

Any serious or long-term problems should always be discussed with your doctor or another suitably qualified health professional. They are not the province of the aromatherapist.

After talking to you, the therapist will select five or six oils that seem most appropriate to your condition. Most aromatherapists use about 40 oils from about 60 or 70 that are generally available.

After sniffing each of those selected for you, you will choose the one you feel is most pleasing. This is because aromatherapists believe that we are intuitively drawn to the oil that will most benefit us.

The essential oil will be diluted in a bland oil such as almond or sunflower and you will be offered a whole or partial body massage, whichever you prefer. The idea is that not only is the massage relaxing but it will also help the essential oil to penetrate the skin and benefit certain parts of the body.

CHOOSING OILS
Among the oils you may be offered, depending on your condition, are lavender and camomile for stress

nd insomnia, marjoram to relax tight muscles and neroli, that is orange blossom, for anxiety. Sandalwood, rose and jasmine could all be used to help you relax while rose is thought to be particularly helpful for women with sexual difficulties. Ylang ylang, from the flower of a South East Asian tree, is used as a tonic while benzoin, from a resin, is said to have a warming, cushioning effect in times of stress.

MASSAGE

At home you can use an essential oil, suitably diluted in vegetable oil, to give either yourself or your partner a massage, as long as neither of you has a medical condition, has been recently ill or has had an accident in which case it could be hazardous. Massage with oils is suitable for stressed or tense but otherwise healthy people. It can simply help you to relax and feel cared for – or it can be a good prelude to lovemaking.

Choose your essential oil to suit your purpose. Try juniper or rosemary to tone tired or mildly aching muscles, ylang ylang, sandalwood or patchouli if you want to stir your senses and marjoram if you simply want a good night's sleep. Remember, massage with oils does not have to involve the whole body.

Although massage with essential oils does not have to involve the whole body, it is a good idea to set time aside for a full body massage

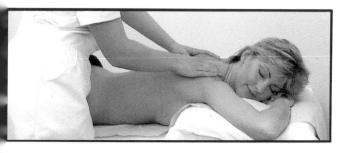

BATHS

Another way to use essential oils is in your bath. Make sure the room is warm and that the door and window are firmly closed so that the vapours cannot escape. Put about six to ten drops of the selected oil in your bath, swish the water gently so the oil forms a film on top, and immerse your body for about ten minutes, breathing deeply. A certain amount of the oil should penetrate your skin and some will be inhaled.

Neroli, lavender, lemon-grass and geranium are particularly soothing, whereas juniper, rosewood and bergamot are stimulating and lavender and camomile should help you sleep. If you want to inhale the vapours from essential oils more directly, you can put a few drops of the chosen oil in a basin of hot water. Lean over and inhale for several minutes. Rosemary is refreshing, eucalyptus and peppermint good for head colds, camphor and eucalyptus for influenza, while cedarwood and benzoin can ease respiratory problems.

Sometimes simply your feet are aching at the end

Massaging your face with a suitable essential oil is an effective and pleasing way to ease away the effects of stress and tension

of the day. Soaking them for ten minutes in a bowl of hot water with a few drops of peppermint oil, lavender or rosemary oil and gently massaging them should soon revive you.

OTHER USES

Often a few drops of an essential oil sprinkled in a room can do much to improve a stuffy atmosphere. Rosewood, lemon and bergamot will all have a refreshing effect. Or if you want to create a special atmosphere for a party, for example, sprinkle a few drops of oil or put a few drops in a bowl of warm water.

And finally, of course you can suit your mood by wearing essential oils as a perfume. Try ylang ylang, jasmine, patchouli or rose.

A combination of various essential oils is often used, particularly for cosmetic purposes and many home remedies for minor illnesses. Should you wish to find out more about combining oils for particular conditions, consult an aromatherapist or an authoritative text. *The Art of Aromatherapy* by Robert Tisserand, published by CW Daniel, 1985 (revised edition) is the most useful reference.

Most essential oils are applied externally. But should you take any of the essences internally (among those which can be taken internally) make absolutely sure they are correctly diluted and that you do not take them on an empty stomach or for longer than the recommended period. Essences can be extremely powerful and should not be given to young children to take internally.

SEX DRIVE

The society in which we live has a strong influence on how we think and feel about sex. But, according to the experts, if you take away all outside conditioning, individuals would have identical sex drives

Biologically, most people start off with the same capacity for sex. The amount of expession that anyone gives to his or her sex drive, however, varies enormously, both from person to person, and also within any one individual from time to time.

BIOLOGICAL DESIRE

The desire to have sex is governed by the circulating levels of the male hormone testosterone which is present in the blood of both sexes. A low level of this hormone can result in little or no interest in sex, but such cases are rare and can be treated.

It may suit some individuals to believe that people are born with different levels of sex drive. Indeed this belief often seems to be borne out by what they see around them, or what they read in magazines about people being under- or over-sexed.

OUTSIDE INFLUENCES

Clinical experience suggests that variations in sex drive are a result of outside influences such as the culture in which we live, or the way we have been brought up to view sex, rather than any biological considerations.

This seems a reasonable view to hold, because many people who go to therapists with a so-called absent sex drive can often be transformed very swiftly into normally-functioning individuals, sexually, simply by helping them undo the damage done to them in their childhood. This usually involves lifting their sexual inhibitions.

SEXUAL CONTROLS

Although we are all basically interested in sex, it would be totally inappropriate if we were simply to give expression to these drives in an uncontrolled way.

Some sexual prohibitions and restrictions are essential if we are to function as a society. But it is when these restrictions stop us functioning as well as we would like that problems arise. We then perceive that we have a low sex drive.

The trouble when discussing sex drive is that it is so difficult to compare one person against another. We tend to think that we are 'normal' in most respects and then find it hard to accept the criticism from our partner that we have a low sex drive.

THE 'NORMAL' COUPLE

Unfortunately, we all have at least some misapprehensions about how much sex is normal, but in reality there are no norms when it comes to sexual activity. 'Normal' for any given couple is what is normal for them, whether they make love seven times a week or twice a month.

It is also very difficult to discuss sex drive in a non-clinical setting because an individual who has gone off sex may well just not want sex with his or her partner but may be having good sex outside the relationship, unknown to the partner. They may be masturbating and fantasizing more than usual because the relationship is not working well.

THE PATH OF THE SEX DRIVE

Males usually reach their sexual peak in their late teens, and at this time several orgasms a day are not unusual. From this age onwards, the male sexual drive falls slowly. But here again, circumstances and conditioning come into play and some 50-year-olds are having as much sex as they did when they were 20 and others may close down on most sexual activity at around 40.

The path of the female sex drive is more difficult to chart. A few have several orgasms a day by one means or another, but this is unusual. Three or four sex acts a week seem to cover the majority of women, whether in the form of masturbation or physical intercourse. A few women are, of course almost totally inactive sexually and have little or no sexual drive for one of several reasons – just as are some men.

Many women find that they become more capable of having orgasms as they mature and, for the majority, their sex drive increases as their inhibition levels fall in their 30s. This means that quite a number of women find that they are at their sexiest in their late 30s and 40s.

The capacity of women for sexual pleasure is almost limitless, but their ability or willingness to exploit it is controlled by their emotions, their upbringing, their education, their partner and their current circumstances.

LOSING INTEREST IN SEX

Although it is impossible to be rigid about what is normal and what is not, on a general basis, it is possible to know in any one individual whether or not their sex drive is down for them. There are many possible causes

of a reduced interest in sex in a person. These include: **Drugs**, including sleeping tablets, steroids, some high blood pressure tablets, some water tablets, and some angina drugs can all cause a provable reduction in sex drive. In certain cases, the type of tablet can be changed to alleviate the problem.

In women, the Pill is often said to reduce sex drive but this is very controversial and research with dummy tablets in controlled trials has found that women on dummy tablets who thought they were taking the Pill were just as likely to become depressed as those who

Male and female sexual peaks do not coincide – he reaches his in his late teens, she in her mid-thirties. This seems to make little difference, however, in a truly loving relationship

really were taking the Pill. There are, however, some women who seem to be depressed on one make of Pill and yet not on another.

Many women take tranquillizers and these can cause indifference to sex. Given that nowadays millions of women are taking tranquillizers at any one time, this is a very large problem.

Depression is the most common of all psychological illnesses and one of the earliest clinical signs of the condition is the loss of interest in sex – and indeed other pleasurable activities. If someone has any of the other signs of symptoms of depression (feeling sad, crying, difficulty in getting off to sleep or waking very early, poor appetite, poor concentration, or a lack of self-confidence and self-respect) he or she should see a doctor at once.

Serious physical disease such as chronic arthritis or

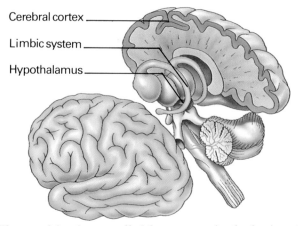

Cerebral cortex
Limbic system
Hypothalamus

The sex drive is controlled by an area in the brain called the hypothalamus. The instinctive patterns of sexual behaviour in humans are modified by other parts of our highly evolved brain. The cerebral cortex that houses our reasoning and learning, and the limbic system that controls our moods and emotions, both modify our sexual response and reduce it from the primitive 'urge' found in animals, thus allowing us to function in a social context and preventing us from becoming visibly aroused by all sexual stimuli

any long-term painful condition can reduce even the sexiest individual's drive for sex.

For any person with a physical, or indeed psychological disease, it is important to realize that many people are simply 'going along' with their current sexual lifestyle – but with little real interest, except to please their partner. For someone in this position, an illness can give them the excuse they are unconsciously searching for to let them off the hook, and some people retreat from sex on the slightest pretext.

Physical and mental exhaustion make most people go off sex. The usual story is that after a rest they bounce back to normal sexual activity again.

Some women go off sex for weeks or months after having a baby, and individuals of either sex can find they want little sex after an operation.

Stress can radically affect a person's ability to function well sexually. A man who has lost his job, a woman who is worried about the pregnancy of her teenage daughter, a bereavement, or even moving home can all be so stressful even to the sexiest person that he or she goes off sex, if only for a while.

Some men find work so permanently stressful that they never actually turn off enough to relax and have sex. Often this can be difficult to sort out because, in fact, the man may be seeking an escape from a poor relationship by overworking.

Guilt can be a real barrier to anyone's normal sex drive and is a cause that is commonly seen by therapists working in this field. Even unconscious guilt can wreak havoc, let alone that of which an individual is aware.

Some people lose their sex drive because of the guilt they feel about something that they have done (an extra-marital affair, for example) and others can even be guilty enough to lose their sex drive for something they have only thought about doing.

Over-romantic views of sex tend to affect women more – particularly many younger women who believe a 'Mr Right' will one day come along and sweep them off their feet. In the meantime, they remain virtually sexless as a kind of sleeping beauty. Occasionally, you find males with the same belief.

Relationship causes are probably the most significant cause in lowering the sex drive of either sex. About a third of all marriages go wrong enough to end in divorce, but possibly another third are diseased but not terminally so. At some time in almost every marriage, a couple will have problems with their relationship and these difficulties can lead to one or both losing their sex drive, if only with their partner.

Affairs are a common reason for a loss of sex drive. With the 'prohibited' partner, guilt prevents the normal sex drive from asserting itself and, when trying to have sex with the spouse, it fails for fear that he or she will be able to tell there is someone else. Failure sexually with another partner can produce a poor level of sex drive in the main relationship.

Every couple experiences bad individual lovemaking episodes occasionally and these can put one or both off sex, sometimes for a long time. A man who pushes his wife too hard to indulge in something she really does not want to do can put her off sex for ages. Any woman who enjoys sex, but fears what she will be obliged to do, is likely to go off sex, if only for a while.

Letting oneself go to seed can affect the sex drive. At least some people who go off sex say that it is becase their partner has let him- or herself go to seed, physically or emotionally. Overweight wives, and husbands who smell of drink are just two examples. Even dirty fingernails can be a turn-off to an otherwise sexy woman as her lover approaches her vulva.

FINDING A SOLUTION

Perhaps the most important starting point is to stop having sex. This takes the pressure off the situation and can, ironically, begin to help matters greatly.

Try to treat the underlying cause. By reading through the above list, it should be fairly obvious what the problem is. If you cannot sort things out between you, seek the help of a trained counsellor.

Start on a programme for making your lives more erotic. Read sexy books and magazines together, watch sexy videos and films, buy some sex toys, share your fantasies with one another, learn how to massage and, if possible, take a second honeymoon.

Masturbate more. This is a very good way of getting the sex drive back. It seems to work particularly well for women.

Return to your courtship behaviour and try to make love rather than just to copulate.

Once the cause has been removed, the sex drive returns in many people within a few weeks, or even sooner. If things do not improve within this time span, seek professional help.

ANXIETY, DEPRESSION AND SEX

Learning to relax in lovemaking minimizes the emotional charge of anxiety and depression, and helps prove that the ups and downs of life need not destroy sexual pleasure

When we feel depressed or worried about something, it is as if our bodies feel it too. A tight knot in the stomach or a clenched jaw are signs that all is not well with our minds. In the same way, a loss of sex drive, or lack of satisfaction in sex, are parts of this link between our minds and our bodies. We have all known times when a furious row with our partner can end up in passionate kisses – and bed. Anger and desire seem to spark each other off. Often, too, lovemaking triggered off by a fight wipes away the hurt, angry feelings – bringing the calm after the storm. But some of the other difficult feelings we have to deal with – worry, depression, stress – may act in a less satisfactory way and become a barrier to sexual enjoyment.

A common example of this is when a man's anxiety about his 'performance' in bed prevents him from achieving an erection. Another is when a woman feels depressed about her body – possibly having an adverse body image, or maybe not having regained her figure after the birth of a baby – and so rejects her partner's caresses.

PINPOINTING THE PROBLEM

Anxiety is not always the acute, nail-biting kind, nor is depression always debilitating. They can simply mean a general lack of confidence, or motivation, so that many situations – including sex – are found difficult.

But most kinds of anxiety and depression do have straightforward causes. They are simply reactions to actual events. It can be difficult, for example, to switch off from money worries and surrender to the sensuousness of sex. Or we may feel too let down by a major disappointment to 'want to play'.

Sometimes, however, the causes of our anxiety or depression may be buried in our unconscious. We feel 'wound up' or deflated, apparently for no good reason. But there probably is a very good reason, if we take the time and effort to look for it. The solution may simply lie in a few minor alterations to our general lifestyle. Or it may be more serious.

CHEMICAL CULPRITS?

Most of us face a certain amount of stress in our lives, but still manage to cope from day to day. For some, though, depression may hit at a much deeper level as though it came 'from inside'. This may show itself in uncontrollable crying, or in feeling unable to face the day at work. Such depression is known as 'endogenous' and those who suffer from it should seek professional help.

The same applies to manic depression. Here, the sufferer is unable to control his or her emotions and slides from frantic activity to deep depressions which make any action impossible.

It is not clear what causes these two more serious forms of depression. Some psychiatrists have linked them to a chemical imbalance in the brain which can be treated by drugs.

Sometimes, too, the more everyday forms of anxiety and depression, which are best treated without drugs, are the result of hormonal fluctuations in the body. Many women know, without counting the days, when they are close to a period, because of the mood changes that they experience. These changes are thought to be caused by an alteration in the levels of hormones which play an essential part in both conception and pregnancy and also affect women's responsiveness to sex.

The effect of hormones on sexuality has been shown by the reactions of some women to the contraceptive Pill. Depression and loss of libido or sex drive have both been connected with the hormone progesterone, a synthetic form of which is contained in the Pill.

It is also known that high levels of testosterone, the 'male' hormone, are linked with increased frequency of intercourse in both sexes.

Unfortunately, an improvement in sex drive cannot be guaranteed by a dose of testosterone. Human beings are more complicated than that. So although anxiety, for example, is clearly linked to high levels of the hormone adrenalin, the solution to most sexual problems does not lie in hormones, but in a better understanding of our emotions.

UNDERSTANDING OURSELVES

If a sexual relationship is unsatisfactory, we may sense that the cause lies in our own or our partner's emotions, but be unsure of what to do about it. The first step is to recognize what is wrong. When either

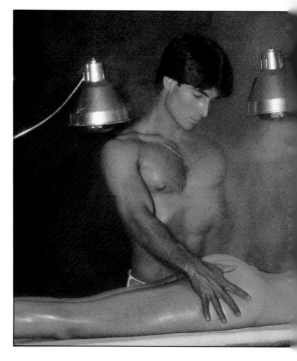

partner feels 'turned off' sex, he or she may put this down simply to tiredness. But often what appears to be a permanent state of exhaustion may be hidden depression.

Depression has sometimes been defined as an absence of energy. The depressed person lacks emotional and therefore physical zest. He or she feels apathetic and passive, unable to summon up much enthusiasm for anything. In this situation it is hardly surprising that there is a loss of interest in sex.

TELL-TALE SIGNS

When we are depressed we often describe ourselves as 'down'. In contrast, the sufferer from anxiety is 'wound up'. An intense inner feeling of nerves on edge, and a tension in the body of which the person concerned may be unaware, are typical signs of anxiety. It is helpful to learn to monitor the signs.

As you read this, you may be showing signs of anxiety – your jaw may be clenched, or you may be sitting with shoulders hunched. Depression will show in a slumped posture and, often, dull eyes and skin. Being aware of our bodily signals is the first step to take in learning to identify feelings in ourselves which we may have suppressed, but which can affect our mind and body if we do not learn to recognize and deal with them at an early stage.

A professional massage (left) is a treat that most of us would enjoy. But sharing a massage with your partner costs nothing, and can be an even more sensual experience. A luxurious bath (above) is another way of helping body and mind to function at their relaxed, sexual best

The same applies if it is your partner rather than yourself who seems to be losing enjoyment in sex. Look for the tell-tale bodily signs. A loving massage may help to stimulate energy-giving blood circulation in a depressed person, or to soothe the tense muscles of the over-anxious, and can often go a long way towards alleviating their state of mind.

But most of all do not forget to talk to each other. Communication plays an important part in minimizing the effects of depression and anxiety, and may help you and your partner towards a better understanding of your underlying feelings.

SELF-HELP

Both depression and anxiety are states which lead us to lose touch with our feelings, both emotional and physical. When we are anxious we tend to shut off feelings which unconsciously frighten us, tensing our bodies as though to ward of a threat. In depression we suppress feelings, and our bodies seem dull and lifeless.

The key to 'turning ourselves on' to the world and to sexual feeling lies in learning to relax. A good start is a little self-indulgence.

POSITIVE PAMPERING

Reserve a few hours completely for yourself. Take a warm, scented bath – do not make it too hot. Massage your body with scented oils, perhaps some of the aromatic oils now on sale in health food and body shops.

At first, keep away from the genitals, then move closer – perhaps stroking the insides of the thighs with an upwards motion. Women can cup the breasts without touching the nipples, men lightly caress the testicles.

This should leave you feeling relaxed and scented. You can then wrap up lightly, and – perhaps with a glass of wine – join your partner in a smooth, freshly-made bed. Any daily cares and worries should be now seem a long way away.

SOOTHING AWAY STRESS

Another effective and enjoyable way to relax is through massage with your partner. These sessions should aim simply at regaining the basic pleasure of touch and physical contact, and should, therefore, concentrate on parts of the body other than the genitals.

When massaging or being massaged, pay particular attention to the areas which tend to reflect tension, such as the face, neck, back and shoulders.

And when you are being massaged, concentrate your mind completely on the sensation you are feeling in the particular part of your body which is being touched. This will help break down the muscular barriers which many people put up around different parts of the body.

Another way of breaking down these barriers is to tense your muscles deliberately and then let go, releasing when your partner rests a hand over the contracted muscle. The feeling should be as though you are letting the tension flow out into your partner's body, and it should leave you relaxed and peaceful.

TUNING IN TO YOUR BODY

For some people, though, simple pampering or relaxation exercises may not be enough to help them lose a feeling of detachment or lack of concentration in sex. This is often caused by hidden anxieties which may lead the mind to 'shut off' from the immediate experience and wander on to unconnected areas.

When this happens, a technique which psychologists call 'shuttling' may help. Here, instead of trying desperately to fix your mind on the here and now, which can itself be draining, allow yourself to withdraw, then 'shuttle' back to the present. In this way you will be able mentally to deal with what was bothering you, without interfering too much with the experience of the moment.

Remember that lack of full enjoyment in sex is often caused by the unconscious desire to 'control' – to have everything ordered in your mind. In this way attention is fixed on the mind rather than the body. So, listen instead to your body, allowing it to throw the switches to full arousal and absorption in sex.

PAINFUL SEX

Painful sex is a very real problem that can rock the steadiest relationship. By finding out the possible causes, the problem can often be overcome

Almost every woman experiences at least one episode of pain on intercourse at some time in her life – it is a simple signal that something, somewhere, is not quite right.

The pain or discomfort felt may have an anatomical cause, be a symptom of infection or disease and/or be psychological in origin.

Medical textbooks tend to divide the reasons for painful sex into emotional and physical causes, but such distinct demarcation is often misleading – the two are often closely related.

Many women who experience painful or difficult intercourse are put off even trying to have sex and some even go off orgasms too. Even quite a mild degree of pain can cause anxiety. This in turn reduces the ability to become aroused and the resulting lack of lubrication causes even more pain. It can become a vicious circle if nothing is done to cure it.

SURFACE PAIN

It is not uncommon for first-time sex to be accompanied by a certain degree of surface pain. And this is particularly likely if the girl has never inserted fingers or a tampon into her vagina, and the hymen has remained rigid and intact.

At the point of penetration for the first time, the muscles of a woman's vagina may automatically go into spasm, partly in anticipation of pain and partly because of the anxiety of new experience.

Early sex may also be uncomfortable because of a lack of lubrication. In non-virgins, such surface pain during intercourse usually comes about as a result of an episiotomy (the incision made between the vagina and the anus during childbirth to aid delivery). Even well-repaired episiotomies can be painful for weeks after giving birth, but less expertly repaired ones can go on being painful for longer.

If a woman has a painful episiotomy scar she should tell her doctor who can examine her to see if the repair was properly carried out. If it was not – the stitches may be too tight – the doctor will suggest methods of stretching the area. In some cases, he or she may recommend that the episiotomy is re-done.

PAINFUL IRRITATIONS

The commonest cause of pain inside the vagina is infection. Various infections can be present even without an obvious discharge.

For women of reproductive years, the most common infections are thrush and trichomoniasis. Thrush is characterized by a curdy, white, thick discharge – it can produce such an intense itching that it is very distressing and can make even the thought of sex a nightmare. Trichomoniasis produces an irritating discharge of a yellowish-green, bubbly fluid. With both infections the vulva becomes swollen and inflamed, and sex is painful.

Both these types of vaginal infection should be properly diagnosed and treated by a doctor. It is also advisable to treat the woman's partner, or the couple can shuttle the infection back and forth between them for weeks or even months.

Other vaginal irritations which may result in painful sex can be caused by certain rubbers in contraceptives, foams, jellies and soaps, and vaginal deodorants.

DEEP PAIN

Deep pain in intercourse can be caused by a retroverted uterus (one which is tilted backwards instead of forwards). If this is the case, the pain is present from the first time a woman has sex. If the pain comes on later, after pain-free intercourse, a pelvic disorder may be the cause, such as pelvic inflammatory disease, endometriosis (when pieces of womb lining come adrift) or fibroids.

Often a doctor can decide fairly easily which is to blame, but sometimes the diagnosis can be difficult to make and he or she will have to recommend a laparoscopy (in which a thin telescopic tube is inserted into the abdomen), so that the pelvic area can be viewed directly. Women with endometriosis usually have other troublesome symptoms such as painful periods and mid-cycle pain.

If a woman's uterus is retroverted, the ovaries are slightly altered in position and can more easily be knocked by the penis or a man's fingers during lovemaking. Retroversion itself, however, is not a disease. It is a variation of normality and usually needs nothing done about it. The best thing is to experiment with different intercourse positions to find those that allow the woman to remain pain-free.

Some women greatly enjoy their man's penis hit-

ting the cervix during intercourse but to others this is painful and they seek to avoid it. Fortunately, it is almost always possible to find a position in which such cervical pain can be avoided.

SEX AND THE MENOPAUSE

In older women, after the menopause, there is a narrowing of the vagina as the lining thins under the influence of falling levels of oestrogen.

The painful intercourse that may result can be prevented (and treated) by increasing the amount of intercourse a woman has. This keeps the vagina supple and helps lubrication to return towards premenopausal levels. This alone can be enough to prevent painful sex.

The cycle can be broken initially by using plenty of KY or a similar lubricating jelly. If this does not improve matters, oestrogen creams work well for most women. And it is also possible, with a little creativity, to find a range of intercourse positions that do not cause the pain.

ALL IN THE MIND

Even if a physical cause for painful sex cannot be found, it does not necessarily mean that the problem has a psychological or emotional origin – although it might. Depression is a relatively common cause of pain, as is marital discord, a fear of pregnancy and many other different reasons.

VAGINISMUS

Mild attacks of difficult intercourse caused by muscle spasm (vaginismus) are common in early attempts at intercourse. And mild or transient attacks are not uncommon in women who have been having perfectly normal, pain-free sex for years.

Vaginismus is the painful spasm of the vaginal and pelvic muscles that occurs in anticipation of penetration. It can occur either spontaneously or as a result of one of the physical causes of painful sex.

As the average girl negotiates her teens, she may explore her vulva and put something (usually a finger or two) into her vagina as she masturbates. This enables her to incorporate her vagina into her body image for intercourse. But some girls do grow up believing that they have a very small vagina. And clinical experience has shown that some women even believe that their vagina does not exist at all. To such a woman, anything pressing between her legs is seen as if it were pressing on an intact surface. Some even describe the pain as 'knife-like'.

A young woman who suffers from vaginismus early on in her sexual life usually goes for help promptly and gets good results quickly. In older couples the problem may show up as infertility – they desperately want a baby, but cannot have intercourse.

WHY IT HAPPENS

The causes of vaginismus are many and are often far from obvious. For the majority of young women who suffer, there is no serious underlying cause – they may be simply apprehensive or guilty, poorly aroused or sexually inexperienced.

But there are also many more deeply hidden causes. These can include a fear of pregnancy, a woman's unconscious perception of her lover as her father, latent lesbian tendencies, a belief that the vagina is too small to take so apparently large an object as a penis, negative sexual conditioning in childhood, falling out of love with a partner, an extra-marital affair, or even just a partner who puts the woman off.

Obviously deep-rooted psychosexual causes of vaginismus need to be sorted out by trained counsellors. And any physical condition that causes pain should be treated by a doctor. But there is still much that a woman who suffers from vaginismus can do herself.

SELF-HELP FOR VAGINISMUS

Very commonly, there is no obvious medical cause, yet the woman continues to experience pain in intercourse, which may cause her to hold back from sex.

With the help of a loving partner, however, she may soon be able to enjoy a fulfilling sex life:
☐ Discuss the problem together. The woman should try to understand her personal background, her early sexual experiences, her relationship with her mother and father, her early fantasies about how children are born, her first factual information about intercourse (especially any mention of pain and bleeding), her sexual fantasies, and how she masturbates

MEN AND PAINFUL SEX

Men suffer from painful sex less commonly than do women; this is partly because the penis is less prone to ailments than is the vagina or the female pelvic organs.

The commonest of the causes of painful intercourse in men are associated with the foreskin. If it is tight and cannot be pulled right back easily, pain is almost inevitable with all but the shallowest of penetration.

Sometimes this condition can be helped if the man or his partner can stretch the foreskin while soaking in the bath until it will pull completely back. If this is not possible, then the man will need to be circumcised. This cures the problem once and for all.

A man may also experience tenderness or pain on intercourse and masturbation if there are small tears in the frenulum (the little ridge of tissue on the underside of the head of the penis).

A few men have deformities of the penis, which cause bending and bowing during erection, and this can be painful during sex.

Infections affecting the tip of the penis or under the foreskin can cause irritation and even pain on intercourse.

An infection of the prostate gland (prostatitis) or even an infection of structures such as the epididymis in the scrotum can cause some pain on ejaculation.

Some young men complain they get aching sensations, usually in the testicles or the groin, following any prolonged periods of sexual arousal without ejaculation. This discomfort is usually relieved by ejaculation.

An uncommon but troublesome cause of painful intercourse in men involves painful ejaculation (where no infection is present), a pain in the groin or even a headache which comes on during sex.

Some men with these problems claim that something is wrong with their semen, and that they have a blockage or something similar. But excessive penile sen-

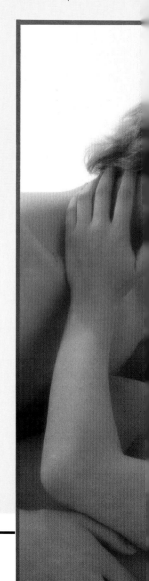

...ations are almost always a sign of an unconscious desire to avoid sex and such cases can be very difficult to sort out even by a trained sexual counsellor.

The possible causes are many, and are often related to unconscious fears of women and sex generally. Some such men, for example, have been brought up to think of semen as a form of excretion and so, quite understandably, cannot readily bring themselves to 'defile' a woman they love with it.

Sometimes sex is painful for the man because the woman's vagina is too dry. This can happen if his partner is insufficiently aroused, or if she has just removed a tampon. This type of friction pain can easily be avoided by devoting more time to foreplay and, if necessary, by using a lubrication gel, such as KY jelly, in her vagina.

□ The next step is for the woman to learn about her vagina. She may have picked up worrying myths as she grew up. Looking at the vulva in a mirror helps. Watching so-called pornographic films may help, too, because it may prove to her that a penis really can go into a woman and give her pleasure

□ If a woman cannot accept the help of her partner she can now slowly and gently start to insert first one fingertip and then eventually a whole finger into her vagina, perhaps while she masturbates. When she can do this easily without pain she can go on to a vibrator or small dildo, gradually becoming more confident until she can happily contemplate her partner's penis

□ Ideally she should engage her partner in the learning process. Then, when she is highly aroused and, if necessary, lubricated with KY jelly, he can persuade her to open her legs wide. He slowly inserts the tip of one finger. If and when her vaginal muscles go into spasm, he stops and keeps his finger still. The woman then contracts her pelvic muscles hard around the

finger, and then relaxes them – as she relaxes, he advances his finger a little further. The tip of the finger is then rotated around the vaginal entrance – not thrust in an out – this would be too intimidating

□ The cycle of insertion, muscle contraction, relaxation and further insertion is repeated until a whole finger can be tolerated without too much anxiety. Once this state is achieved, progress can be very rapid.

The secret is not to go rapidly for intercourse, but rather to return to this level of penetration and then to increase the number of fingers or to use a vibrator or dildo. Intercourse should not be attempted until the woman feels totally happy about it, and the man should not thrust until she feels ready for him to do so. This calls for patience on the part of the man, but it is worth it – for the future happiness of both partners.

COMMUNICATING ABOUT SEX

Many couples can live together for years but never really talk. Yet communication is vital to any relationship – and one of the essential ingredients of good sex

Sex is a very private subject for most people – especially when it involves our own personal sexuality, rather than discussing sex in a general way. Even within a close, truly loving relationship, many people feel awkward about declaring things about their sexual needs, desires and anxieties.

The joy of a close personal and sexual relationship is that a couple can discuss and share each other's fears as well as sexual desires. But all too often – although sex may be enjoyable and good – there is a lack of communication. A couple who can succeed in overcoming this communication gap will almost certainly find that the physical and emotional sides of lovemaking will become so much better.

There are many reasons why communicating about sex is so difficult. One problem is that we tend to make assumptions about sexuality – in our attitudes to what we believe men and women want and need, and on an individual level within our close relationships.

Not communicating about sex is at the heart of countless problems and arguments within long-term relationships.

HAVING SEX AND MAKING LOVE
Having sex – simply copulating – with someone is not very difficult, and not very fulfilling. But making love is probably the ultimate in communication between two people. The couple who have learned from each other will know the difference between the two:

☐ Copulation is essentially self-centred – it is a form of sexual release that takes little account of the other person's sexuality. Making love is partner-centred and highly personalized

☐ For most people who copulate, it is an almost entirely genital activity that requires little other commitment. Making love involves not only the genitals, but the whole personality

☐ Copulation usually pays little or no heed to a

partner's needs and preferences; making love does
☐ Someone who 'copulates' is unimaginative and has little insight into his or her partner. The reverse is true for those who make love
☐ Copulation has limited horizons, making love has none
☐ Should failure occur when copulating it can be a disaster, but to the couple who make love, it is no great problem – they know they can work things through, and that things may well be better again tomorrow
☐ Copulation is primarily a way of relieving sexual tensions, whereas making love is the most intimate form of interpersonal communication. It is based on a deep knowledge of each other's needs and involves much self-revelation.

TIME TO TALK

Clinical experience and many couples' personal explorations of their relationships have highlighted some ways to break down the barriers to communicating about sex.

MAKE TIME
Many people who go to marital and psychosexual counsellors complain that they never talk, nor even spend much time doing anything together. They then wonder why their relationship is withering.

It is a good idea to be quite disciplined when it comes to communicating about sex. Because it is difficult, it tends to be crowded out of a busy life. One answer is to make a date with each other to really talk to each other.

Try to make it fairly early on in the evening so that you are not both exhausted and likely to become irritable. It may be a good idea to go out – as being on neutral territory can help greatly. Go for a walk together, to a pub or to a restaurant for a simple meal.

Talking to each other in bed is just as important as, if not more than, talking to each other over the breakfast table. And often, inhibitions are shed along with clothes, making it easier for a couple to communicate at a deep level. A couple who use their bed not just for making love, but as a place where communication barriers do not exist, will be able to build and maintain a strong and healthy relationship

TALK THE SAME LANGUAGE
One of the problems of communicating about sex is that we often use different words, and think that we know what our partner thinks about something even though we have never actually asked.

Make a list of key sexual words such as breast size, oral sex, semen, testicles and clitoris. Then, write (privately) your own words for these 'medical' terms. In another column write your main thoughts about them – just notes will do.

Now swap your pieces of paper and go through each item, sharing your new-found knowledge about each other's ideas and talking about it.

COMMUNICATE PHYSICALLY
It might seem strange to discuss massage in the context of communicating with each other, but it is a vital tool in two ways.

First, communication between lovers *is* physical, and sensual massage is a good learning tool. But more important is that the sharing and caring that takes place during massage is a solid foundation for any other form of communication about sex.

Someone who cares enough about you to pleasure you so lovingly in a physical way becomes well worth listening to and taking seriously. And the simple 'instructions' that are given by your partner during sensual massage are good ways of becoming aware of his or her needs (both emotional and physical) and doing something about them.

The couple who take the time to massage each other in this way are also much less likely to have destructive

arguments. Because they are tuned in to each other's needs, they can either prevent rows occurring or are loathe to let small disagreements blow up into serious confrontations.

APPROACHING THE 'NO-GO' AREAS

Much hostility in a relationship can arise over 'no-go' areas. These can be such subjects as oral sex, mothers-in-law, schooling, politics and religion.

For many couples, every time one of these subjects comes up, one or both of the partners skirts around it – usually because they hold very differing views which, if aired, would lead to a fight or silence.

Obviously, no two people can agree about everything, but a good friendship can withstand a fair amount of disagreement. There are often no absolute answers to the problems being discussed, and it is important to remember that one person's view is of as much value as another's.

The thing to do is to be sure that you both know what the 'no-go' areas are, and then to try to work through them slowly and lovingly. You might be closer together on them than you thought.

Do not forget that attitudes change as the years go by and as people mature. Even if you knew what your partner thought about oral sex, for example, ten years ago, this might not apply now. It is essential to be dealing with your partner on the basis of real knowledge, not outdated assumptions.

When you reach an area about which you cannot agree, accept it. Understand that if your relationship is good, it will stand quite a lot of disagreement – provided that you do not attack each other's personalities for being different.

If you have many 'no-go' areas you might benefit from seeking professional help, if only because a couple who disagree on most things will almost cer-

tainly find it very difficult to sustain a deep emotion: and fulfilling sexual relationship.

Once people begin serious discussions about thei 'no-go' areas, they often find that they are not as ba or as numerous as they had previously thought.

Many couples who seek professional counsellin: find that they think more similarly about lots of thing than they had ever realized. Often, the 'no-go' area have become symbolic battle grounds for other prob lems in the relationship and are not really a problem ii themselves.

AVOID FULL-SCALE ROWS

Although it can be difficult to discuss sex, it is essentia to prevent small disagreements and differences from blowing up into full-scale rows.

Reward your partner's efforts by taking time to massage his cares away. Straddled over his buttocks you will be in an ideal position to massage his shoulders and back. Pleasuring your partner in this way will let him know you love him, and is an ideal way of demonstrating your emotions on a physical level

It is very easy for a couple to start discussing something which is a problem, and then for one partner to widen the scope of the argument to include all kinds of other things that 'need to be said' or 'got off the chest'. Before the couple know where they are, it is the middle of the night, and one of them ends up storming out to sleep in another room or leaves the house. At the worst extreme, physical violence can sometimes be the unfortunate outcome of such major confrontations.

Be careful. Hurtful things said during such rows

tick in the memory and are difficult, or impossible, to remove. A thirty-second outburst can take years to mend, especially if it attacks the individual's personality or innate sexual style.

VALUE FRIENDSHIP

When you set about discussing a sexual topic, always remember that your partner is probably your best friend and that you should not do anything to harm the friendship. This may mean holding your tongue sometimes. It is all very well dumping your troubles on to your partner, but if she or he cannot cope, and does not know how to handle them, have you really made progress?

Total honesty is not always the best policy, especially when it comes to affairs or even to certain fantasies. Be loving about what you reveal, and be sensitive as to how much your partner can cope with.

Many people misuse their friendship. A boss who is impossible, a bad business deal or a row with the children can all be upsetting. This is perfectly understandable, but many people then bring out these battles and woes and heap them on to their partner.

There is, however, a limit to what any individual should be expected to handle on someone else's behalf. Instead of expecting your partner to cope with all your personal difficulties, it is probably better to try to deal with these problems yourself – turning to your partner for emotional support, rather than expecting them to solve your problems or to bear the brunt of your frustrations and anger.

At times, a loving friend can be the ideal person at whom to let off steam. But if this becomes a habit, beware, because it can wear away at even the best friendship. Perhaps it would make sense to seek professional help if you find yourself bringing out your problems on your partner repeatedly. It is very easy to push even a loving, friendly partner into a position in which he or she says 'I've had enough'.

This might not mean that they will actually walk out, but they might do so metaphorically. Such an in-

dividual then becomes remote and will not communicate about anything, least of all sex, for fear of having to take on another load of trouble. The relationship can slide slowly downhill.

BEHAVE IN A MORE LOVING WAY

If you act more lovingly towards your partner you will find that you communicate about sex more openly, more often and more successfully.

When a man says 'I'd like an early night tonight', he does not necessarily mean that he is desperate for sleep. It may be his indirect way of saying 'Let's have sex'. If the woman does not know this, she cannot be blamed for saying 'OK, you go and I'll see you later, if you're still awake'.

Many couples start off their lives together with all kinds of private language and communication skills. Unfortunately, these can be lost through laziness, lack of practice and boredom. Partners who always behave in a loving way seldom fall into this trap because they keep topping up their fund of goodwill, show each other signs of affection all the time, and find it easier to withstand criticism and failure when it occurs.

Making love is a continuous process that is an important part of every successful couple's life. No one can spend all day having intercourse, and most people would not want to, but we can make love in the widest sense of the word.

Enjoyable intercourse grows out of this mood, and each partner knows (because they are so well tuned in to each other) when the other wants sex and when they do not. Such couples share a secret language, often know what each other is thinking and feel 'as one' much of the time.

For many couples this will sound like a fairy story, but it is not. It is achievable by any couple who want to make it happen. It does, however, need working at – like anything worthwhile. You have to invest time and effort or you will see no return.

'SECOND HONEYMOONS'

A second honeymoon, or sensual holiday, can last for an evening, a day, a week or more. There is only one rule – devote the time solely to each other, and agree not to fall into your usual routine. This is time for expanding your horizons. Be more adventurous, try something new, make love in a new way or in a new place and so on.

You can take a holiday at home, go away for a weekend or go the whole way and have a holiday abroad. Whatever you do, go back to courtship behaviour and rediscover each other. Look for the unexpected, and make the most of your time together.

When you return from your 'holiday', build in any new experiences into your relationship, so that your day-to-day life is enriched. Take it in turns to plan these holidays, and see if you can have one several times a year – even if it is simply an evening out or a weekend away together. It need not be expensive to be successful.

CONTRACEPTION

*Despite the availability of family planning and an
increasing range of contraceptives, millions of women
throughout the world still risk unplanned pregnancy
because they and their partners do not use regular or
reliable contraception*

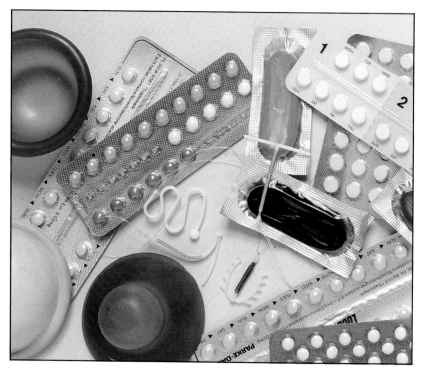

In 1987 there were nearly 200,000 legal abortions
performed in the UK; this figure increases annually,
and the number of unintended pregnancies remains
stubbornly high.

One reason is that information about contraception
is often not reaching the people that most need it. As
a result, couples and individuals often make the
wrong decisions about the methods they choose, use
them badly, or abandon them altogether. Others are
not using contraception at all and simply taking a
chance that they do not get pregnant.

This is not really surprising since information
about contraceptive methods is changing all the time.
As methods are tested and researched, more risks and
side effects come to light and the more confusing it all
becomes – for doctors as well as the consumers.

Choice becomes even more complicated as scientific research points to limiting medical methods of
contraception to particular ages and groups of women.

At the same time women have learned to understand and appreciate their bodies far more and are less
inclined simply to accept what they are prescribed.
Increasingly, they are attracted by methods which

they see as more natural, in keeping with the general
trend towards a more natural lifestyle.

SHARING THE CHOICE

With the arrival of the Pill and IUD (Intra-Uterine
Device) in the 1960s, women took responsibility for
contraception and were relieved to have the means of
preventing pregnancy under their own control. But
many women now feel resentful that they shoulder all
the risks and problems, while more men feel unhappy
that they have no role to play.

Time and time again, studies show that men's in-
tentions in terms of sharing responsibility for contraception are often very positive. Unfortunately, these
same studies show that for most men there is a wide
gap between intention and practice.

There is no ideal contraceptive, nor is there likely to
be for decades. But good methods do exist. They all
have advantages and disadvantages, and the way individuals or couples assess these very much depends on
their lifestyle and attitudes to sex.

For many people there will be a different 'best
method' at different times of their life. For couples the

CONTRACEPTIVE METHODS AND EFFECTIVENESS

Information from leaflets and Fact Sheets published by the UK Family Planning Information Service (September 1989)

METHOD	EFFECTIVENESS
THE COMBINED PILL (triphasic and biphasic pills/Everyday Pill)	99% (if taken properly)
MINI-PILL	99% (if taken properly)
INJECTABLE CONTRACEPTIVES (Depo-Provera/Noristerat)	Over 99%
IUD	97–99%
DIAPHRAGM or CAP (plus spermicide)	85–98% (with careful use)
SPONGE	75–91% (with careful use)
SHEATH	85–98% (with careful use)
'SAFE PERIOD' (body-temperature method)	80–98% (with careful use)
FEMALE STERILIZATION	Occasional failure: 1 in 200–1 in 1,000*
MALE STERILIZATION	Occasional failure: 1 in 1,000

Effectiveness rates for reversible methods refer to the number of women out of 100 using the method for a year who do not get pregnant. Post-coital effectiveness rates refer to the number of women out of 100 who do not become pregnant after using post-coital methods.   * Depending on method used.

olution to sharing the responsibility may be to alternate between male and female methods.

Doctors and nurses can help you make a choice, and counselling services are gradually becoming more accessible to men as well as women, but in the end the decision has to be yours. A good choice of contraceptive can help you enjoy a relaxed sex life as well as protecting against unintended pregnancy.

THE PILL

When most people refer to the Pill, they mean the oral contraceptive which contains two hormones, oestrogen and progestogen, that stop women ovulating.

The Pill became available in the early 1960s and it gained popularity, after initial problems, to become the most used method of birth control and almost synonymous with contraception. But in the last 20 or so years a great deal of information has been collected on the effects of the Pill on women's health.

Some of this information is inconclusive and confusing, but it has resulted in more thought being given to minimizing side effects and the production of a second generation of contraceptive Pills which contained much lower doses of hormones.

THE PILL AND THE RISKS

To some extent it has also become possible to identify those women who might run risks from taking the Pill, such as smokers, those who are overweight or those with high blood pressure.

Since the publication of reports in October 1983, suggesting possible, but unconfirmed, links between taking the Pill and breast and cervical cancer, women are increasingly questioning that crucial balance between reliability and safety.

The great attraction of the Pill has always been its reliability together with its convenience. For many

Sheaths, the only contraceptive product available for men, can be bought readily from any chemist

couples the Pill is the only method which allows them to be completely spontaneous in their lovemaking.

Many women are trying to weigh up the plusses and minuses of taking the Pill. The most serious condition linked with the Pill is thrombosis, although the risk is very small unless you smoke or are overweight. Other side effects include depression, weight gain, loss of sex drive and headaches, although these can often be stopped by changing to a different Pill. It is worth remembering, however, that the Pill may protect against some diseases such as cancer of the ovaries and rheumatoid arthritis. And it is certainly the most convenient form of contraception at present.

THE MINI-PILL

For some women looking to minimize the health risks of Pill-taking, a move to the mini-Pill will provide a good solution. Mini-Pills contain only one hormone, progestogen, and the dose is lower than the progestogen dose in the combined Pill. They do not stop ovulation but prevent pregnancy in other ways, such as thickening the mucus at the entrance to the cervix to make it difficult for the sperm to penetrate.

As it does not contain oestrogen the mini-Pill is not thought to contribute to the risks of thrombosis, nor have mini-Pills been implicated in the recent cancer scares. On the other hand, they are less effective, and if a pregnancy does happen there is some risk of it being outside the womb – most probably in the Fallopian tubes. Women taking the mini-Pill also tend to suffer from irregular, or break-through, bleeding.

Mini-Pills must be taken every day at exactly the same time each day to be effective. They are usually considered most suitable for older women and breastfeeding mothers, but are not yet widely prescribed.

LONGER-ACTING METHODS

Depo-provera is a synthetic progestogen which is given by injection, usually into the muscle of the buttock. It is absorbed over a period of three months and stops ovulation.

Use of Depo-provera as a contraceptive has been controversial, and for many years it was only licensed in Britain for short-term use in special circumstances. In 1984, however, it was given a licence for long-term use and is slowly becoming more readily available.

The controversy has arisen partly because of unpleasant side effects such as irregular and frequent bleeding, weight gain and delays in return of fertility, and partly because of unsubstantiated fears of breast cancer and cancer of the lining of the womb.

There is concern that Depo-provera is sometimes given without proper explanation, so that women are

A chat with a counsellor to discuss the various methods may make the final decision easier

misled about possible side effects and sometimes suffer badly until the effect of the drug wears off.

The advantages of Depo-provera are its high reliability and ease of use. Most family planning experts, however, do not see it as a first-choice method of contraception, but rather as a useful addition to the range of contraceptives suitable for those unable to use other methods.

There is another injectable hormone called Noristerat now available, which lasts for two months and is used as an extra precaution after a vasectomy.

IUD, OR COIL

An Intra-Uterine Device (IUD) is a small 2.5cm (1in)-long flexible plastic device, now usually wound with copper, which is inserted into the womb by a doctor.

Coils come in a variety of different shapes and are

MALE PILLS AND OTHER MALE METHODS

Probably the most intriguing possibilities for contraception lie in the development of a male Pill.

Magazine surveys show that men have a variety of reactions to the idea of shouldering the responsibility of contraception by taking a pill every day.

Women, too, while wanting to shift the responsibility, question how dedicated men would be in taking it regularly. After all, it is not the man who gets pregnant if he forgets to take it.

A male Pill is actually more difficult to 'design' than the female Pill because there is no single event – like the release of the female egg – on which to work.

The most promising male Pill so far has come from China and was discovered by accident when it was noticed that in rural areas, where cotton-seed oil was used for cooking, the men had become infertile.

The first clinical trials on the plant extract gossypol, responsible for the infertility, started in China in 1972 and were reported six years later. The results were very encouraging, the effectiveness was nearly 100 per cent and there were few side effects.

Further research carried out by the World Health Organization (but which has been abandoned) showed that side effects were more com-

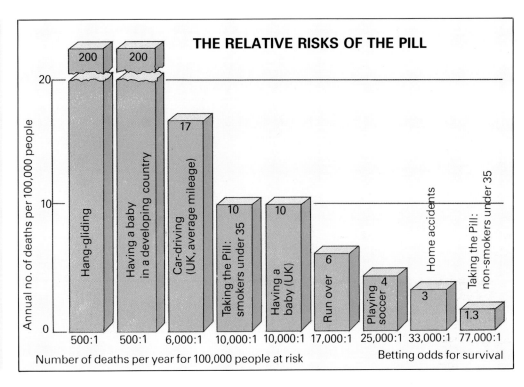

THE RELATIVE RISKS OF THE PILL

Annual no. of deaths per 100,000 people

Activity	Deaths	Betting odds for survival
Hang-gliding	200	500:1
Having a baby in a developing country	200	500:1
Car-driving (UK, average mileage)	17	6,000:1
Taking the Pill: smokers under 35	10	10,000:1
Having a baby (UK)	10	10,000:1
Run over	6	17,000:1
Playing soccer	4	25,000:1
Home accidents	3	33,000:1
Taking the Pill: non-smokers under 35	1.3	77,000:1

Number of deaths per year for 100,000 people at risk

normally replaced every two to five years, depending on the type. Although no one knows exactly how an IUD works, it prevents an egg from implanting in the womb lining.

Like the Pill, the coil was introduced in the 1960s, but has never achieved the same popularity. One reason for this was that early coils were not usually a first choice for women who had not had a child, for they were rather large in relation to the size of the womb.

More recently, copper-wound coils are smaller, but now there are different reasons why these are not recommended to women who have not had children. The problem is that the presence of a coil makes a woman more susceptible to pelvic infection which can be difficult to deal with and which could affect her ability to conceive later on.

The failure rate of the coil is about the same as the mini-Pill and, like the mini-Pill, pregnancies that do occur could be ectopic (occuring outside the womb).

One of its main disadvantages is that it often causes heavier periods. There may also be bleeding between periods. One of the main advantages is that, once fitted, there is no further involvement by the woman, except to check now and then that it is in the correct place by feeling the threads. An internal check-up by your doctor every year or so is essential.

BARRIER METHODS

Men and women started using barriers of various kinds to prevent pregnancy thousands of years ago.

Currently available are the diaphragm, cervical cap, vault cap and vimule cap. They are all made of soft rubber and fit over the neck of the womb (the cervix).

mon than first thought, including feeling weak, digestive problems and loss of sex drive.

The conclusion seems to be that gossypol itself will not be the male Pill of the future, but something similar may be developed instead.

Other male Pills could be developed from existing drugs, such as one used for hypertension and at present on trial in Israel. This particular drug acts as an 'ejaculation inhibitor'.

Alternative possibilities being researched include the injection of the synthetic hormone – 19-nortestosterone – which is used by some athletes to build up their muscles. Unfortunately, however, the drug has the strange side effect of reducing the testicles to half their normal size.

A mixture of the

hormones oestradiol and testosterone rubbed into the abdomen has also been unsuccessful as in trials it caused the men's partners to grow moustaches.

A male version of the 'releasing' hormone nasal spray and a mix of hormones introduced by a tiny pump have had no success so far.

INTRA-UTERINE DEVICES (IUDs) AND BARRIER METHODS

THE CHOICE:
IUDs (and applicator), the sponge, diaphragm, vault cap and cervical cap

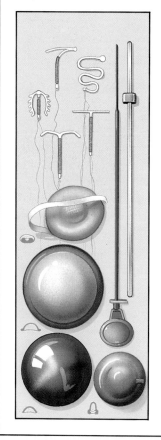

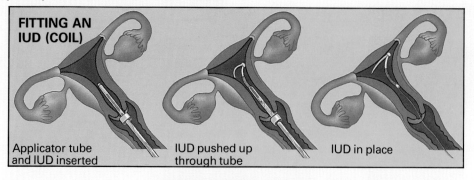

FITTING AN IUD (COIL)

Applicator tube and IUD inserted

IUD pushed up through tube

IUD in place

The IUD is fitted by a doctor. It is threaded into an applicator, which is inserted into the vagina and through the cervical opening. The IUD is passed through the applicator tube into the womb

Diaphragms and caps must be used with a spermicide, and initially fitted by a doctor or nurse, who gives instructions on how to use them. The contraceptive sponge works on similar principles

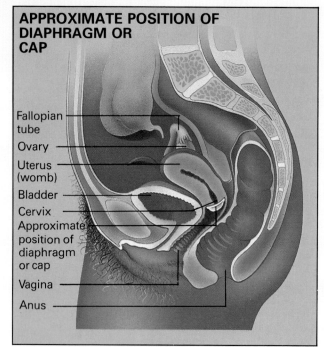

APPROXIMATE POSITION OF DIAPHRAGM OR CAP

Fallopian tube
Ovary
Uterus (womb)
Bladder
Cervix
Approximate position of diaphragm or cap
Vagina
Anus

They are used with spermicide cream or jelly, and inserted before lovemaking to form a barrier to sperm.

The newest barrier is the contraceptive sponge. Even though it is less reliable than the diaphragm, and therefore only suitable for women for whom pregnancy would not be disastrous, it overcomes some of the main objections to diaphragms and caps.

A major complaint by women is that barrier methods are too messy, interfere with spontaneous lovemaking and look unattractive. The sponge, which like the cap must be left in place for at least six hours after lovemaking, is impregnated with spermicide and after one use thrown away.

The male sheath is making a comeback. It is a reliable barrier method which rarely has any side effects. Today's sheaths are finer than ever before and often ribbed for increased sensation.

'SAFE PERIOD' METHODS

These are usually used by couples who have objec-tions to other methods for religious or other reasons. They are becoming increasingly popular with women who do not want to use medical or mechanical methods to avoid pregnancy. And as women become more aware of changes throughout their reproductive cycle, they are drawn to methods that are finely tuned to their own needs.

'Safe period' methods aim to pinpoint when a woman is most fertile and to avoid intercourse at this time. She will have to note signs of ovulation by taking her temperature every day (body-temperature method) or examining her cervical mucus (Billings method).

Careful record-keeping is essential, as is high motivation by both partners, with the acceptance that there will be times when they cannot have intercourse. These methods do need to be learned and are not suitable for women with irregular periods or for a while after childbirth.

'Safe period' methods do not give the reliability that most couples demand. The effectiveness is increased when the temperature method is combined with the Billings method and other signs of ovulation, but the failure rate is still high.

Most people have heard about the 'morning-after' Pill, but fewer know about the post-coital IUD, which is another option.

The post-coital Pill is in fact a special dose of the contraceptive Pill containing oestrogen and progestogen, which is taken within 72 hours of intercourse. The fitting of a coil within five days after intercourse is the alternative.

Morning-after methods have become generally available and endorsed for safety in recent years. They are, it should be stressed, only for use in an emergency – when contraception has not been used or has been used but has failed.

The post-coital Pill method involves taking a special dose of hormones under a doctor's supervision. However, it will only work for the one occasion. Sometimes side effects such as nausea, and occasionally vomiting, are experienced. Once fitted, the post-coital coil will ensure continuous protection.

STERILIZATION

Female sterilization and male vasectomy are intended as permanent methods of birth control. They involve relatively simple operations that close the Fallopian tubes in a woman, and the tubes through which sperm travels in a man.

A vasectomy is usually done under local anaesthetic and takes a few minutes. Female sterilization takes longer and can be done under general or local anaesthetic.

There are several ways female sterilization can be carried out, the most common being by laparoscopy when the Fallopian tubes are blocked with rings or clips. Neither the male nor female operation affects the production of hormones responsible for sexual drive, so sexual feelings should not be changed, unless they are improved by removing the risk of pregnancy.

Sterilization was once a last resort chosen by couples who had had many children. Today, it is increasingly chosen by couples who have decided that they have completed their family. In many countries one in five women in the fertile age range have been sterilized or their partners have had a vasectomy. It is seen nowadays as a positive and responsible step.

However, in a time of increasing marriage breakdown, there are also more requests for reversal. But reversal operations are frequently not effective, so sterilization operations really should be regarded as permanent and irreversible.

THE 'SAFE PERIOD' METHODS

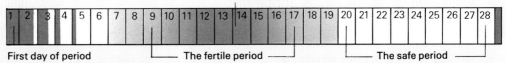

The principle of safe period methods of contraception is to learn to predict and recognize the time of the month when you are most fertile, and to avoid intercourse at that time. Sex is thus restricted to 'safe' days, when you are less likely to conceive.

A woman is most likely to get pregnant at and around the time of ovulation – when the egg is released from the ovary into the Fallopian tube. This usually occurs about two weeks before the start of the next period, but there are various ways that a woman can pin-point the precise moment more accurately.

Since sperm can live for up to five days inside a woman, and an egg can live for about two days, a woman must not have sex for at least five days before ovulation and for several days afterwards. Calculating the time of ovulation (when sex should be avoided) can be done in several ways:
□ The body-temperature method
□ The Billings (mucus) method
□ The calendar method
□ Combinations of these methods

The body-temperature method The woman takes her temperature every morning on waking up, and keeps a special chart. Immediately before ovulation, body temperature drops slightly – after the egg is released, it rises to a higher level than in the previous week.

The Billings (mucus) method This method works on the principle that ovulation can be detected by changes in cervical mucus. The woman is taught to examine her mucus and to recognize changes – such as increased amount and 'wetness'.

The calendar method The woman is shown how to calculate when she is most likely to ovulate by keeping a long-term record of her menstrual cycle. On its own this method is *very* unreliable and is not recommended.

Combined methods Combining methods and learning to recognize other 'symptoms' of ovulation increases the reliability. With all these natural methods, skilled guidance is essential. See your doctor or family planning clinic for advice.

These techniques are most successful for women who have regular periods. Anything which makes periods irregular – from the recent birth of a baby to a change of routine – makes the time of ovulation difficult to predict. Taking pain-killing drugs can alter body temperature and consequently make the 'temperature method' rather unreliable.

SEXUAL DISEASES

Sexually transmitted diseases are on the increase throughout the world, and young people form a high proportion of those affected. But if diagnosed early some of these infections can be cured

Any disease that can be passed on from one person to another by sexual contact is called a sexually transmitted disease, or STD. In the past the term VD (short for veneral disease) was much more commonly used, and usually referred to gonorrhoea and syphilis, the more serious of the diseases, apart from the killer disease AIDS, which is discussed fully later in the book.

For many people, VD was not merely a term describing an infectious disease transmitted sexually – it was regarded as something that was only caught by people who indulged in immoral behaviour. This attitude has changed a great deal in recent years, so that today STDs, and departments of genito-urinary medicine where they are treated, are usually thought of with less embarrassment than in the past.

WHO SUFFERS?

Anyone can catch an STD by oral and anal sex as well as by vaginal intercourse; in most cases the treatment for the infection is not painful or difficult, but as with most diseases, the earlier it is diagnosed, the easier it is to cure.

Generally, the most severe consequences of neglected STD fall upon women and babies. Women are far less likely to have the recognizable symptoms that make early diagnosis easy. That is why the follow-up of contacts by an STD clinic is so important.

Not surprisingly, some 60 per cent of those infected worldwide are under 24. The effect on young women can be particularly devastating if the untreated disease leads to infertility. So, if you think you could have caught an infection, even though you have no symptoms, go for a check-up anyway – nobody is going to criticize you for being safe rather than sorry, and it is better to put your mind at rest.

SYPHILIS

Syphilis, one of the most serious of all STDs, is becoming less common in Great Britain and the western world generally, while increasing in the developing world. There are about 20 to 50 million cases in the world every year. There were 1,727 cases reported in Great Britain in 1987, over 21 per cent fewer than in the previous year – with nearly twice as many men as women contracting the disease.

WHAT IS SYPHILIS?

Syphilis is caused by a corkscrew-shaped organism which is present in the blood and body fluids of an infected person. It can only live in the warm environment that the body provides. The likelihood of your contracting syphilis if you have sex with an infected person is thought to be about one in two – particularly when it is in the early stages.

When the disease is passed on (by contact with a sore or ulcer), a hundred or more of the minute organisms, called triponemes, pass through the skin. After only half an hour they have passed to the lymph nodes in the groin and next they pass into the blood stream and are distributed to the whole body. It takes about three weeks before the body's defence mechanism begins to work against them.

THE FIRST SYMPTOMS

The first symptom of syphilis is a raised pimple on the vagina or penis (although it can sometimes occur on the mouth or anus from oral or anal contact).

Next, hard tissue forms around the pimple. The pimple becomes a painless ulcer or sore from which fluid oozes, and finally heals leaving a scar, usually taking about three weeks to do so.

Most people seek treatment when the sore appears; the doctor will take a sample of the fluid from the sore to examine under a microscope and will also look to see if the lymph nodes of the groin are swollen.

The doctor will also take blood tests to see if antibodies to the organisms have been manufactured by the blood.

EFFECTS ON THE UNBORN CHILD

Transmission of syphilis to an unborn baby occurs by way of the placenta. A blood test done, for example, in the first ten weeks of pregnancy, can diagnose the disease in the mother before it is passed on to the baby – which does not happen until after the twentieth week. She can be cured with penicillin and produce a perfectly healthy baby.

TREATMENT

The chances of curing early syphilis by penicillin or other antibiotics are excellent, and even the advanced disease can be arrested. Daily injections of penicillin (together with Probenecid which maintains high levels of the antibiotic in the bloodstream) are given for about ten days, or a single dose can be injected into a muscle. Alternative antibiotics are given to those allergic to penicillin.

GONORRHOEA

Gonorrhoea is much more common than syphilis – about 50,000 new cases are diagnosed in Great Britain each year. It is the third most common STD, after non-specific genital infections and thrush, but much more common than herpes.

More than half of gonorrhoea cases are among under 24-year-olds, with three to five times as many cases among young men as among young women. Today there are probably between 200 and 500 million new cases every year in the world.

WHAT IS GONORRHOEA?

The gonorrhoea organism is small and bean-shaped, and is passed on by sexual intercourse – oral and anal as well as vaginal. It can therefore be passed from the urethra of a man, to the cervix, urethra, throat or rectum of his partner. It can be passed to a male as well as female partner. A woman can pass it on to the urethra of her male partner during penetration.

Since the organism (gonococcus) dies very quickly outside the human body, it is virtually impossible to pass it on without sexual intercourse. So you need not worry about catching it from a lavatory seat or towel. But if you do have sexual intercourse with someone

One of the most important elements in the treatment of STDs is the tracing of contacts, particularly as many women have no symptoms

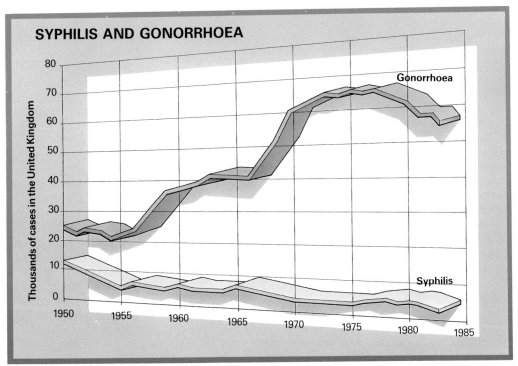

SYPHILIS AND GONORRHOEA

Thousands of cases in the United Kingdom

who has gonorrhoea, you have more than an even chance of catching it.

THE SYMPTOMS
The symptoms are different in men and women. While only one man in ten is symptomless, over half the women who develop the disease have no symptoms.

The first signs for a man occur between three and five days after contact with an infected partner. They start with a tingling of the man's urethra, followed by a thick, creamy-yellow discharge, which drips from the penis. At the same time there is a burning pain on passing urine.

Although at first he feels well in himself, if the infection is not treated and spreads, he may well begin to suffer from fever and headaches within ten to fourteen days. Infection can then travel to the prostate gland, the bladder, the testes or the epididymis. Scarring of the epididymis – the two long narrow tubes where sperm mature before they are ejaculated – can cause permanent sterility if both are affected.

Symptoms of gonorrhoea in a woman may include vaginal discharge or a burning feeling when passing urine. One painful complication occurs when the glands which supply secretions to keep the vagina moist become swollen and tender.

If the infection is not treated, it may spread upwards, often during menstruation, and affect the Fallopian tubes. This may happen in as many as one in ten women who contract gonorrhoea, and is accompanied by fever, headaches, and severe pelvic pain. The inflammation of the tubes, known as salpingitis, can be serious enough to need emergency hospital admission, and the resultant scarring and blocking of the tubes can lead to permanent sterility.

TREATMENT
A positive diagnosis, found by microscope examination of penile discharge, or of a smear taken from a woman's urethra, vagina or cervix, is followed by treatment with penicillin. If oral sex has taken place, a swab is taken from the throat, and if anal intercourse has occurred, one is taken from the rectum.

Treatment today usually consists of one large dose of penicillin in tablet form, together with Probenecid which maintains high levels of the antibiotic in the blood stream. While treatment is taking place, it is very important to avoid alcohol and sexual contact, usually for a matter of weeks, until all signs of the infection are gone and the patient is pronounced clear.

A week following treatment, more swabs are taken and checked for gonocuccus. If none is present the man is considered cured, but a woman needs to be checked again, after her next period.

PREVENTION
For both syphilis and gonorrhoea, the condom may provide a degree of protection, and it is accepted that the diaphragm or cap can protect the cervix from infection. Passing urine after sex may also help a woman to avoid gonorrhoea, although none of these measures guarantees protection.

NSU IN MEN
There were over 166,000 cases of non-specific genital infections reported in British clinics in 1985, and the numbers have been rising each year.

The most common non-specific infection in men is non-specific urethritis (NSU), also called non-gonococcal urethritis. Urethritis is an inflammation of the urethra. It is termed non-specific, when no particular cause (such as gonococcus which causes gonorrhoea) can be found. Although various germs may be responsible for NSU, in about half the cases an organism called chlamydia is present.

Because women have a shorter urethra than men, they seldom develop NSU itself, but the germs can infect the cervix without producing any symptoms.

When a man catches NSU, the infection usually starts about a week or two after sexual contact. He experiences pain on passing urine, and feels the need to go more often. He also has a discharge from his penis – a discharge which looks exactly like that of gonorrhoea and can only be differentiated by microscopic examination.

TREATMENT AND TRACING
A number of antibiotics can be used to treat NSU. The most commonly prescribed are tetracyclines. Tablets are taken over a period of a week or more, and during this time alcohol should be avoided. It is also important that there is no sexual contact and that sexual partners are traced as soon as possible.

A check-up is usually carried out after a week to confirm that gonorrhoea is not present, and again after a further week or so, to check that the infection is cured. If the infection is not quickly treated, the organism (usually chlamydia) may spread to other organs.

When the bladder is infected, urinating becomes very difficult and painful. If it reaches the prostrate gland there is pain in the pelvic area. The infection can spread further to produce conjunctivitis and the slow development of arthritis. The arthritis is sometimes accompanied by fever, and a general feeling of being unwell, and is known as Reiters syndrome. It is usually cured after a few months, but further attacks can lead to permanent damage to the joints if nothing is done to treat them.

GENITAL HERPES
The number of cases of genital herpes diagnosed each year is steadily rising. In Britain there are over 20,000 cases annually, which makes it the sixth most common STD. There has been a great deal written about this so-called 'new' disease. Yet the herpes virus has been around for hundreds of years, and blood tests show that over half of all adults have been infected with the virus – although most of them have no symptoms.

THE TWO TYPES

There are two types of herpes simplex virus, known as type 1 and 2. The first usually causes cold sores around the mouth and nose. Type 2 usually causes sores in the genital and anal area, but can be spread to the mouth. The two types of virus are very similar and can only be told apart by tests in a laboratory.

Most people have built up antibodies to the type 1 virus by the time they are adults, although most of them will have had no symptoms. Fewer will have built up this resistance to type 2 virus in childhood and adolescence, as it is usually passed on by sexual contact.

It is known that herpes can be passed from the mouth to the genital area. When an adult is infected with the simplex 2 virus, there is about an even chance he or she will develop no symptoms.

HERPES SYMPTOMS

The first symptoms of an attack occur within seven days of genital contact. A man will feel a tingling or itching along his penis (or anus) and a woman around the vulva. Sometimes there are 'flu-like symptoms, with headache, backache or a temperature.

Very quickly small, painful, reddish bumps appear in the places where there was itching. By the next day they have become small blisters. These can be very painful, particularly during the first attack, and for the woman the whole area may become swollen so that it is difficult to pass urine. Sometimes the blisters are not visible, and go unnoticed inside the vagina or rectum.

Next, the blisters burst and leave small red ulcers that crust over and heal in a week or so. The area is infectious for about a week after the ulcers have healed, and the virus can be passed on by sexual contact, or by touching, during this time.

RECURRENT ATTACKS

For about half of those who have a first attack of herpes, it will be their last. But for the other half, recurrent attacks happen with varying frequency. What triggers this off is still uncertain and may vary from person to person. Possible triggers are:
☐ stress
☐ hormonal changes
☐ friction during intercourse
☐ sunbathing or using sunbeds
☐ tight clothes or nylon underwear.

MEDICAL TREATMENT

If you think you are having an attack, go to your doctor or special clinic. Diagnosis is made by taking swabs, and the results can be ready within 24 hours.

Although there is no known absolute cure, there are drugs which make the sores less painful, and one drug, acyclovir, which effectively treats the initial attack. This is usually taken by mouth, but is sometimes used as an ointment. It does not, however, seem to prevent or effectively treat future attacks – although

For many people the first attack of genital herpes is often the last – but others may suffer recurrent attacks. If this happens to you, look closely at your lifestyle. Is stress – even something as common as travelling in the rush hour – acting as a trigger?

there is some evidence that it can help ward them off if used immediately when an attack seems imminent.

Suggestions for relieving the painful area include:
☐ bathing in a salt solution
☐ applying an ice-pack to the sores
☐ sitting in a warm bath with potassium permanganate in it
☐ leaving sores exposed to the air as much as possible
☐ dabbing sores with witch-hazel or surgical spirit to dry them out.

Occasionally a woman finds urinating too painful to bear when she has an attack of herpes. She can have a catheter temporarily inserted into her bladder, or she may find relief by passing urine in a warm bath.

LIFE AFTER HERPES

Although herpes is very painful, and recurrent attacks unpleasant, it need not be the end of your sex life.

There is a very small risk of passing it on when you have not got sores, and there are many other ways of giving pleasure to each other when you do. It is a good idea to talk about it with your partner, and if you need more support, there are a number of self-help groups around that will provide it.

AIDS

The world faces a major epidemic of a disease with a hidden dimension, for the AIDS virus can be carried for years without symptoms becoming evident. Despite worldwide concerted efforts, no solution is predicted for the short term, although changes in sexual behaviour can mitigate the situation

Much of the hysteria about AIDS that is gripping the world, particularly the West, is generated by society's attitudes towards some of those groups most likely to be affected – homosexuals, bisexuals and intravenous drug users.

This has resulted in an outbreak of hysteria as devastating in its way as the disease itself, which has earned the tags of AFRAIDS and AIPS (AIDS Induced Panic Syndrome). Children have been barred from classrooms, dentists have refused to treat gay patients and cameramen have boycotted interview sessions featuring victims.

The disease itself has confounded doctors and scientists alike since it was officially recogized in July 1981 in San Francisco, and a cure is not expected in the near future, despite extensive research being carried out throughout the world.

WHY AIDS KILLS
The acronym AIDS stands for Acquired Immune Deficiency Syndrome which spells out about as much and as little as we know about the disease. It is *acquired* and not inherited; it strikes at the *immune* system, the body's natural defence against hostile invading organisms; it produces a *deficiency* in its ability to fight infection; and it is a *syndrome* – a collection of symptoms which seem to occur together and very probably have the same cause.

AIDS-RELATED DISEASES
Victims die not from AIDS itself, but from one of a host of diseases to which the human body deprived of its immune system can fall prey.

Chief among these are Kaposi's sarcoma (a rare and disfiguring skin cancer) and a type of pneumonia (*Pneumocystis carinii pneumonia*) hardly ever seen except in cases of AIDS. Together or separately, these two diseases have caused about three-quarters of the deaths of AIDS victims in both Britain and the United States of America.

UNKNOWN ORIGIN
Equally puzzling is the origin of AIDS. Many researchers believe the virus was perhaps passed from animals to humans in day-to-day contact.

Monkeys in Africa, pigs in Haiti, even sheep in Iceland have all been singled out as possible one-time hosts of the virus, but no one really knows how and why it claimed humans as its victims.

There is mounting evidence that AIDS is in fact an old disease from Africa, where the cancer Kaposi's sarcoma is thought to have been known long before the current outbreak.

AIDS IN THE USA
Wherever it came from, the disease has spread extremely rapidly over long distances in a very short

As with most living organisms, the AIDS virus must kill in order to procreate and survive. Unfortunately, its natural prey – the T4 cell – is part of the immune system. And while the virus is as fragile as a soap bubble outside the human body, once it reaches the blood stream it becomes, to date, impossible to destroy

space of time. The problem is that whereas most diseases increase arithmetically (2, 4, 6, 8 and so on) AIDS increases exponentially (2, 4, 8, 16, 32), and this is what has led to the cliff-face rise in the numbers affected. In America, five cases of *Pneumocystis carinii pneumonia* in Los Angeles and 26 cases of Kaposi's sarcoma in New York and California heralded the arrival of the disease in the summer of 1981.

THREAT TO HETEROSEXUALS

By the end of July 1989, over 100,000 cases of AIDS had been officially notified in the USA and up to 56,000 deaths from the disease had been recorded. It is believed that the rapid increase in the number of cases in previous years was due to the fact that some homosexuals were considerably more promiscuous than heterosexual men or women. However, as the latest figures for gonorrhoea show that incidences within the gay community are declining – whereas heterosexual cases are still increasing – it can be assumed that homosexual promiscuity has declined. This, together with increasing awareness of safe sexual practices, has made doctors hopeful that the increase in gay AIDS cases will decline.

AIDS IN THE UK

Hot on the heels of the American outbreak of the disease came its British appearance, and although the numbers involved are far smaller, the rate of increase in the numbers of AIDS sufferers in the United Kingdom has been equally dramatic.

The first case of AIDS in the United Kingdom was reported in December 1981, with the first death, that of a 37-year-old man, on 4th July 1982. By July 1989 the number of AIDS cases reported in the UK stood at 2,561 and the number of AIDS-related deaths at 1,352.

AIDS WORLDWIDE

By 31st July 1989 the number of AIDS cases notified to the World Health Organization (WHO) had ex-ceeded 172,000, although WHO estimates put the true number of AIDS sufferers worldwide at between 300,000 and 350,000.

Russia has finally acknowledged that it does have the beginnings of an AIDS problem, but the governments of other countries, particularly those dependent on their tourist trade, are keeping quiet about the actual incidence of the disease. Undoubtedly, AIDS is no respecter of borders – cases are being identified in developing nations as in the West, in small towns and in the country, as well as in larger cities.

NOT A HOMOSEXUAL DISEASE

Although AIDS has been dubbed by some as the gay plague and has even been described as being the result of the wrath of God brought to bear on homosexuals, it is by no means exclusive to the gay population, nor even the male population.

In Europe and the US, male homosexuals have made up the majority of victims to date, but other high risk groups include intravenous drug users, haemophiliacs using blood products, bisexuals and prostitutes. In the US and UK a number of sufferers are heterosexual men and women, proof of the fact that anyone who has sex is now at risk.

Outside of the western world, the concentration of AIDS in the gay population has been far less of a feature of the disease. In Central Africa, for example, where as many as one in 10 people are affected in some areas, AIDS is spreading rapidly through heterosexual contact and women are just as likely as men to fall victim to the disease, particularly prostitutes. This may be because of poor standards of hygiene in hospitals and clinics. But it may also be the result of the widespread practice of anal intercourse as a form of contraception in some African countries.

VIRUS ISOLATED

When people were first stricken by AIDS, doctors were mystified and the actual cause of this deadly disease was only isolated in 1985. The culprit is a virus

Sexual transmission
Usually entering the bloodstream via the vulnerable linings of the rectum or urethra – although transmission may be by other means – the AIDS virus hunts down T4 lymphocytes (white blood cells)

Fatal attraction
Receptors on the T4 cell, designed to pick up hostile invaders, lock on to special chemical markers on the virus's surface. Now the T4 cell will begin to release antibodies, but to no avail

THE SAFER SEX CODE
1. Only solo sex is guaranteed safe.
2. Avoid any contact with your partner's semen, bodily fluids or blood.
3. Have sex where you do not orgasm inside your partner's body, or if you feel you must do so, use a condom.

Supplied by the Terence Higgins Trust.

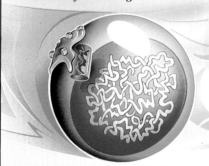

Insertion
As the antibodies begin their attack, the virus discards its outer coat. Now the core of the virus insinuates itself into the cell. Since the core contains RNA and not DNA, the cell is unaware of the danger

Assimilation
Once safely in place, the virus continues to fool its unsuspecting host by using an enzyme to change its RNA into DNA. This genetic material is treated by T4 cells as if it were its very own

which attacks the very cells which protect us from infection. This rod-shaped bug has been labelled the HTLV III virus (or human T cell lymphotropic virus, Type 3) by American scientists, and LAV (lymphaedenopathy associated virus) by French scientists. They have now compromised and the virus is known as LAV-HTLV III. Since the isolation of the original virus, another, more virulent, strain of the disease has been identified and others may exist.

How the AIDS virus spreads from one person to another is still not completely understood. Scientists have isolated it in most body fluids of AIDS victims – in blood, semen and saliva. But because the virus can be isolated in a laboratory test tube does not mean that it can be passed on through contact with all these fluids. AIDS is predominantly a blood-borne disease, although semen is also a likely carrier.

What is clear is that those in normal daily contact with AIDS victims are not necessarily in danger.

ANAL TRANSMISSION
The most common method of transmission is still through anal intercourse. The reason why anal intercourse allows the virus to cross over from one host to another is because the membranes of the rectum are much more delicate than those of the vagina, and hence far more likely to tear and bleed.

Unlike the vagina, the walls of the rectum allow fluids to pass through into the blood stream, so viruses from contaminated sperm could enter another person's body in this way.

There are two other ways in which the virus might be spread by blood to blood contact; by exchanging and using infected needles, a common practice among intravenous drug users; and by transfusing contaminated blood or blood products.

OTHERS AT RISK
Haemophiliacs have found themselves in a high risk group because of their treatment with the blood clotting agent, Factor VIII.

However, these two routes of transmission – blood transfusions and contaminated Factor VIII – should have been blocked by the introduction of tests for all blood donors and of heat-treating all blood to kill off any AIDS viruses present. These measures have been mandatory in the UK since September 1985.

MANY SYMPTOMS
When they do develop, the symptoms of AIDS are those of an array of diseases to which the immune deficient victim has fallen prey, making it difficult to tell whether someone actually has the disease. These include swollen glands in the neck, armpit or groin, weight loss, high fever and night sweats, diarrhoea and persistent coughs or shortness of breath.

There may also be skin changes with pink or purple flattish blotches or bumps occurring on or under the skin, inside the mouth, nose, eyelids or rectum or blemishes in the mouth.

Where any of these symptoms occur alone, or even in twos and threes, it is extremely unlikely that AIDS will be found to be the cause, and because the fear of AIDS can be almost as debilitating as the disease itself, it is important to seek medical advice.

death
AIDS DNA may lie hidden for up to
years within the T4 chromosomes.
... and why it becomes activated remains
...tery – but when it does, the cell begins
...ke copies of the virus and dies

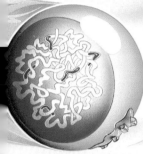

DNA – *found only within the cell nucleus, it stores the genetic code and can (uniquely) replicate itself*
RNA – *found throughout the cell, it can act as a messenger for DNA in synthesizing the protein chains that are part of the human body*

COMPLETE CURE NOT YET IN SIGHT

As yet, the prospects for the prevention and cure of AIDS look none too hopeful.

No known cure has yet been found for the disease and the best that can be done, medically, for victims is to help alleviate the symptoms. Nor is there any effective vaccine at present, and according to scientists there is no chance of there being one in the near future.

The virus probably has several different forms, each capable of mutating (changing), which makes the development of a vaccine difficult. Many of the drugs currently being tested as possible cures for AIDS are aimed at stopping the virus reproducing after it has entered the body, but progress is slow. According to a report in the New England Journal of Medicine, doctors have isolated the virus in the brain and spinal fluid from AIDS sufferers. The implica-

tions are that the virus 'hides' in the brain – and this could make eradication difficult, though probably not impossible.

Despite the anxiety among health care workers, and those involved in caring for AIDS victims, their chances of contracting the disease themselves seem remote. Apart from one case in the UK of a nurse who contracted the disease by accidentally innoculating herself with a small amount of blood from an AIDS patient, there have been no known cases of the disease being contracted at work by doctors and nurses.

It is, however, known that an infected mother can pass on AIDS to her unborn child, possibly through the placenta or else during the actual birth when blood is lost by the mother.

VIRUS NOT NECESSARILY FATAL

As yet there is no test which shows categorically whether a person has AIDS. Anyone who has come into contact with the virus will make antibodies to it, and will show up as 'antibody positive'.

But although the presence of antibodies gives no protection against the disease, only 5–10 per cent of those who are found to have LAV-HTLV III antibodies in the blood go on to develop a fatal case of AIDS.

Some will develop milder, less life-threatening infections, and a sizeable number may develop no obvious symptoms at all.

AIDS CARRIERS

Exactly what makes one person develop the disease while others remain unaffected is not known exactly, but carriers – those who have antibodies without symptoms – will still be capable of passing the virus to others, who in turn will stand much the same chance of developing AIDS.

The other worrying problem about AIDS is that symptoms make take anything from two, possibly as long as seven, years to emerge, which means that sufferers may unwittingly be infecting a large number of other people before realizing they have the disease.

One of the most distressing facts about the AIDS virus is that it can lie undetected for some years before the carrier shows any symptoms. Thus the virus can be passed unwittingly from one person to another, as there is no way of telling who is infected during this dormant period

INDEX

PICTURE CREDITS

Art Directors Photo Library: 185. Paul Beattie: 20 (l, cl), 21 (tl, tr, cr), 22 (tc, tr, c, cr), 23 (c, bl, br), 24, 25 (tc, tr, c, cr), 26 (tl, cl), 27 (l), 28 (l, br), 29 (tr, c, br), 30 (r), 31 (l), 32, 33 (t), 34 (l, cr), 35 (t), 36 (t, c), 141, 143. Steve Bielschowsky: 122–123, 124, 125, 126, 127 (l). Steve Bicknell: 158. Bruce Coleman Ltd: 179 (bl). Alan Duns: 155. Ray Duns: 176, 177, 178–179 (t). Mary Evans Picture Library: 160 (bl). Image Bank: 130 (bl), 148, 166–167. Dave King: 8–9. Pat Kraus: 43. David Lloyd: 152, 153. Ranald Mackechnie: 4–5, 6–7, 10 (l), 11 (cr, br), 12, 13, 14, 15, 16, 17, 18, 19, 20–21 (c), 22–23 (t), 25 (br), 26 (br), 27 (br), 27–28 (c, b), 30 (l), 31 (br), 33 (b), 34–35 (b), 36 (b), 37 (br), 38–39, 40–41, 42, 44–45, 46, 47, 48, 49, 50–51, 52 (cr), 52–53 (b), 56–57, 59 (t), 60–61, 62, 64–65, 66 (tl), 69 (tr), 70–71, 72 (tl), 76–77, 78–79, 80, 83 (c), 84, 85, 88 (tr), 90–91, 92–93 (b), 94–95 (b, r), 98–99, 100–101, 102–103, 104–105 (b), 114–115, 116, 117 (tr), 119 (cl), 127 (c, br), 134, 135, 136–137, 138, 139, 140, 142, 144, 145, 146–147, 150–151 (b), 162, 165, 168, 169, 170–171, 172, 173, 174, 175, 192. Helen Pask: 106–107, 108–109 (t), 111, 112–113 (t). Colin Ramsay: 10–11 (c), 52–53 (c). Rex Features: 149, 151 (tr). Steve Smith: 54–55. Frank Spooner Pictures: 160 (cl). Zefa: 159 (bl), 161 (tr, cl), 182–183.

ARTWORK CREDITS

Frank Kennard: 37 (tl, tr). Trevor Laurence: 179 (tr) adapted from *The Pill* by Dr John Guillebaud (OUP), 181. Tony Lodge: 180. Patricia Ludlow: 103 (br), 104–105 (t). Chris Lyon: 164 (tl). Howard Pemberton: 58–59, 60, 63, 66–67, 68–69, 72–73, 74–75, 80–81, 82–83, 86–87, 88–89, 92–93 (t), 94–95 (c), 96–97, 108–109 (b), 110, 112–113 (b), 116–117, 118–119, 120–121, 132–133. Robinson: 188–189 (b).